Illuminating the
PARTICULAR

Roman B. J. Kwasniewski

Serial #A04136

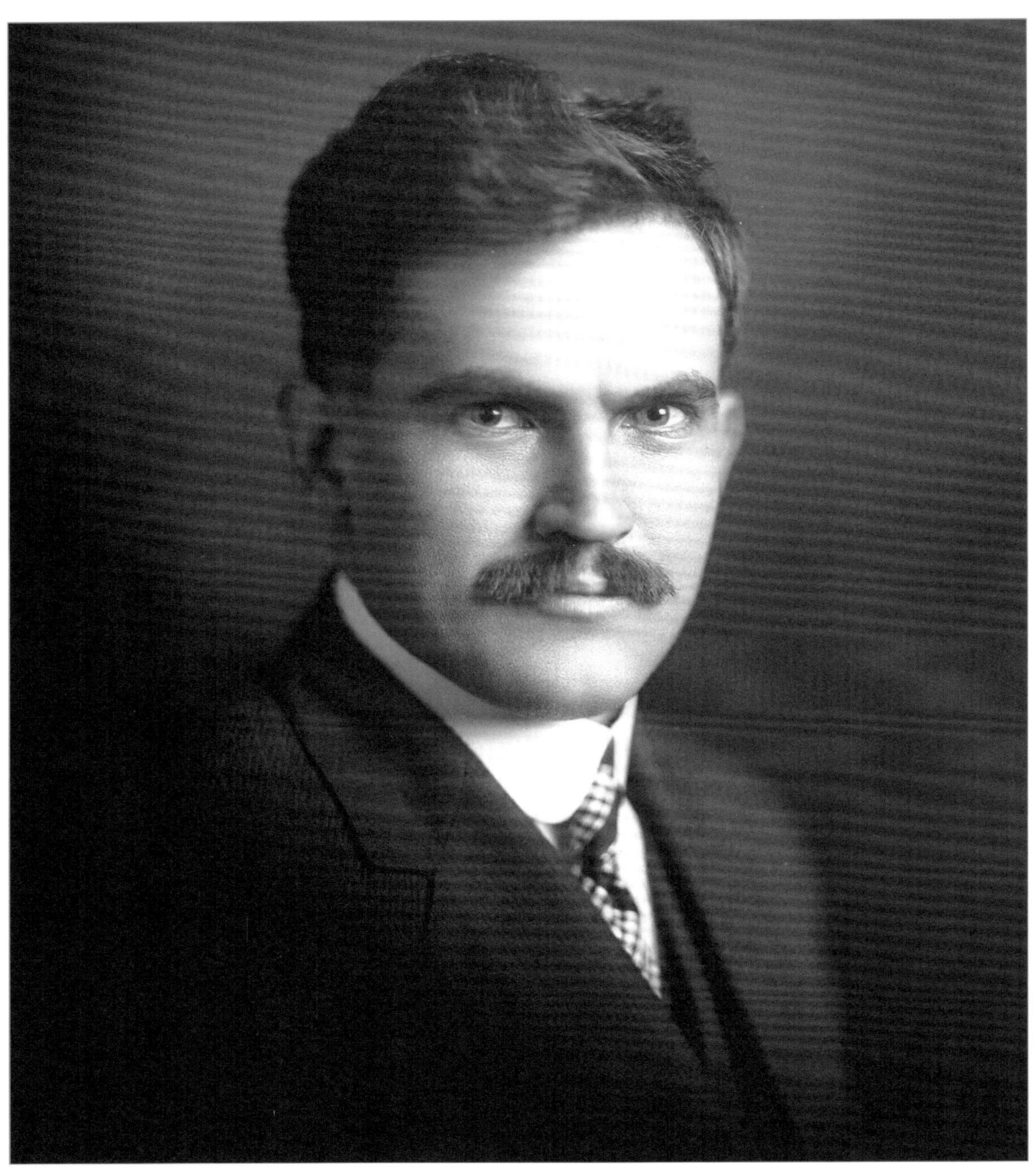

PUBLISHED WITH SUPPORT FROM THE GREATER MILWAUKEE FOUNDATION

GRANT AND ROSEMARY BEUTNER FUND

Illuminating the Particular

Photographs of Milwaukee's Polish South Side

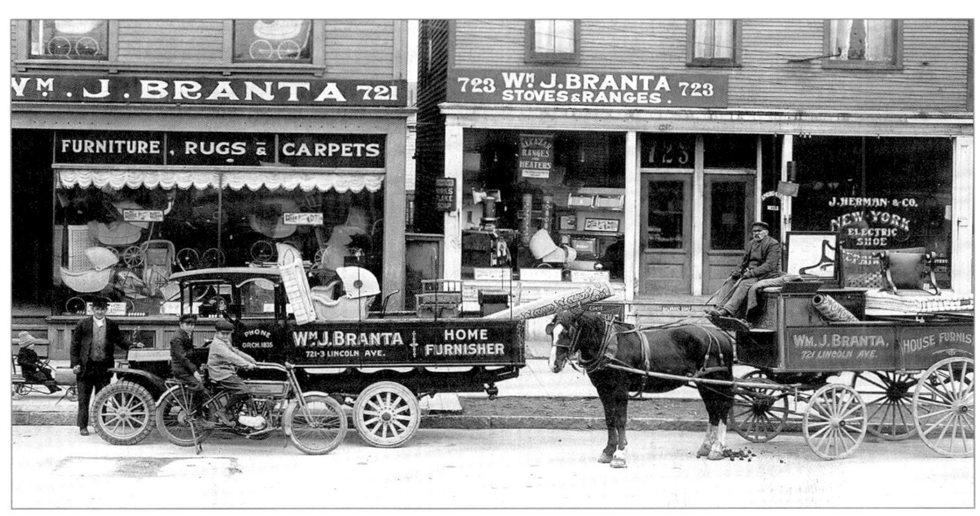

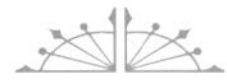

Christel T. Maass

Introduction by John Gurda

Photographs by Roman B̦. J. Kwasniewski

Wisconsin Historical Society Press

Madison

Published by the
Wisconsin Historical Society Press

Publications of the Wisconsin Historical Society Press are available at quantity discounts for promotions, fund raising, and educational use. Write to the above address for more information.

For more information about the Roman B. J. Kwasniewski Photographic Collection, or to order copies of any photographs in this book, contact the Archives by mail at: University of Wisconsin–Milwaukee Libraries, Archives,
P.O. Box 604, Milwaukee, WI 53201;
by phone at (414) 229-5402; or by e-mail at archives@uwm.edu.
Or visit the UWM Libraries at 2311 East Hartford Avenue in Milwaukee.

Printed in Canada
Designed by Timothy O'Keeffe

∞The paper used in this publication meets the minimum requirements of the American National Standard for Information Sciences—Permanence of Paper for Printed Library Materials, ANSI Z39.48-1992.

05 04 03 5 4 3 2 1

Library of Congress Cataloging-in-Publication Data

Maass, Christel T.
Illuminating the particular : photographs of Milwaukee's Polish South Side / by Christel T. Maass ; with introductions by John Gurda; photographs by Roman B.J. Kwasniewski.
p. cm.
Includes bibliographical references and index.
ISBN 0-87020-347-9
1. Polish Americans--Wisconsin--Milwaukee--History--20th century--Pictorial works. 2. Polish Americans--Wisconsin--Milwaukee--Social life and customs--20th century--Pictorial works. 3. Immigrants--Wisconsin--Milwaukee--History--20th century—Pictorial works. 4. Immigrants--Wisconsin--Milwaukee--Social life and customs--20th century--Pictorial works. 5. Milwaukee (Wis.)--History--20th century--Pictorial works. 6. Milwaukee (Wis.)--Social life and customs--20th century--Pictorial works. 7. Milwaukee (Wis.)--Ethnic relations--20th century--Pictorial works. I. Kwasniewski, Roman B.J., 1886-1980. II. Title.
F589.M69P765 2003
977.5'950049185--dc22
2003014728

ISBN: 0-87020-347-9

Publication of this book was made possible, in part, by a major gift from the Greater Milwaukee Foundation—Grant and Rosemary Beutner Fund. Additional funding was provided by Merchants & Manufacturers BanCorp.

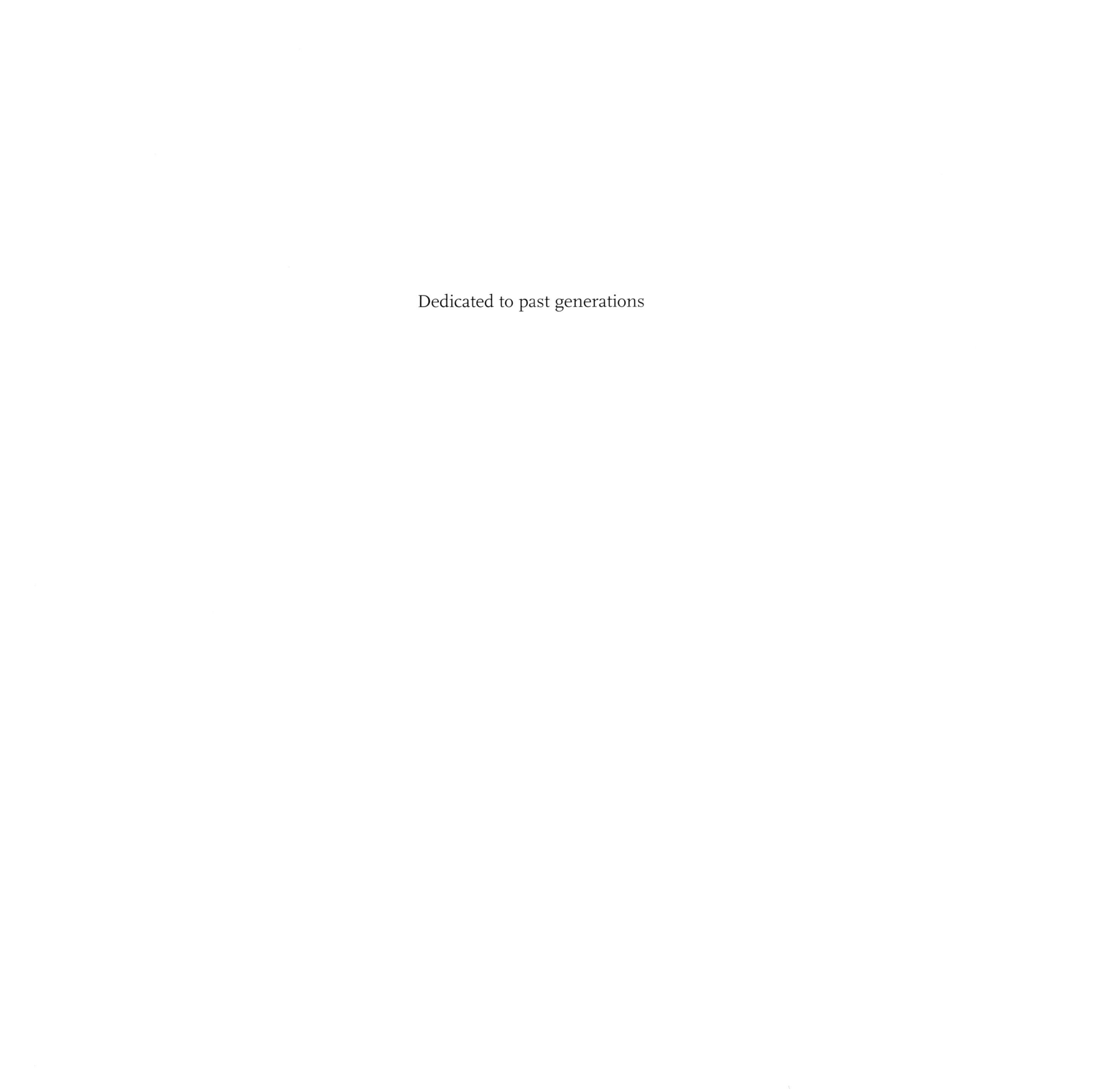

Dedicated to past generations

CONTENTS

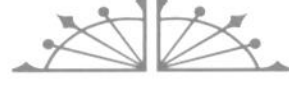

MILWAUKEE'S SOUTH SIDE, 1920

This map highlights streets on Milwaukee's South Side in 1920, a time when photographer Roman Kwasniewski was quite active. Most of Kwasniewski's customers lived in the vicinity of his Lincoln Avenue studio, and the vast majority of Kwasniewski's nonstudio photographs were also taken in this area. In 1926 the city began a project to rename and renumber Milwaukee's streets. By 1930 the project was completed, and changes were in place. In cases where street names have been changed, this map shows the historic names followed by the modern name in parentheses. Street name changes are also noted throughout the text.

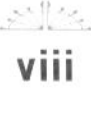

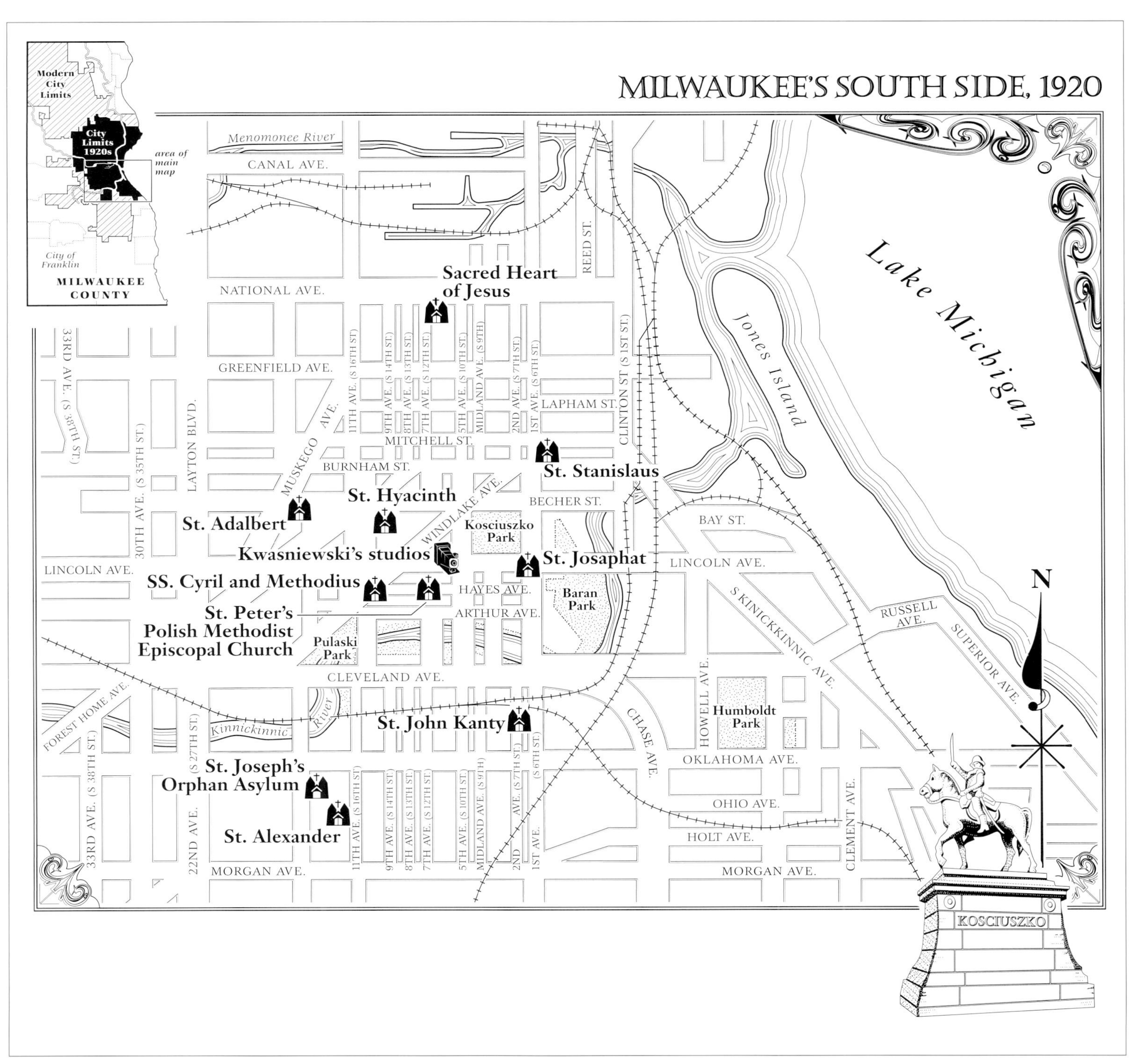

Map by Amelia Janes, Midwest Educational Graphics

AUTHOR'S PREFACE

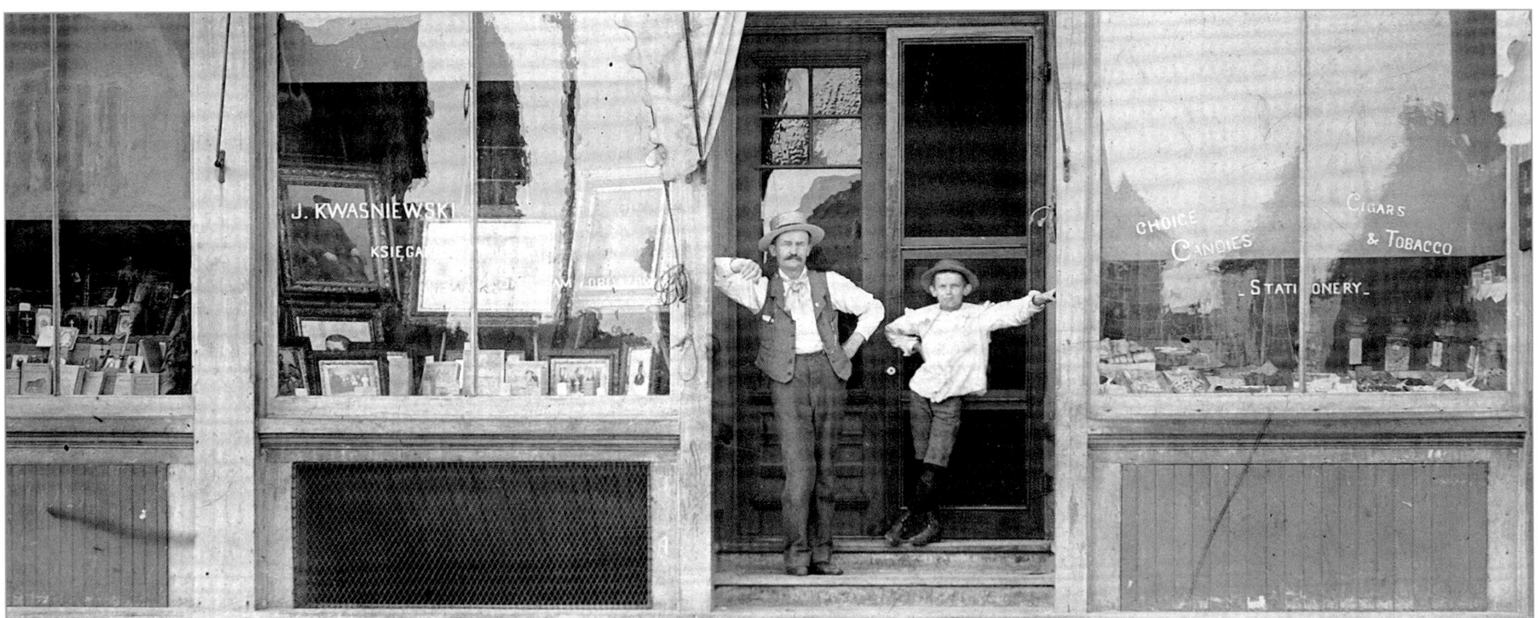

Roman Kwasniewski may have become interested in photography as a profession while helping out in his father's shop. This photograph shows Roman with his father, Jozef, outside the family business on Becher Street in 1897.
Serial # 01073

As an archivist I've seen the pleasure that something as simple as a photograph can give to others; on one occasion, I even received a punch on the arm when an excited researcher found a photograph from the Roman B. J. Kwasniewski Photographic Collection that he could use in his master's thesis.

Roman B. J. Kwasniewski, a son of Polish immigrants, used his camera to document life in his South Side Milwaukee neighborhood during the early decades of the twentieth century. Born in Chicago in 1886, Roman was the only child of Jozef and Wanda Kwasniewski. After the family moved to Milwaukee in the 1890s, Jozef established a lithography and printing business on Becher Street.

Roman assisted with his father's business until 1913, when he struck out on his own as a photographer, establishing the Park Studio at 554 Lincoln Avenue (today 1010 West Lincoln Avenue). In 1916 Kwasniewski built a new studio down the street at what was then 568 Lincoln Avenue (now 1024 West Lincoln Avenue).

The majority of Roman Kwasniewski's business consisted of studio photography. Family portraits, wedding pictures, and photographs marking religious occasions, such as First Communions and confirmations, are his most predominant works. Kwasniewski also took his camera into the community, capturing scenes of life on the streets, local businesses, pictures of homes, classrooms, and cultural, social, and recreational activities. Milwaukee's South Side Poles were devout Roman Catholics, and Kwasniewski's photographs reflect the powerful influence of the church in the community. Kwasniewski closed the Park Studio in 1947.

Shortly before Kwasniewski's death in 1980, Adele and John Kaczmarowski, Roman Kwasniewski's daughter and son-in-law, approached the University of Wisconsin–Milwaukee (UWM) to determine its interest in purchasing Kwasniewski's photographic collection. Financial assistance from Polanki—the Polish Women's Cultural Club of Milwaukee—and the support of Professor Donald Pienkos of UWM's Polish Studies Program made possible the collection's transfer to the university. In 1991 Ron and Barbara Nelson, who had purchased Kwasniewski's old studio, donated an additional set of glass-plate negatives and photographs that they found in the building. The Roman B. J. Kwasniewski Photographic Collection consists of more than twenty-five thousand glass-plate negatives and five thousand prints.

The images reproduced in this book maintain the integrity of Kwasniewski's original photographs. In many instances, however, the reproduced photographs have been cropped somewhat, mainly to eliminate unsightly edges, usually a result of the glass-plate negative emulsion, dark areas, empty space, excess sky, ceiling, road, and the like.

I consulted numerous sources for information about the photographs and the events surrounding them. A selected bibliography is included at the end of this book, but several sources that I most relied upon are worth mentioning. The best source on Milwaukee's Poles from Kwasniewski's time period, and one that I frequently consulted, is *We, the Milwaukee Poles,* compiled by Thaddeus Borun. I also used Milwaukee city directories to track individuals, their places of

Kwasniewski's first studio was located at 554 Lincoln Avenue (today 1010 West Lincoln Avenue). Kwasniewski took this photograph, which he identified as a "test plate," in February 1914.
Serial # A04030

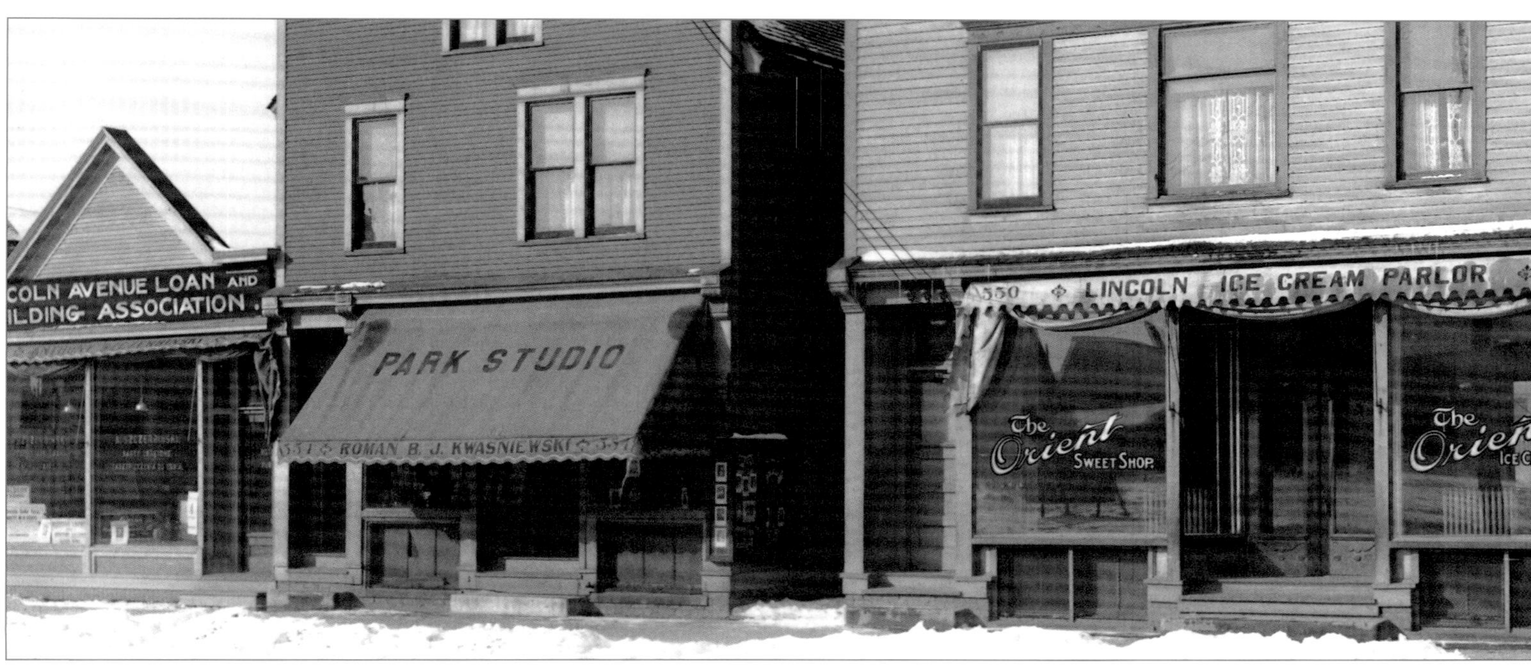

residence, and their occupations, as well as to locate businesses and the dates that they existed.

Kwasniewski himself left much of the information identifying his photographs. He usually recorded on his glass-plate negative sleeves the name of the individual, institution, or business that ordered the photograph; their address; the date; a serial number, which could also be used to date the photograph; and occasionally, other brief details. Sometimes one of Kwasniewski's photographs provided clues about another. For example, a second photograph from another angle might include a business that in turn helped identify where the first photograph was taken. Kwasniewski's detailed information about his photographs was entered into a database during the collection's processing. This database, which allows researchers to search by name, address, topic, or date, is available in the archives at the UWM Libraries.

I was involved in the processing of the Roman B. J. Kwasniewski Photographic Collection and with various activities to promote it, including displays in the Milwaukee area and at the Wisconsin State Capitol in Madison. In the fall of 1996 I began contributing a monthly photo and caption column, "A Glance at Yesteryear," to the *Small Business Times*, a paper for business owners in southeastern Wisconsin. Many of the business-related photographs that I used for that column came from the Kwasniewski collection. This book includes photographs and captions from those columns, as well as additional photographs from the Kwasniewski collection, covering a wider range of subjects.

I hope you will enjoy this look at the past.

—Christel T. Maass

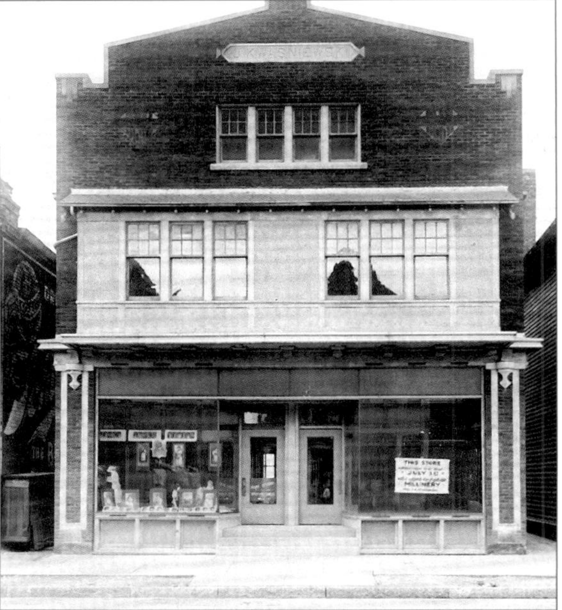

Kwasniewski built his second studio in 1916 at what was then 568 Lincoln Avenue (now 1024 West Lincoln Avenue). This photograph was probably taken in 1917, shortly before Salomea Kozlowski opened the millinery store next door.
Serial # A04027

ACKNOWLEDGMENTS

I would like to thank the following individuals for their support and assistance in making this book possible.

Tim Ericson, assistant director for archives and special collections at the UWM Libraries; Ewa Barczyk, associate director of the UWM Libraries; and Peter Watson-Boone, director of the UWM Libraries, supported this project. Ewa Barczyk also assisted with Polish translations, and Tim Ericson reviewed the completed manuscript.

My current and former colleagues in the UWM Libraries' Archives Department—Leslie Heinrichs, Kathy Koch, and Mark Vargas—provided advice and were sounding boards for ideas. They kindly listened to me express my frustration when I found a particularly interesting photograph but did not have a story to go with it, and they put up with me when I asked more questions than any of us were able to answer. My husband, Terry Rindt, an accountant, helped with statistical calculations, answered my military-related questions, and took the first look at my rough drafts.

Others answered questions and helped in small steps along the way: Tim Cary, archivist at the Archdiocese of Milwaukee; Patti Day, librarian in the American Geographical Society Library at UWM; Rebecca Littman, music librarian at the UWM Libraries; Donald Pienkos, UWM political science professor; and Chan Harries and Amy Schindler, archives interns at UWM.

Special thanks to the folks at the Wisconsin Historical Society, especially Michael E. Stevens, state historian, for his great timing in inquiring whether anything had ever been done with the Kwasniewski photographs just when I was trying to find a publisher, as well as for his work to make this book possible. Thanks also to J. Kent Calder, editorial director, Diane Drexler, managing editor, and Masarah Van Eyck, developmental editor, for taking this publication through the production process.

Special thanks also to Milwaukee historian John Gurda for writing the general introduction and the introductions to each chapter.

I am also grateful to David Niles of the *Small Business Times* for publishing the "A Glance at Yesteryear" columns and for unknowingly providing the stepping stone for this larger undertaking.

Last, and perhaps most important, thanks to those individuals who had the foresight to preserve the Roman B. J. Kwasniewski Photographic Collection.

INTRODUCTION

More than two hundred thousand Milwaukeeans trace their family roots to Poland. That is enough to make Milwaukee one of the capital cities of Polish America, a place where Pope John Paul II is revered, the polka is mastered at an early age, and you're never far from cold beer and good kielbasa. Milwaukee's Polonia (Polish American community) is larger than those in Cleveland, Buffalo, and Pittsburgh, and in proportional terms, it is on par with the colonies in Chicago and Detroit. Within metropolitan Milwaukee, only residents of German or African ancestry make up a larger percentage of the population.

Roman Kwasniewski photographed this distinctive community during a formative period in its development. He was most active in the years between World War I and World War II, particularly the 1920s and 1930s—a time of head-spinning economic prosperity and then economic collapse, of growing ethnic maturity that gave way to systemic social change. What Kwasniewski created, apparently without forethought, was a community portrait that is uncommonly complete,

This was the reception area of Kwasniewski's Park Studio as it looked in April 1917.
Serial # A04005

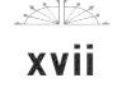

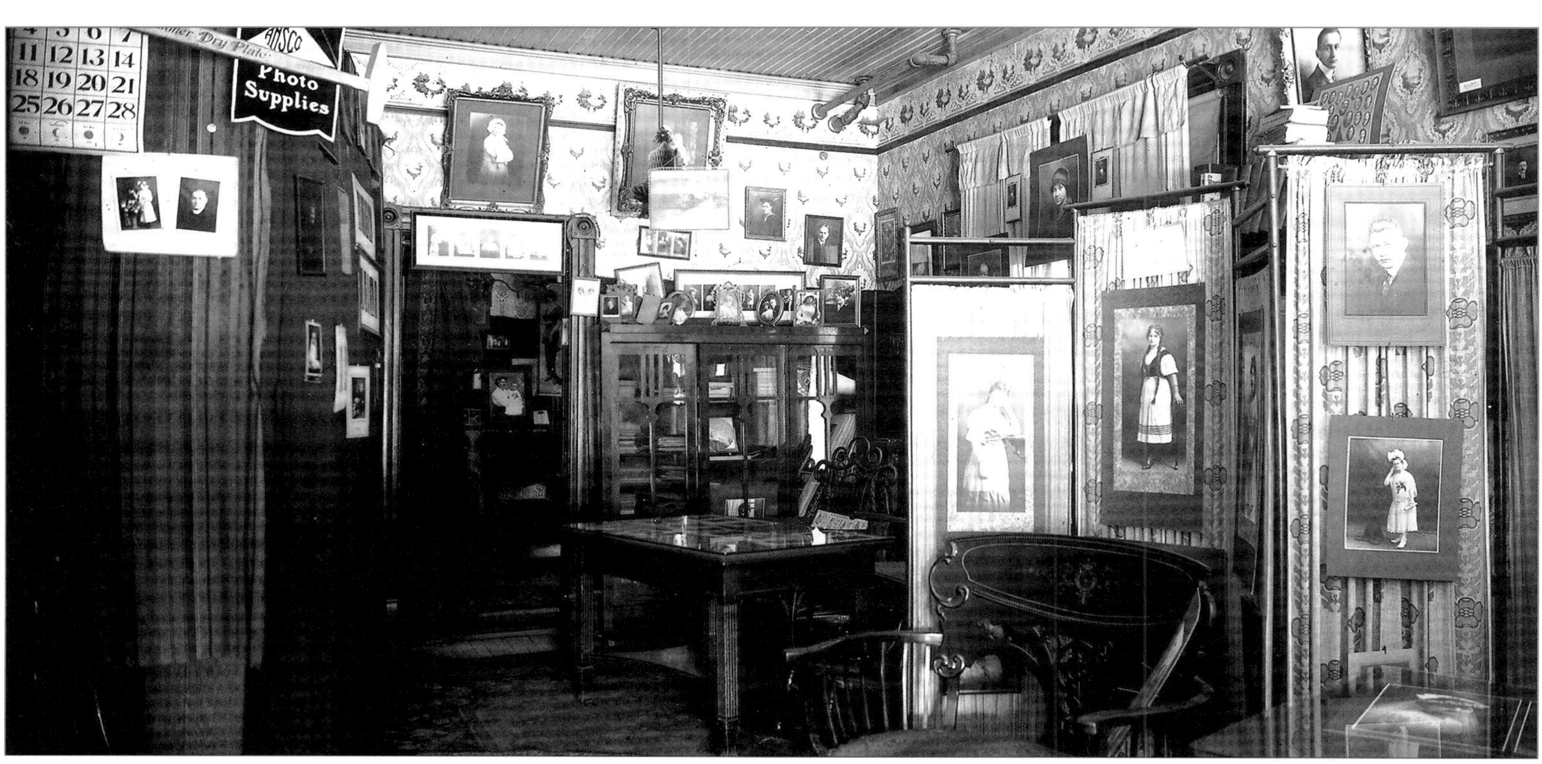

technically superb, and compelling in its humanity. Few neighborhoods in America, ethnic or otherwise, have been chronicled in such loving detail.

The community that appears in Kwasniewski's prints predates his arrival by several decades. In the half century following 1870, more than 3.5 million Poles left Europe for the United States. Most were impoverished peasants facing diminished prospects at home and looking across the ocean for greater opportunities, particularly in the rapidly industrializing cities of the northern United States. There was a political dimension to their movement as well. Once a major power in central Europe, the Polish state had ceased to exist in 1795, when Russia, Prussia, and Austria carved it into three dependent territories. Conditions in western, or German, Poland—the ancestral home of more than 80 percent of Milwaukee's Poles—were especially harsh. Military conscription and cultural repression made emigration an obvious choice.

A significant number of America's Polish newcomers came to Milwaukee, and they came unusually early. In 1866, only two decades after the city was chartered, thirty Polish families organized the parish of St. Stanislaus. It was the first Polish Catholic congregation in urban America, and it was followed two years later by the nation's first Polish Catholic school. The parish's original home was a modest brick building on the near South Side, purchased (for $4,000) from a group of German Lutherans. In 1872 the immigrants built a church of their own design on nearby Mitchell Street. The twin-spired Gothic landmark is still the center of parish life.

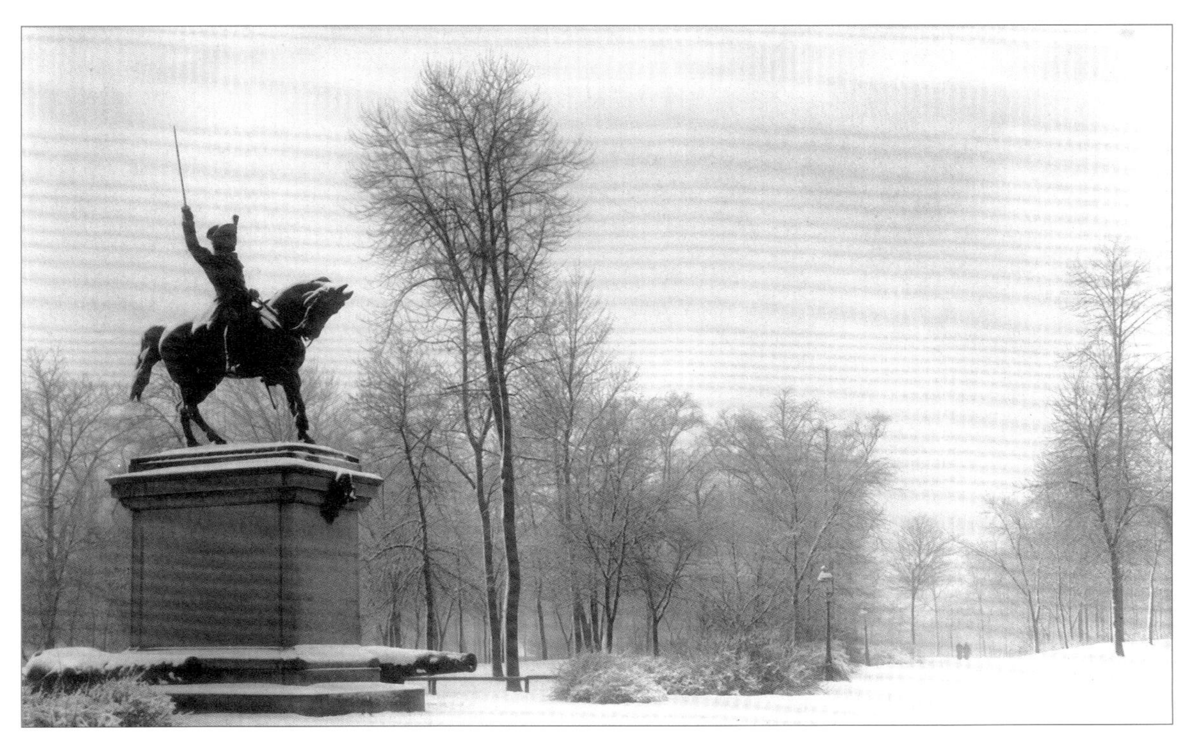

This peaceful winter scene was taken in Kosciuszko Park. Photographer Roman Kwasniewski's Park Studio was located nearby. The Kosciuszko Monument, which appeared as a popular backdrop in many of Kwasniewski's photographs, honors Revolutionary War hero General Thaddeus Kosciuszko, who was one of General George Washington's outstanding aides and one of the founders of the West Point military academy. Undated.
Serial # A15300

With "St. Stan's" as its anchor, Milwaukee's Polonia continued to make history. In 1874 the Kosciuszko Guard was commissioned as America's first Polish military company. In 1878 a saloon keeper named August Rudzinski became the nation's first Polish American to win municipal office, taking a seat on the Milwaukee County Board. In 1888 the irrepressible Michael Kruszka launched the *Kuryer Polski*, a newspaper that proved to be the country's first successful Polish daily.

Polish Milwaukeeans set any number of precedents, but their status as pioneers did not mask the poverty that most families endured. Although they arrived early, the immigrants came to a city whose pecking order was firmly established. Yankees—transplants from New York and New England—exercised an influence entirely out of proportion to their numbers, even though they were vastly outnumbered by German-speaking residents. Milwaukee, in fact, was already the most German city in America, and Teutonic newcomers were shaping its cultural and economic life decisively. The Irish, despite their poverty, were a potent force in local politics. Polish immigrants, after depleting their reserves in crossing to America, had little choice but to start at the bottom.

What that meant, in the later nineteenth century, was jobs in local industries—the foundries, tanneries, packing houses, iron mills, and increasingly, manufacturing plants that were driving Milwaukee's economy. The work was generally hard and often hazardous, not to mention poorly compensated. A laborer of the 1880s could expect to earn only one dollar for a standard twelve-hour day—roughly $1.50 an hour in modern terms—with no vacation, no health insurance, and no pension.

Although their economic struggles were unending, the Polish immigrants did something that took their neighbors by surprise: they built homes of their own. Throughout American urban history, the newest groups have generally occupied the oldest houses, settling in hand-me-down neighborhoods on the fringes of the nation's downtowns. The Poles broke that unwritten law. "Usually the first money they can call their own is put into the purchase of a lot," reported the *Milwaukee Sentinel* in 1874, "on which they mean to erect a house as soon as possible. They have a strong prejudice against paying rent." Reflecting the Old World belief that land, not money, is the key to security, the immigrants bought lots that were painfully small by modern standards—only twenty-five or thirty feet wide—and covered them with simple frame cottages resting on cedar posts.

The result was an unusually dense settlement pattern that got even more dense with time. In Milwaukee and elsewhere Polish immigrants displayed a genius for additive architecture. As the years passed and finances permitted they used heavy jacks to lift the original cottages several feet off their foundations and then underpinned them with brick or block half-basements. Single-family homes became duplexes practically overnight. Known locally as Polish flats (or in the parlance of the building inspectors, English basement duplexes), the two-stage houses covered block after block on the city's expanding periphery. In 1902 Milwaukee was one of the most densely built cities in the country, trailing only Boston and Baltimore, and its densest neighborhoods were those developed by Polish immigrants.

My grandmother's family typified the trends. Mary Heft Gurda's father died of tuberculosis when she was only nine, leaving her mother to raise six children on a washerwoman's wages. What saved the family from ruin was the fact that they had five living units in the two buildings on

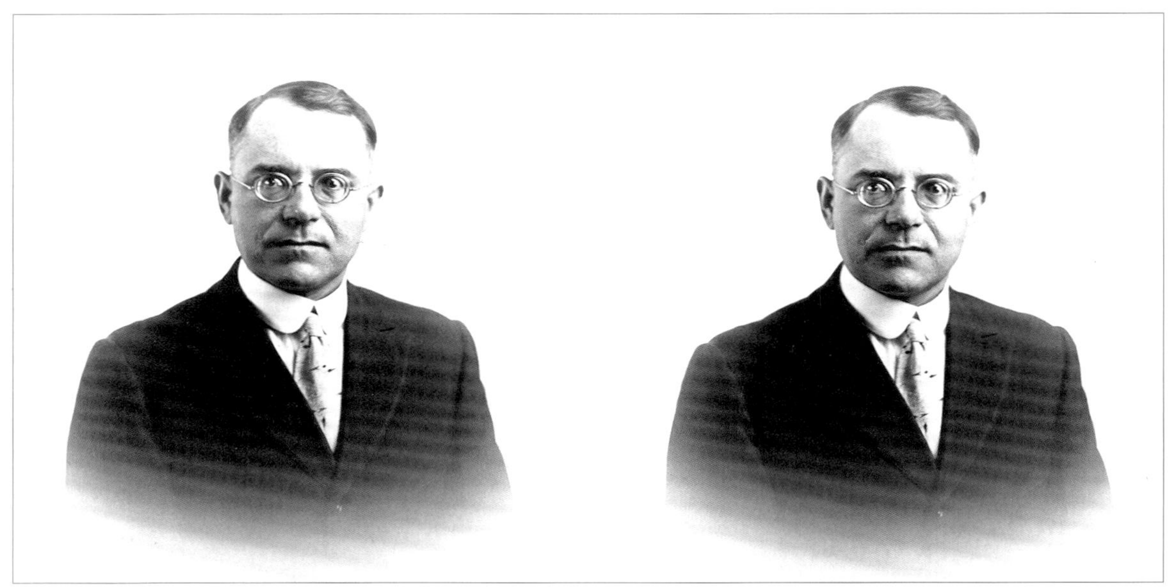

Much of Roman Kwasniewski's business consisted of routine portraiture as well as photographs needed by immigrants for their citizenship papers. These naturalization photographs of Joseph Szedziewski, taken in 1932, are typical of this part of his work. The original glass - plate negative contained two images, from which the client would chose one. ***Serial # 31435***

their cramped South Fourteenth Street property. One (the smallest, of course) was for their own use; the others provided rental income. There was no shortage of playmates. When my grandmother was a girl, a total of twenty-seven children lived on her little lot—enough for three baseball teams!

Polish flats were most numerous on the South Side, particularly in the blocks south of Greenfield Avenue. That area was the heart of Milwaukee's Polonia, accommodating at least three-fourths of its population. A second stronghold developed on the city's East Side, near the intersection of Brady Street and Humboldt Avenue, where jobs in the tanneries, flour mills, and other industries lining the nearby Milwaukee River attracted workers. The neighborhood's linchpin was St. Hedwig's Church, established in 1871 as Milwaukee's second Polish congregation. An entire community grew up literally in the shadow of St. Hedwig's. When the East Side's Polonia was filled to overflowing, younger families moved across the river and developed the neighborhood known today as Riverwest.

Milwaukee's third Polish settlement was one of the most unusual in America. In the 1870s fishing families from the Kaszuby region on the Baltic seacoast began to settle on Jones Island, the windswept peninsula at the mouth of the Milwaukee River. German-speaking Pomeranians and a scattering of other groups joined the Kaszubs in making Jones Island the regional capital of commercial fishing. The islanders harvested two thousand tons in a good year, a mixed catch of trout, whitefish, perch, chubs, and sturgeon. The Lake Michigan fishery supported a community whose population peaked at sixteen hundred near the turn of the twentieth century. Jones Island was a picturesque jumble of fish sheds and drying reels at the water's edge and jerry-built houses set on meandering dirt roads in the interior. (There were also eleven saloons on the island at one particularly wet point in its history.) While their countrymen across the river filed through the plant gates of the city's major industries, the Kaszubs continued a way of life they had known for centuries in their homeland. Jones Island was the closest thing Milwaukee has ever known to a genuine urban village, and it lasted until the 1920s, when the city took the land for harbor facilities and a sewage-treatment plant.

The Polish flats on the mainland and the cottages of the Jones Island fisherfolk were undeniably modest; they reflected the best efforts of a group that could, for the time being, afford nothing better. But the modesty of Polish Milwaukee's houses stood in stark contrast to the majesty of its churches. St. Stan's was the mother parish of more than twenty Polish Catholic congregations, and their steeples stand as benchmarks in the outward expansion of the city's Polonia. Viewed together, the churches are a distinguished ensemble. Despite their poverty, Polish immigrants showed a penchant for grand ecclesiastical architecture, and no church was more imposing than the Basilica of St. Josaphat. Built with materials salvaged from the Chicago Post Office, this Romanesque marvel was completed in 1901. The parish had nearly twelve thousand members at the time—probably the most of any congregation in the state, regardless of faith—and the church they built is still the city's largest. But St. Josaphat was a parish of the poor. It took until 1925—nearly a quarter century—for the congregation to pay off its debt, and only then was work on the interior pushed to completion. In 1929 Pope Pius XI declared the church a basilica, the ecclesiastical equivalent of all-star status. St. Josaphat was only the third basilica in the country.

Completing such a glorious church in 1901, even without a finished interior, was a mark of institutional maturity, a clear signal that Milwaukee's Polonia was here to stay. As immigrants kept crossing the ocean, the ranks of the community continued to swell. By 1906 there were nearly seventy thousand Polish Milwaukeeans—a number exceeded only by the Germans—and the Polish vote had become a decisive factor in local politics. The community's fortunes were further bolstered by World War I. The conflict was disastrous for local German culture (sauerkraut was rechristened "liberty cabbage"), but the Allied victory was an unmixed blessing for expatriate Poles. In 1918 Poland became a free nation for the first time since 1795. Basking in the reflected light of a free homeland and growing slowly more prosperous in the freedom of America, Polish Milwaukeeans had much to celebrate.

It was at this point that Roman Kwasniewski entered the picture. Born in Chicago in 1886, Kwasniewski moved to Milwaukee with his parents as a child and stayed for the rest of his life. His father, Jozef, operated a printing business on Becher Street, near the heart of the South Side's Polonia. Roman worked with him until 1913, when he opened the Park Studio on Lincoln Avenue near Tenth Street. Named for nearby Kosciuszko Park, the studio won a loyal following on the South Side. Kwasniewski typically worked with a 5 x 7 view camera that produced glass-plate negatives of remarkable clarity; most modern digital images look like pixelized mud by comparison. In 1916 the Park Studio moved to new quarters down the block, and Roman Kwasniewski remained in business there for the next thirty-one years.

Studio photography was the core of Kwasniewski's business. Legions of South Siders posed before the obligatory Victorian backdrops in his studio, generally to mark important life passages: First Communions, confirmations, graduations, weddings, and anniversaries. But the photographer also took his camera into the community. Kwasniewski's images are an exhaustive collection

In this detail from a panoramic photograph, Milwaukee historian John Gurda's father (with the white tape on his shoe), along with other Company K members, posed at the dedication of a Polish veterans' home in 1931.
Serial # A15495

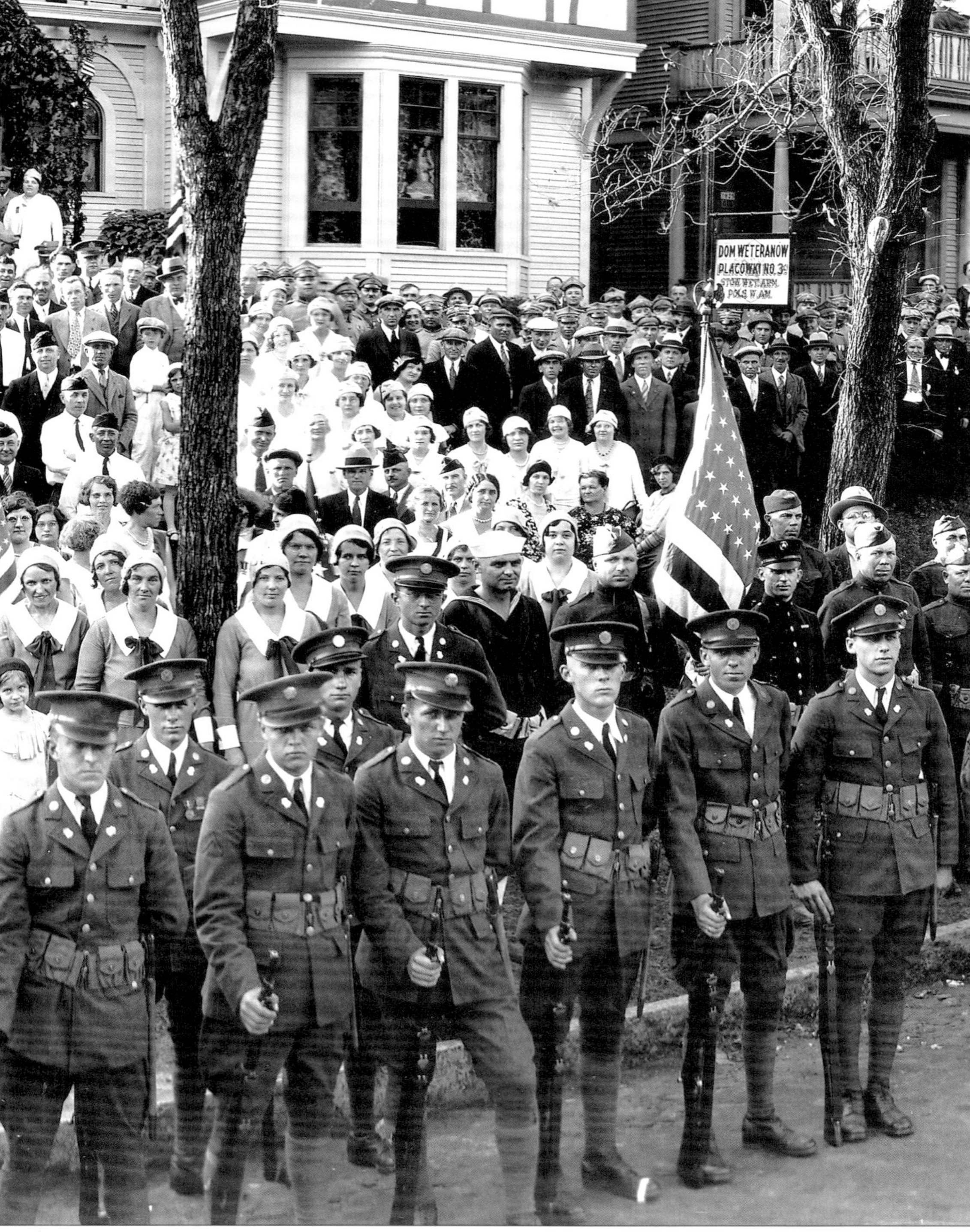

of the mundane, the celebratory, and the picturesque. If a new bridge opened or a new church was built, Kwasniewski was there. If a family wanted a permanent record of a backyard birthday party or a festive Christmas gathering, they called Kwasniewski. He was a fixture at grand openings and ground breakings, at pageants, plays, and parades. He captured masons at work, babies in carriages, corpses in caskets, foundry hands on the job, nuns in full habit, and soldiers going off to war. For literally thousands of families and organizations on the Polish South Side, Roman Kwasniewski was the photographer of choice for decades.

This was clearly a man who was deeply engaged in the world around him. In addition to the carefully crafted images he made for a living, Kwasniewski photographed snowstorms, cloud formations, rural scenes, and arrangements of leaves that he found interesting. Family history and photographic invention were other passions. In his free time the photographer took an active part in Polish fraternal societies, South Side business associations, and church and school groups. In perhaps his most surprising role, Kwasniewski was the agricultural editor of the *Kuryer Polski*.

But photography was the pursuit that defined Roman Kwasniewski for posterity. It is important to note that he was neither an artist nor a photojournalist but a photographer for hire. The vast majority of his images were made for clients who wanted a permanent and pleasing record of something important to them. The emphasis, therefore, is on the positive. But it is equally true that there were many positive moments to celebrate in the 1920s. Kwasniewski photographed a community on the rise, a group whose members were rapidly pulling away from the poverty of their early years. The proud businessmen, the well-fed children, and the confident couples in their Sunday best all reflect a definite upward mobility. Even in the 1930s, when Kwasniewski's commissions were fewer and farther between, the theme of forward progress is apparent.

Kwasniewski also photographed a community in transition. The vitality of Polish culture on the South Side is obvious in his images of dramatic societies and altar guilds, fraternal groups, and dance troupes. But automobiles, motion pictures, radios, marcelled hair, and other icons of the 1920s are perhaps even more prevalent in the collection. Buoyed by the Allied victory in World War I, climbing into respectability, Polish South Siders were embracing modernism. What these pictures show is a community welcoming the seeds of its own demise, the products of mass production that would promote a mass consciousness completely foreign to the insular reality of the South Side before World War I.

Kwasniewski's camera captured it all from the perspective of a single ethnic group in a single neighborhood in a single midwestern city, but his photographs have a resonance that carries far beyond Milwaukee's Polish South Side. By illuminating the particular in such satisfying detail, his images throw light on the generalities of life in America during the early decades of the twentieth century. What we see, reflected in a distant mirror, is ourselves.

Perusing the collection can be a journey of personal discovery for anyone with roots on Milwaukee's South Side. Kwasniewski's photographs include one of my own father, all of twenty years old, at the dedication of a Polish war veterans' home, standing proudly in his Company K uniform with a carbine at his side.

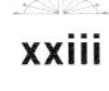

A closer look at the database turned up an even earlier picture of my father with his siblings, and a bevy of cousins, including one who ran a saloon on Lincoln Avenue. The same experience awaits hundreds of Milwaukee families.

And what became of all the people who gaze out at us from inside that distant mirror? Most have long since gone under the hill, but their children and grandchildren, myself included, are still on the scene. Like their counterparts in other American ethnic capitals, most Polish Milwaukeeans are by now several generations removed from Europe. For many, particularly those of blended heritage, ethnicity has become largely a matter of surname and perhaps Christmas customs. But a significant number take part in a rich organizational life whose focal point is the Polish Center of Wisconsin. Dedicated in 2000, the Polish Center is an elegant new building that overlooks a small, pristine lake in suburban Franklin. Its halls are well used for meetings, banquets, concerts, and cultural exhibits—including the photographs of Roman Kwasniewski.

The building is also a final realization of the upward mobility that Kwasniewski began to capture on film in the 1920s. There is a subtle irony in its design. The center is modeled after the great manor houses of eighteenth-century Poland, complete with a cavernous entrance hall like those the nobility used to greet their guests. What the Polish Center expresses is a triumphant sense of arrival: a people who left Europe as peasants have become, in the crucible of American democracy, the landed gentry. I suspect that Roman Kwasniewski would not be the least bit surprised.

—John Gurda

CHAPTER ONE

Neighborhood

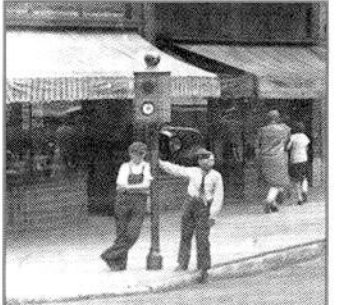
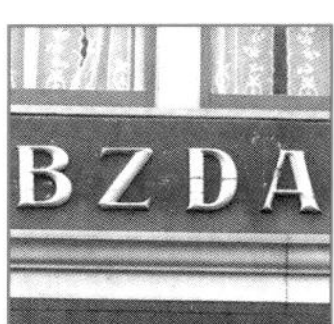

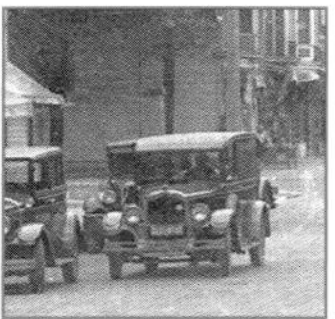
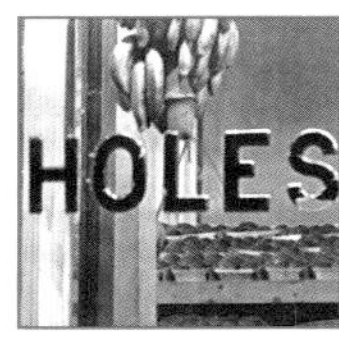

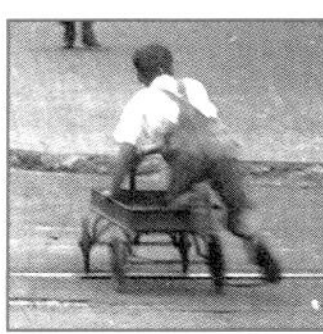

Roman Kwasniewski lived and worked in an extraordinarily small world. The heart of the South Side's Polonia in his day was bordered by what are now First and Thirty-fifth Streets between Greenfield and Morgan Avenues—an area of just over six square miles. Although he traveled farther afield on occasion, Kwasniewski did most of his work within the confines of that neighborhood. It was, and is, a distinctly low-rise section of the city. To the north, east, and west were industrial districts that provided local residents with jobs. Streetcar-oriented commercial streets crossed at regular intervals: Greenfield Avenue, Lincoln Avenue, Muskego Avenue, and most important of all, Mitchell Street. For generations of South Siders, "going downtown" meant shopping on Mitchell Street. Dubbed "the Polish Grand Avenue," it generally ranked third among Milwaukee's retail districts in sales volume, trailing only Wisconsin (formerly Grand) Avenue and North Third Street.

Although its edges were industrial and its seams were commercial, the heart of the neighborhood was intensely residential, a thick carpet of Polish flats, alley houses, and in the blocks south of Oklahoma Avenue, Milwaukee bungalows. Corner saloons abounded, and practically every block had its butcher shop, bakery, or grocery store. Parks provided welcome respite from the density of the South Side. The three largest were named for community heroes: Generals Thaddeus

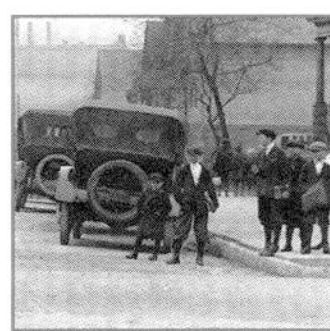
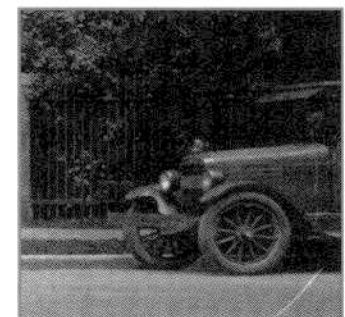
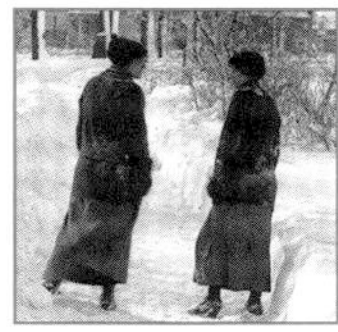
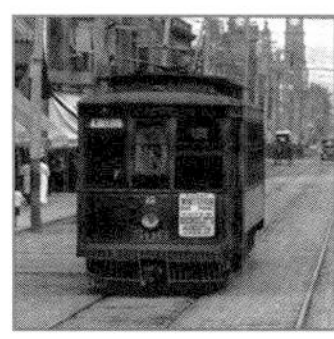
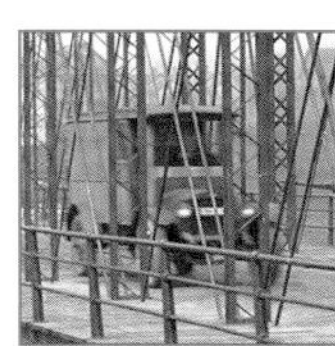

Kosciuszko and Casimir Pulaski, both prominent figures in the American Revolution; and Reverend Felix Baran, the long-time pastor of St. Josaphat.

The South Side was an unusually self-contained community, a separate settlement that would have been Wisconsin's second-largest city if a rift had somehow opened at the Menomonee Valley. From its profusion of small businesses to its abundance of small homes, the South Side was built at the human scale, and the human dimension is a constant in Roman Kwasniewski's photographs.

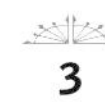

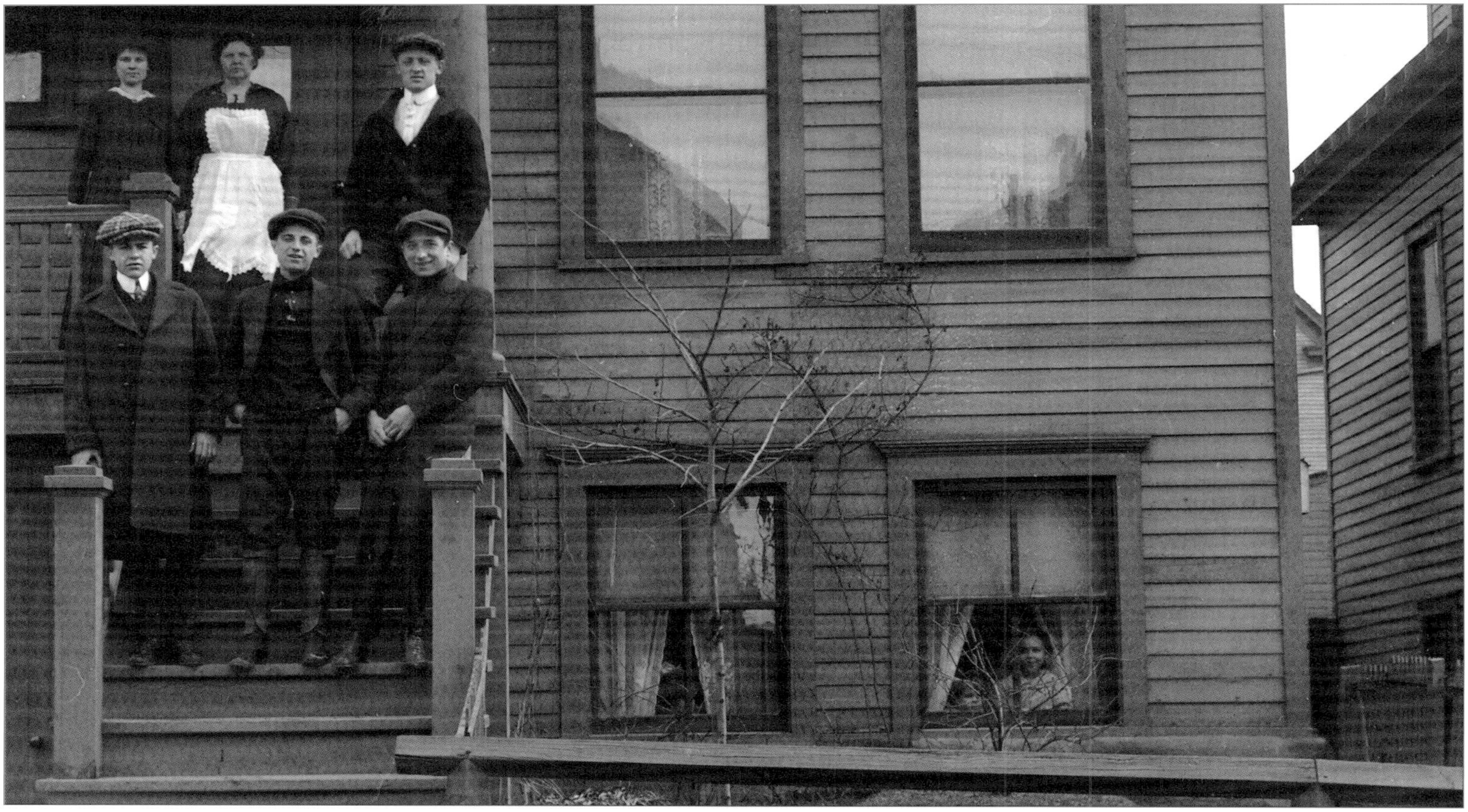

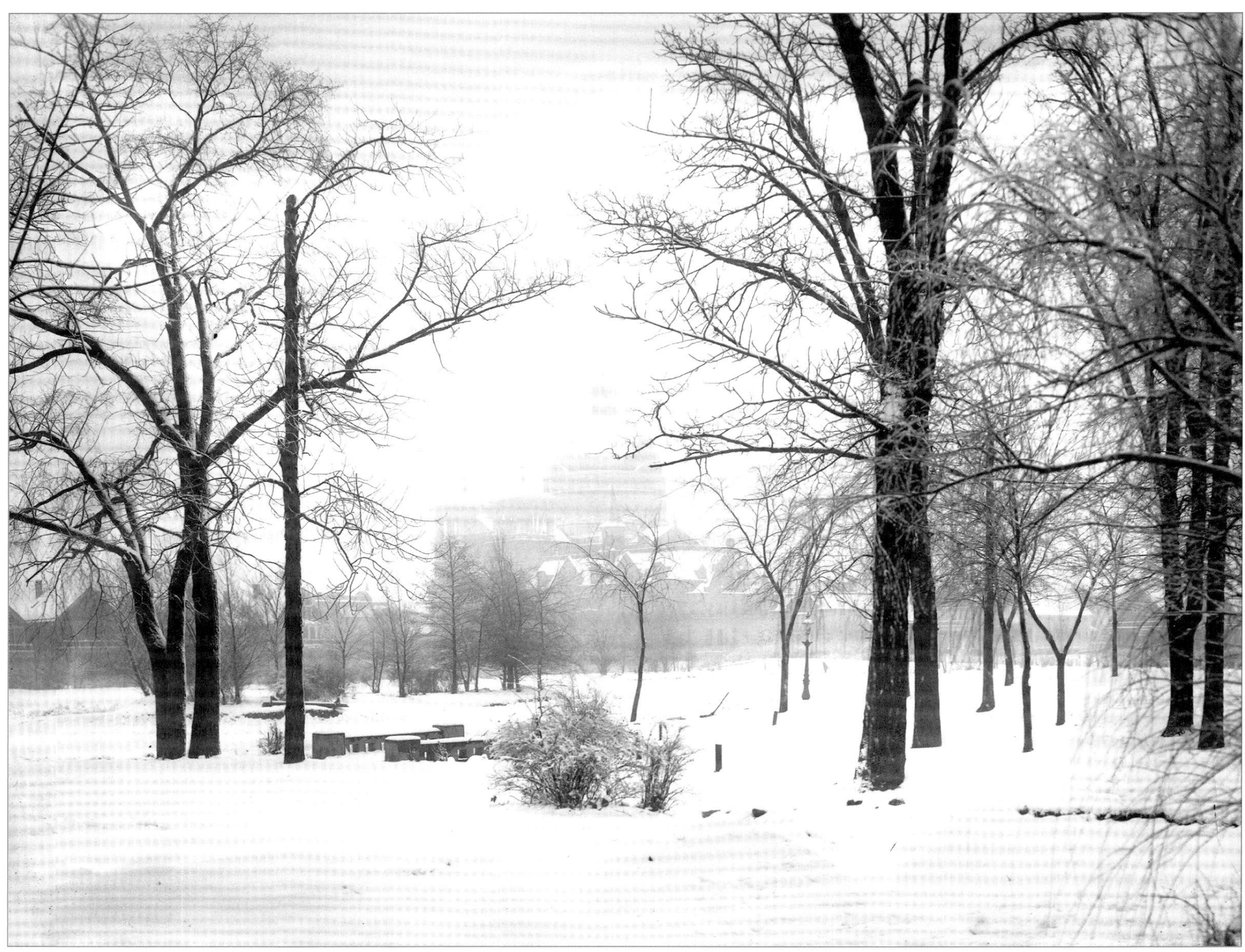

A snowstorm on March 16, 1913, blanketed Kosciuszko Park and the Basilica of St. Josaphat, leaving this idyllic wintertime scene. The Basilica of St. Josaphat, dedicated in 1901, is one of the most magnificent buildings on Milwaukee's South Side.
Serial # A07336

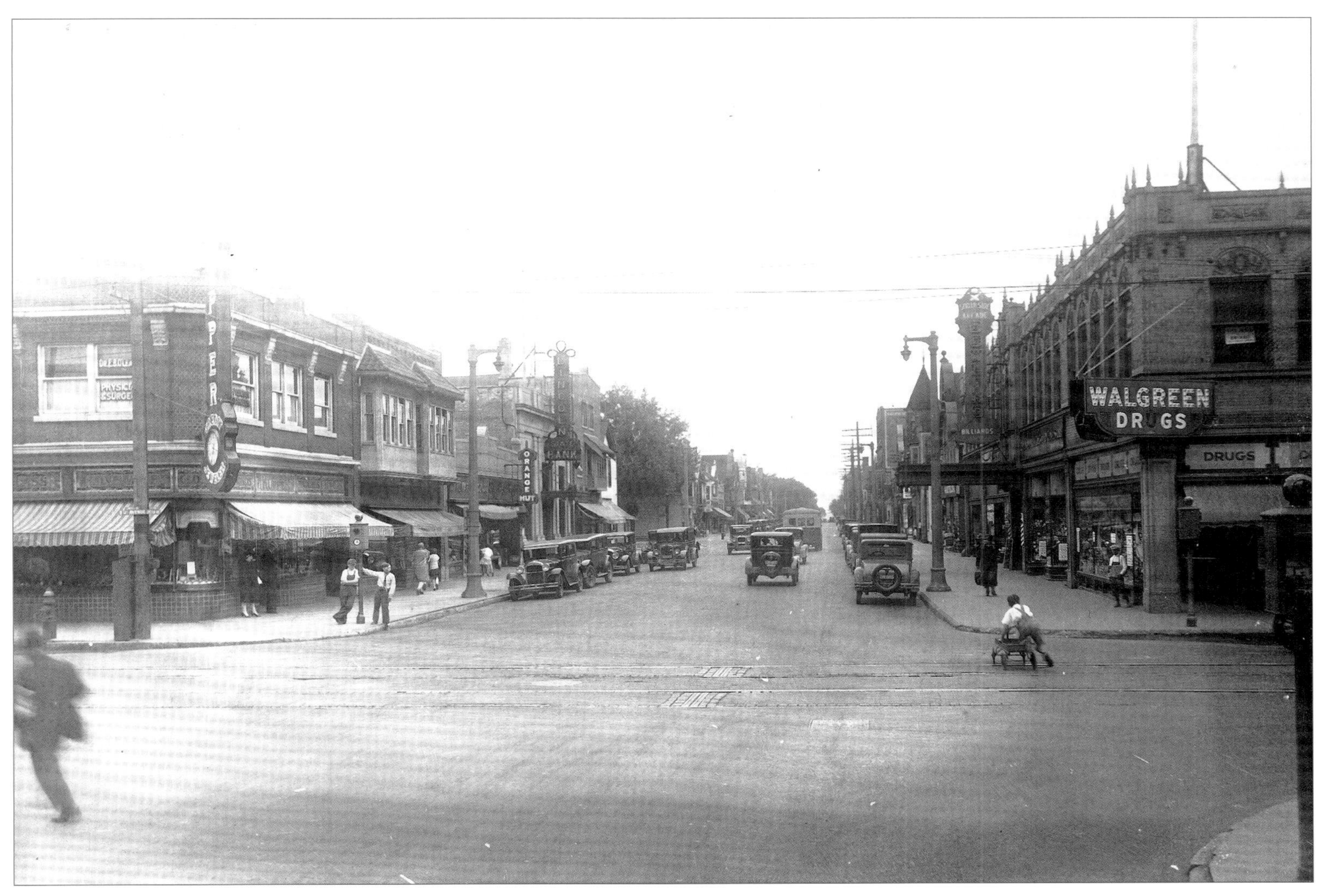

Looking east on Lincoln Avenue from the corner of Eighth Avenue (shortly thereafter renamed South Thirteenth Street) on a busy June afternoon in 1930. Lincoln Avenue and Mitchell Street were the main commercial areas on Milwaukee's South Side. *Serial # 29681-1*

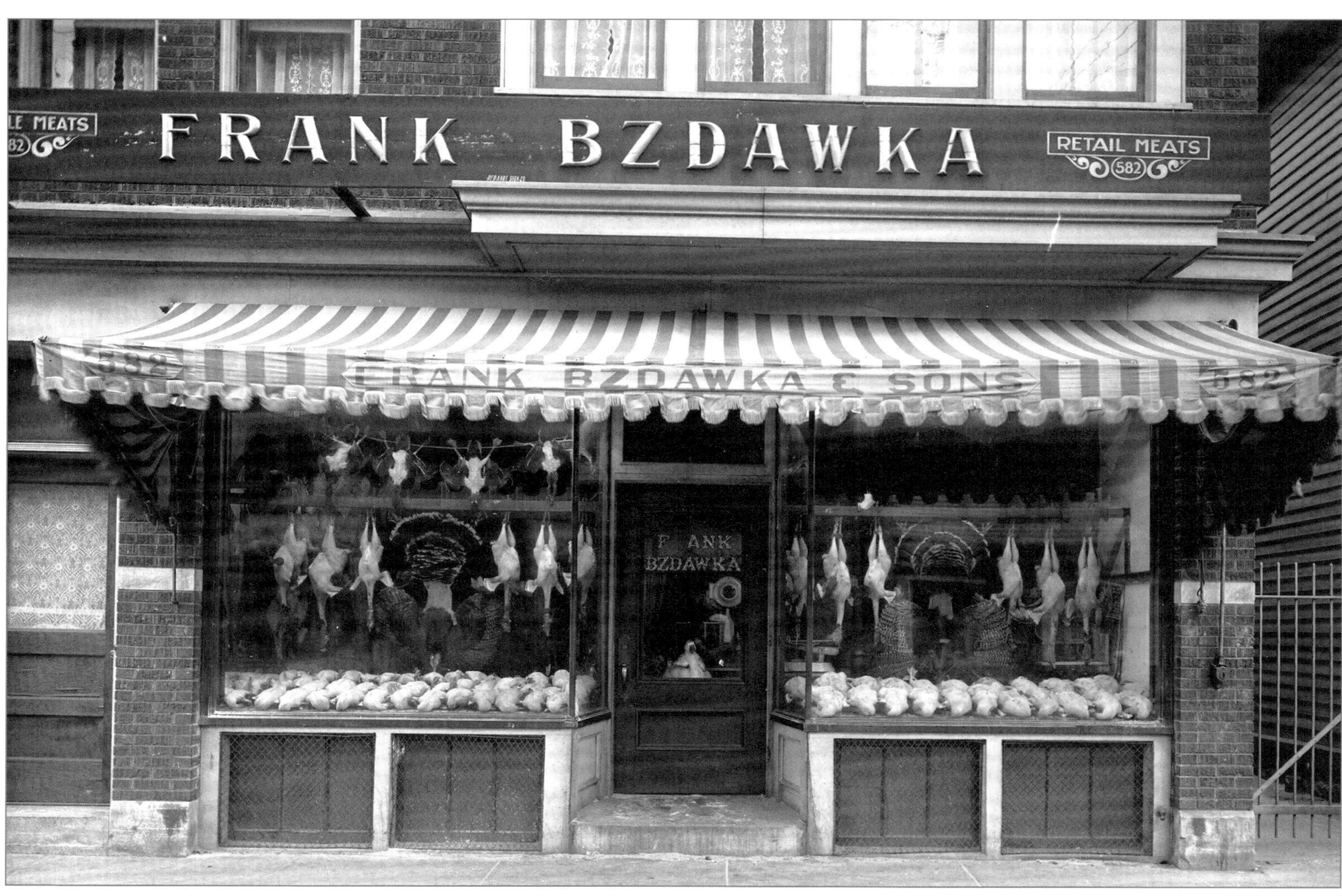

In late 1927 the "show window" of the Frank Bzdawka meat market on Lincoln Avenue featured birds with feathers hanging amid fowl ready for the frying pan. A duck can also be seen peeking out of the door window. ***Serial # 27003***

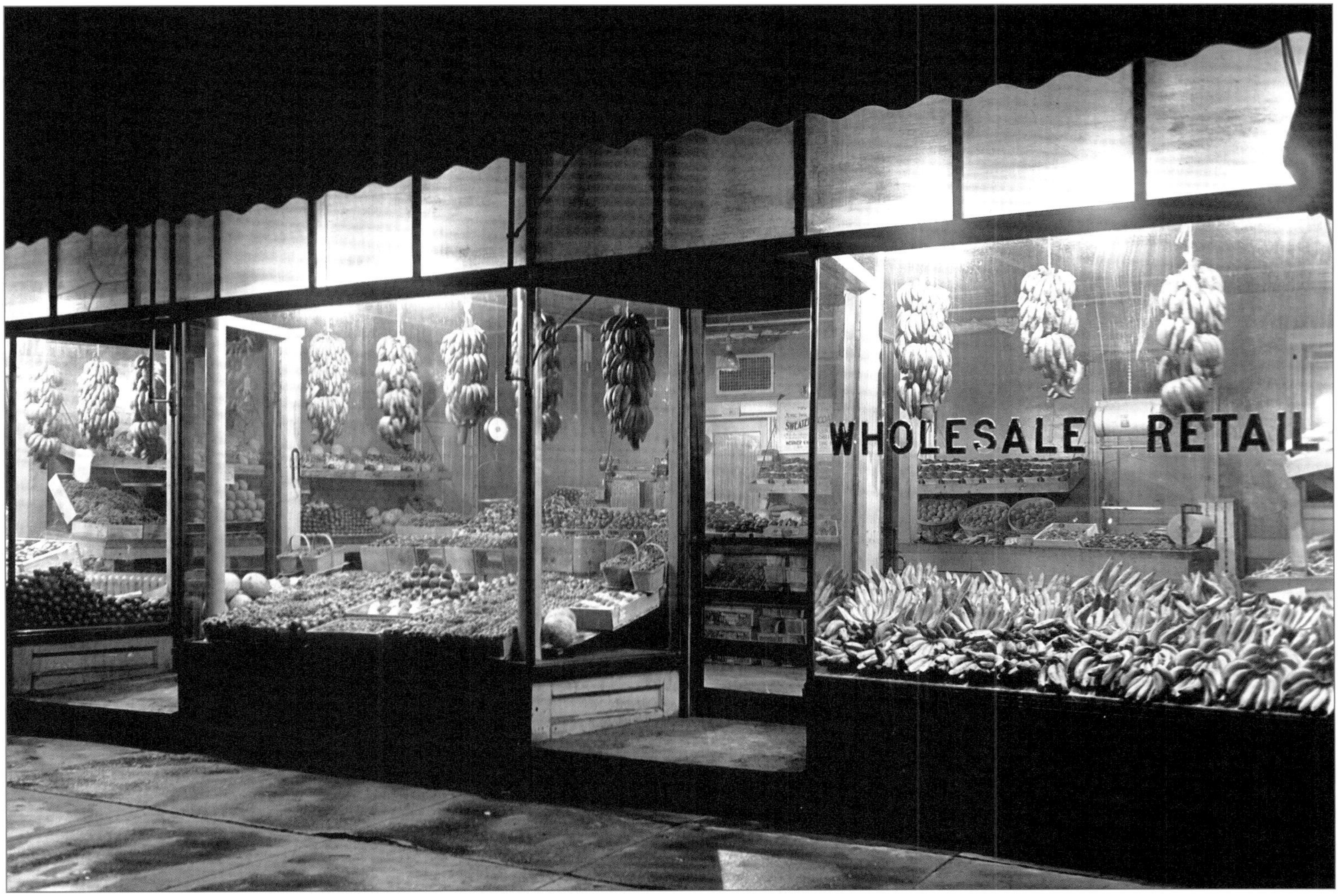

Roman Kwasniewski rarely took photographs of his neighborhood after dark. He captured this image of the well-stocked Lincoln Fruit Store in 1925, as bright lights illuminated the interior and reflected on the wet sidewalk outside.

Serial # 24816-1

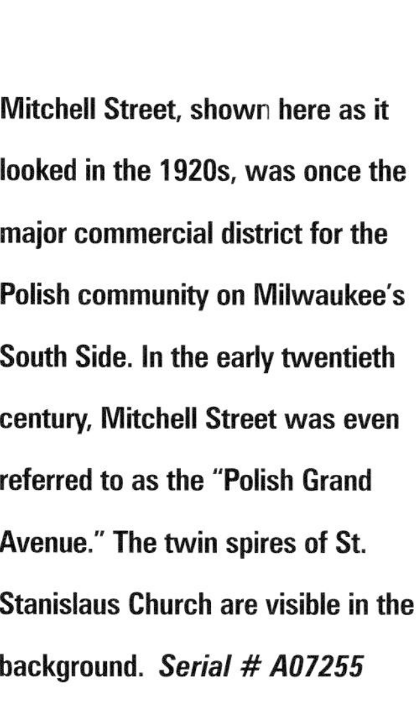

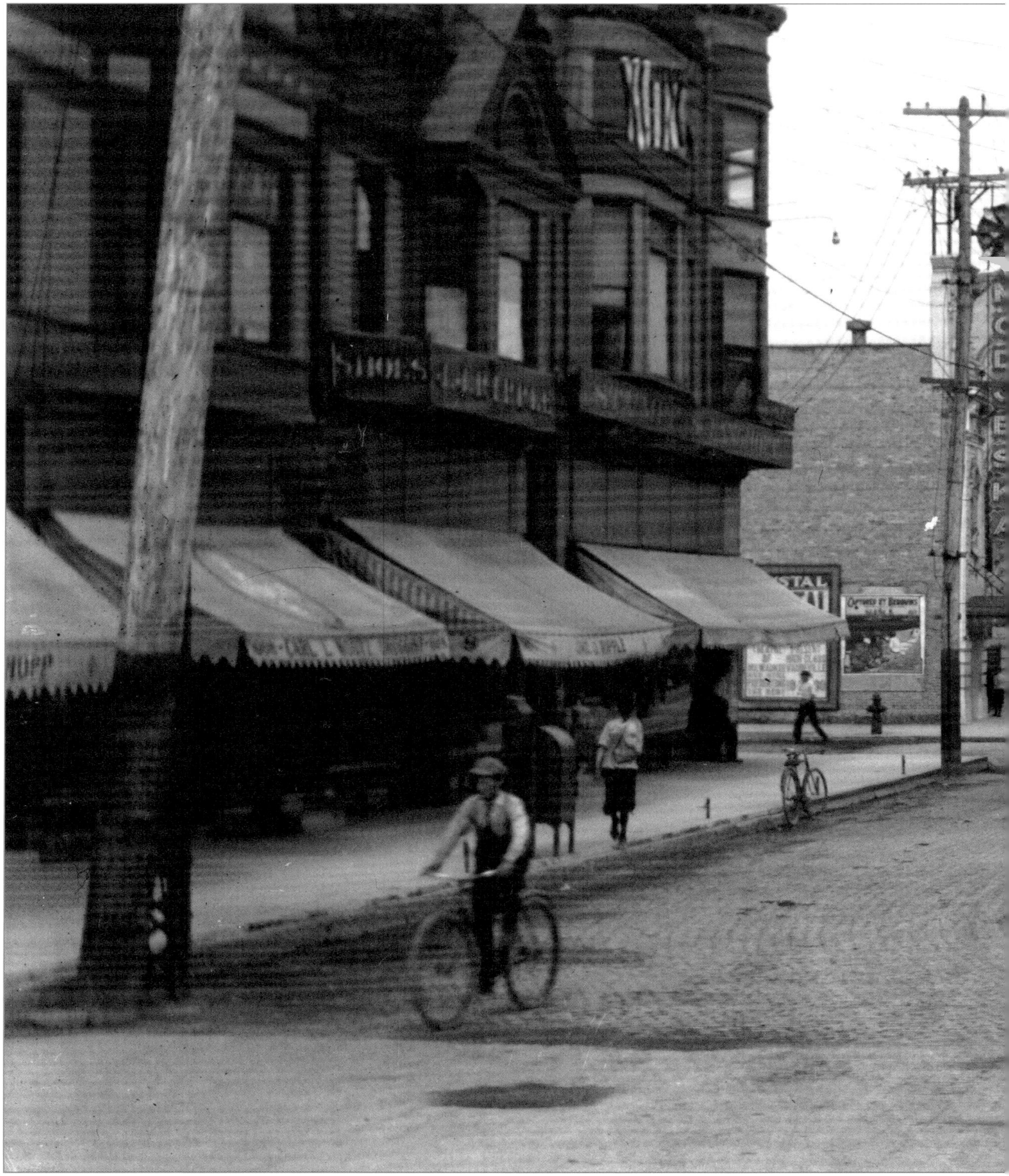

Mitchell Street, shown here as it looked in the 1920s, was once the major commercial district for the Polish community on Milwaukee's South Side. In the early twentieth century, Mitchell Street was even referred to as the "Polish Grand Avenue." The twin spires of St. Stanislaus Church are visible in the background. ***Serial # A07255***

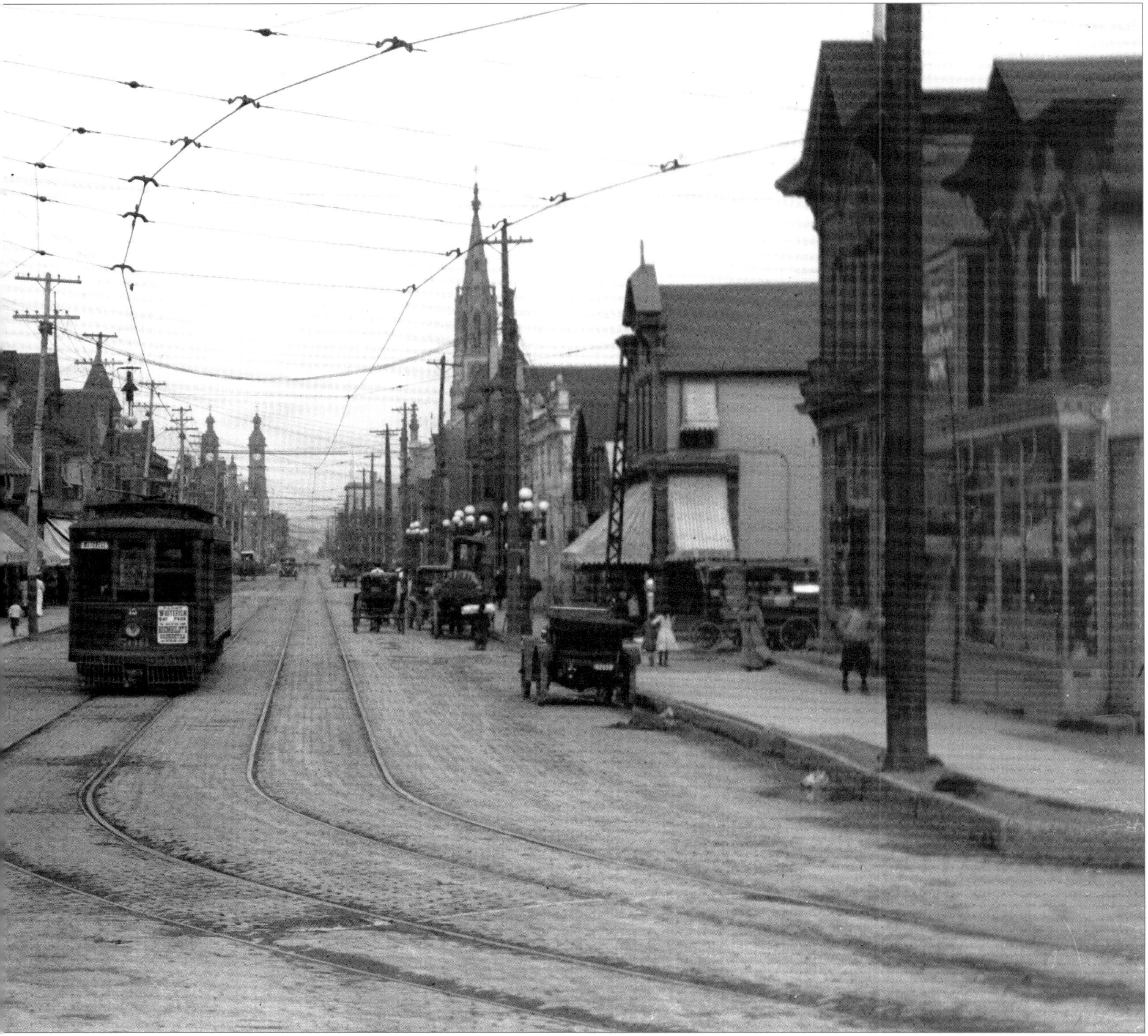

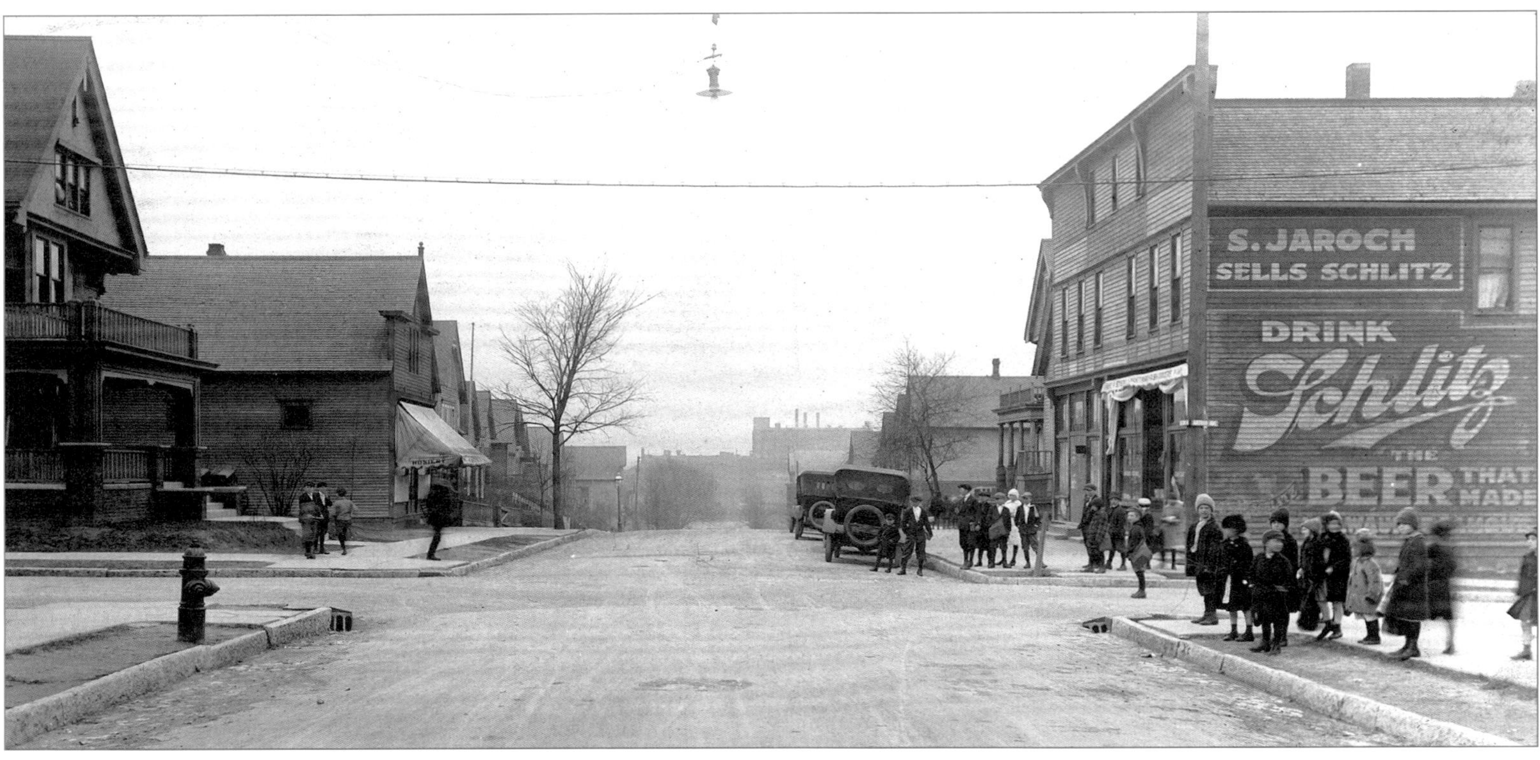

Perhaps the children standing on the corners of Second Avenue (later South Seventh Street) and Arthur Avenue on this day in the early 1920s were waiting while their parents called on Stanley Jaroch, who sold Schlitz, "the beer that made Milwaukee famous." ***Serial # A15315***

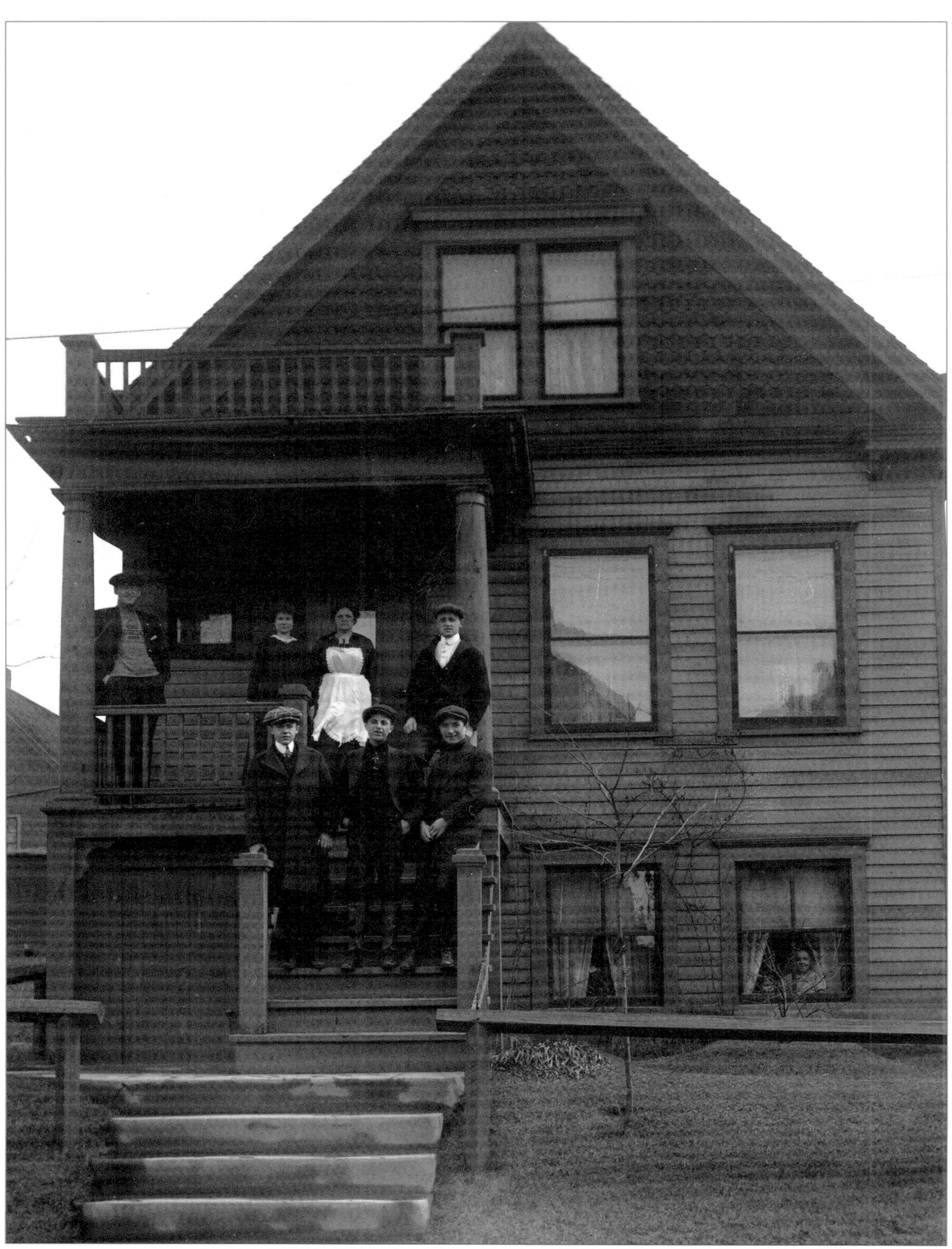

This family posed on the steps of their raised, or "Polish," flat while youngsters inside the house watched out of a lower window. Houses of this type are typically found in the formerly Polish areas on Milwaukee's South Side. It was common practice for the Polish immigrants of the area to purchase wooden houses that they raised to create a basement apartment when additional space was needed. Undated. *Serial # A06279*

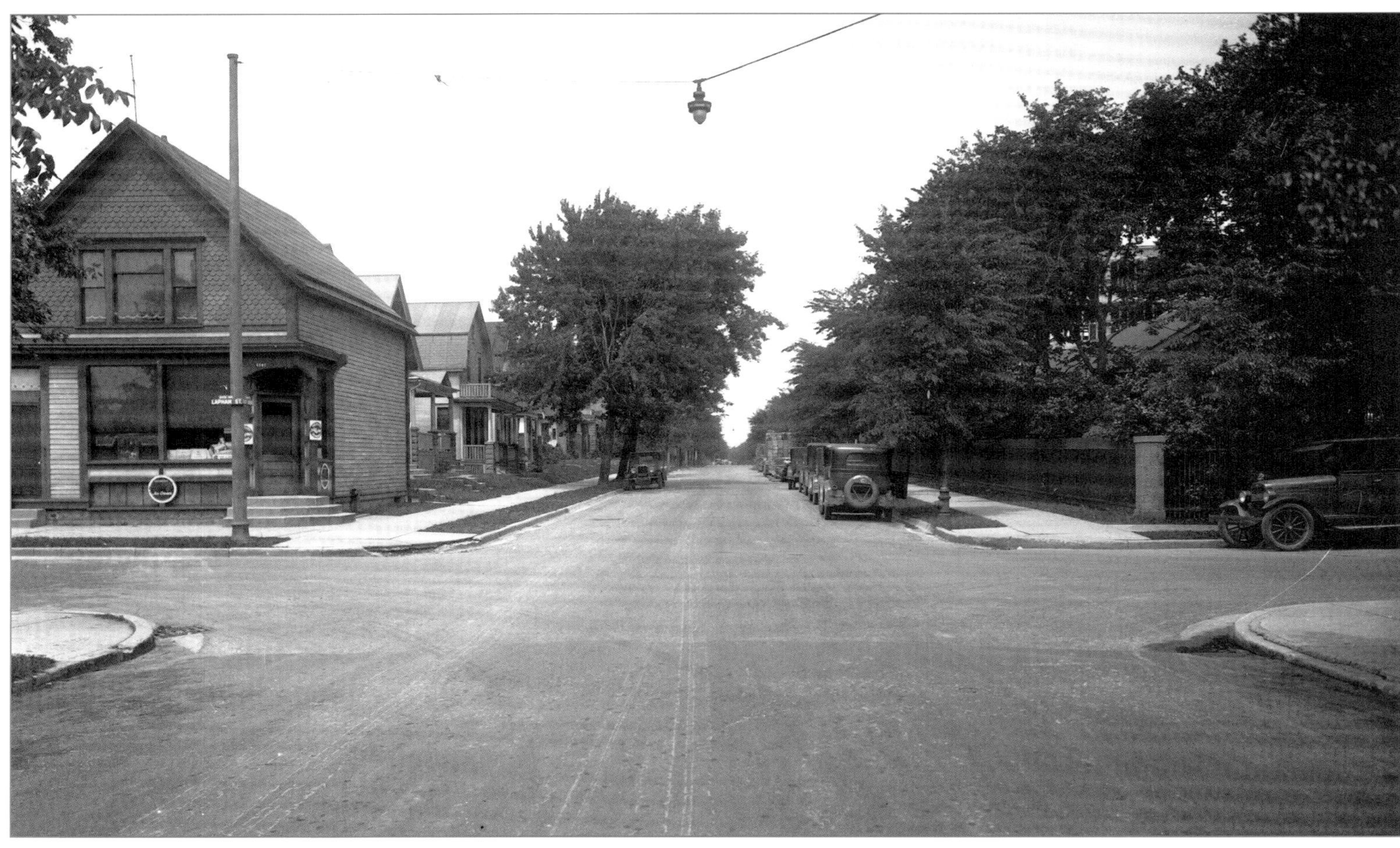

This June 1928 photograph shows a pleasant, tree-lined Lapham Street neighborhood with a corner business establishment.

Serial # 28551

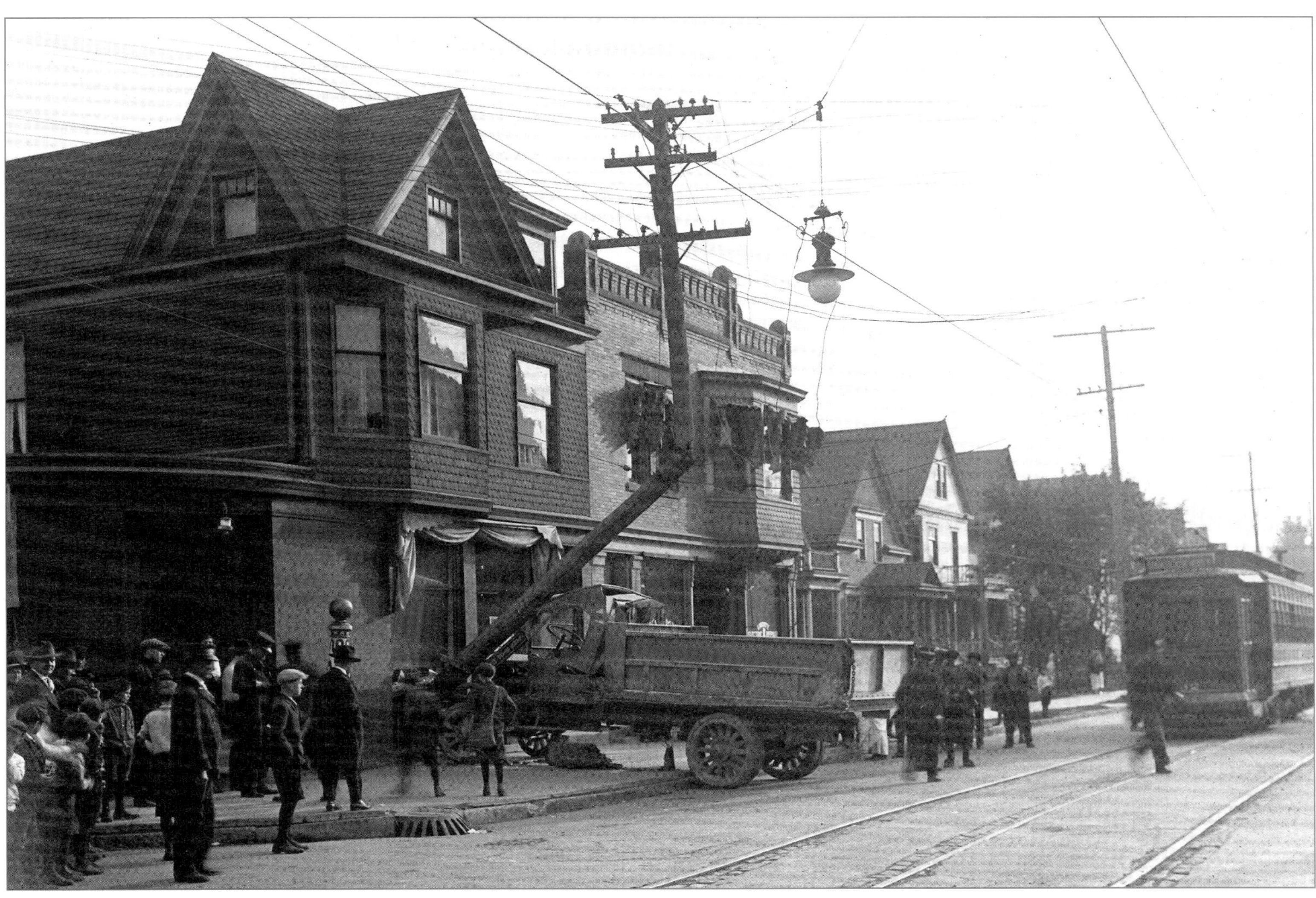

Kwasniewski was often called on to take photographs for insurance purposes. Accidents were unavoidable, especially when modern vehicles had to share the roadway with streetcars and horse-drawn wagons, not to mention pedestrians. This accident occurred near the corner of Becher Street and Windlake Avenue around 1921. The sign on the pole that was hit reads "Cars Stop Here," adding a touch of irony to the scene. ***Serial # A07151***

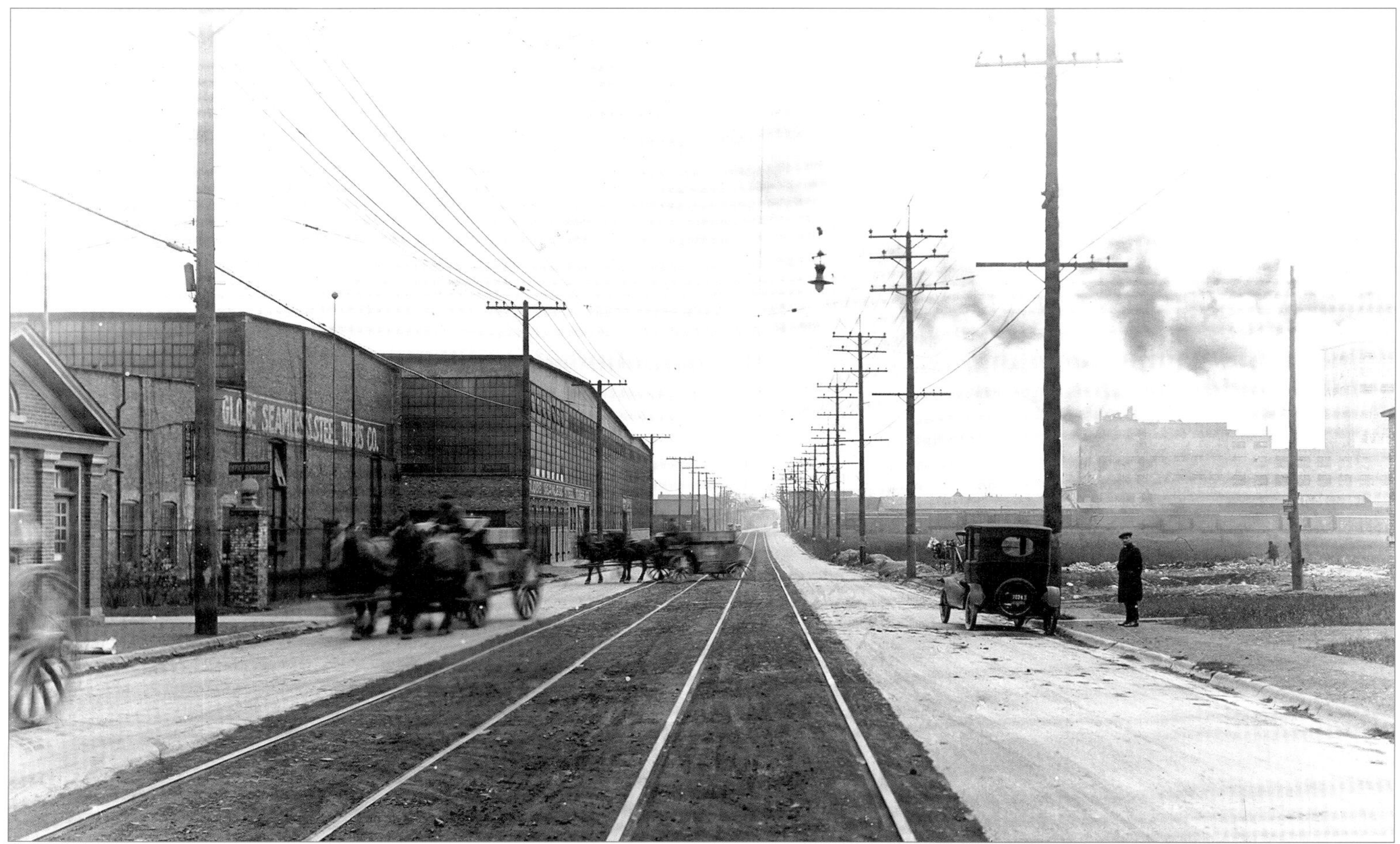

By 1922 the Burnham Street and Thirty-third Avenue (now South Thirty-eighth Street) area was undergoing widespread industrial growth. Foundries like the American Metal Products Company and the Globe Seamless Steel Tubes Company, as well as construction, malting, and milling companies, were located in this part of Milwaukee. At that time, the local industrialist drove his automobile to work, while most employees took the streetcar. The Chicago & North Western Railway had shipping lines in the area, yet local deliveries were still made with horse and wagon. ***Serial # 20189***

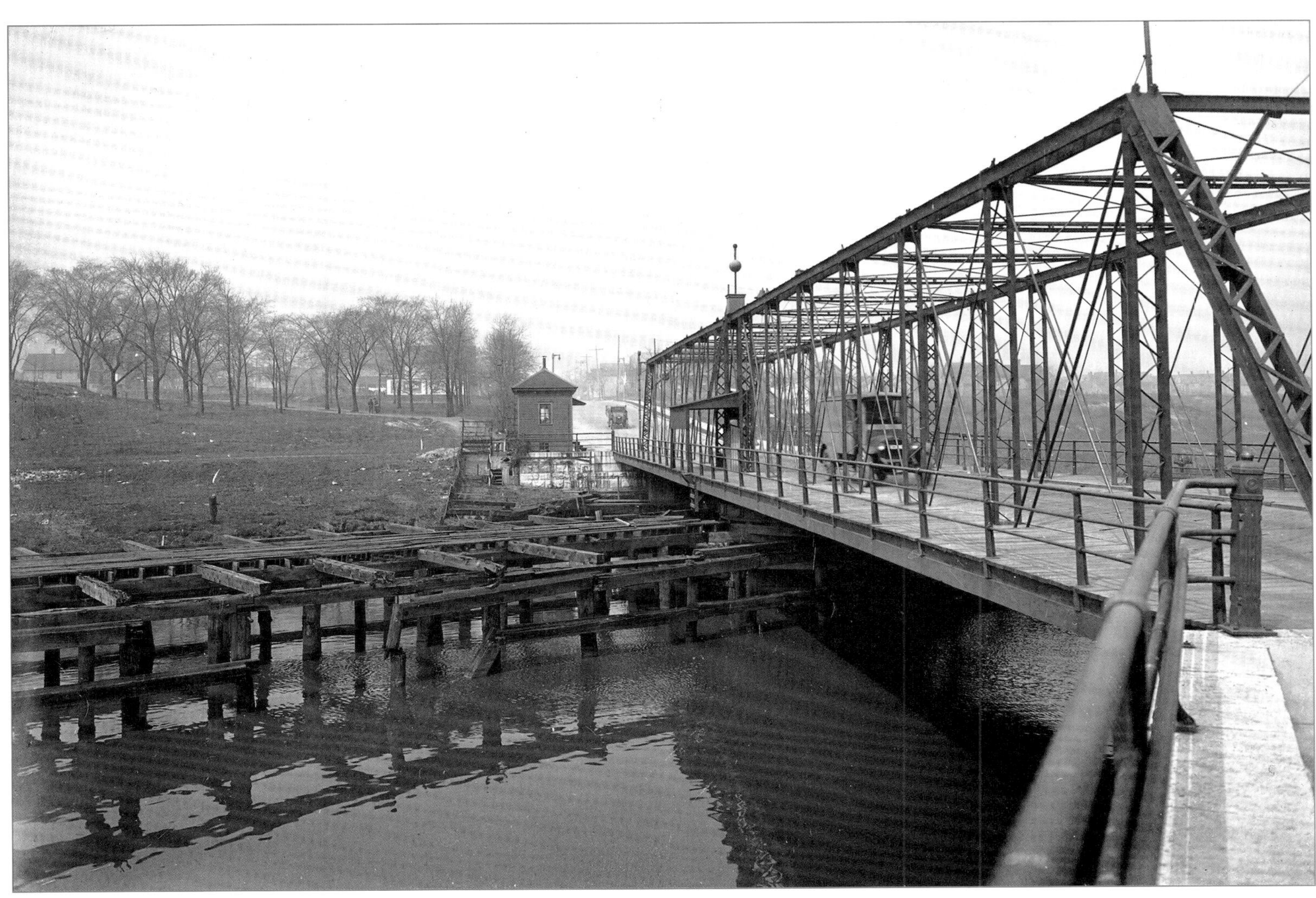

Kwasniewski captured this view of the Lincoln Avenue bridge from the east in April 1924. The bridge crosses the Kinnickinnic River. Baran Park is in the left of this photograph. ***Serial # A07252***

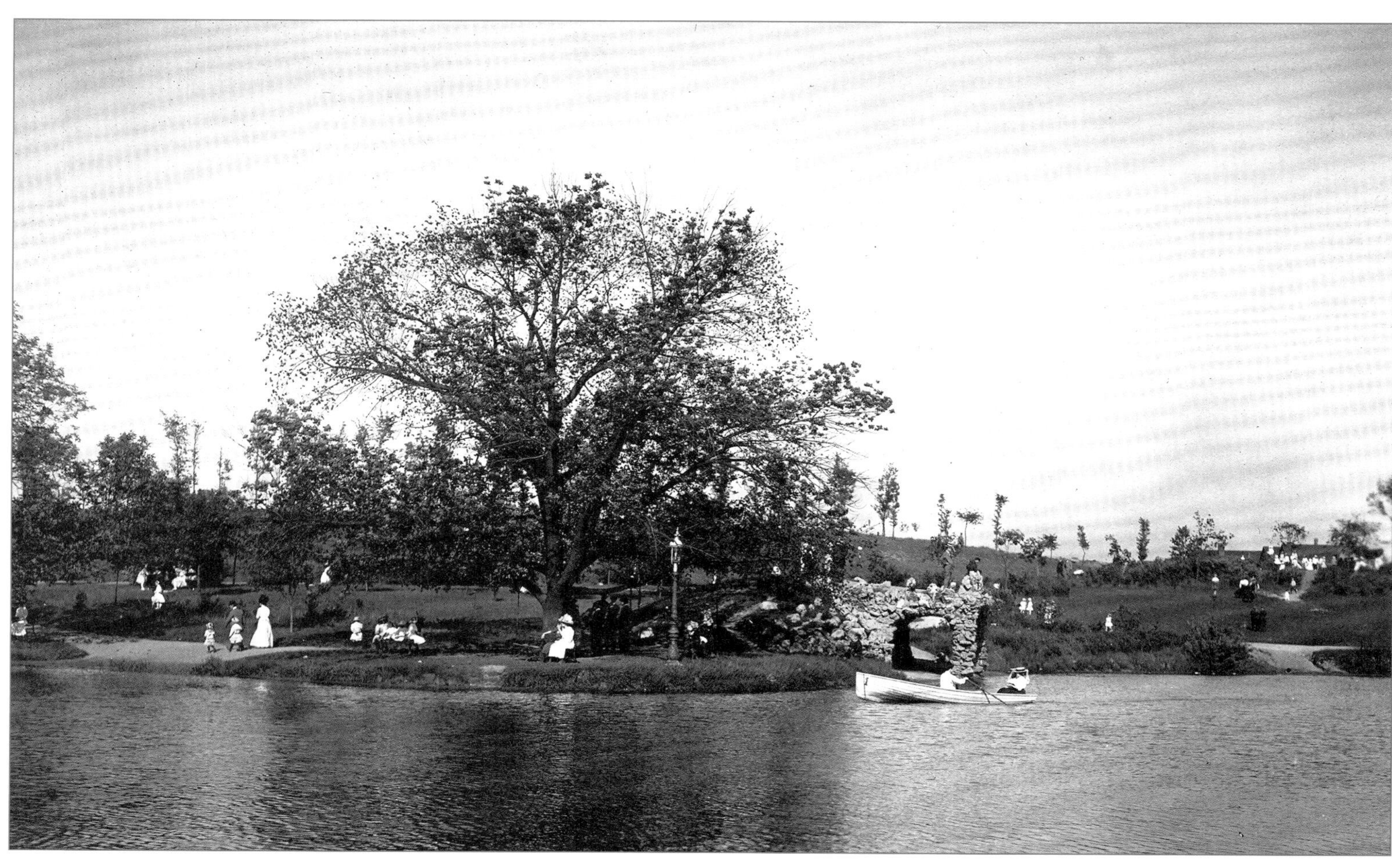

April 18, 1912, was a pleasant day for a boat ride or a stroll through Kosciuszko Park. ***Serial # A04373***

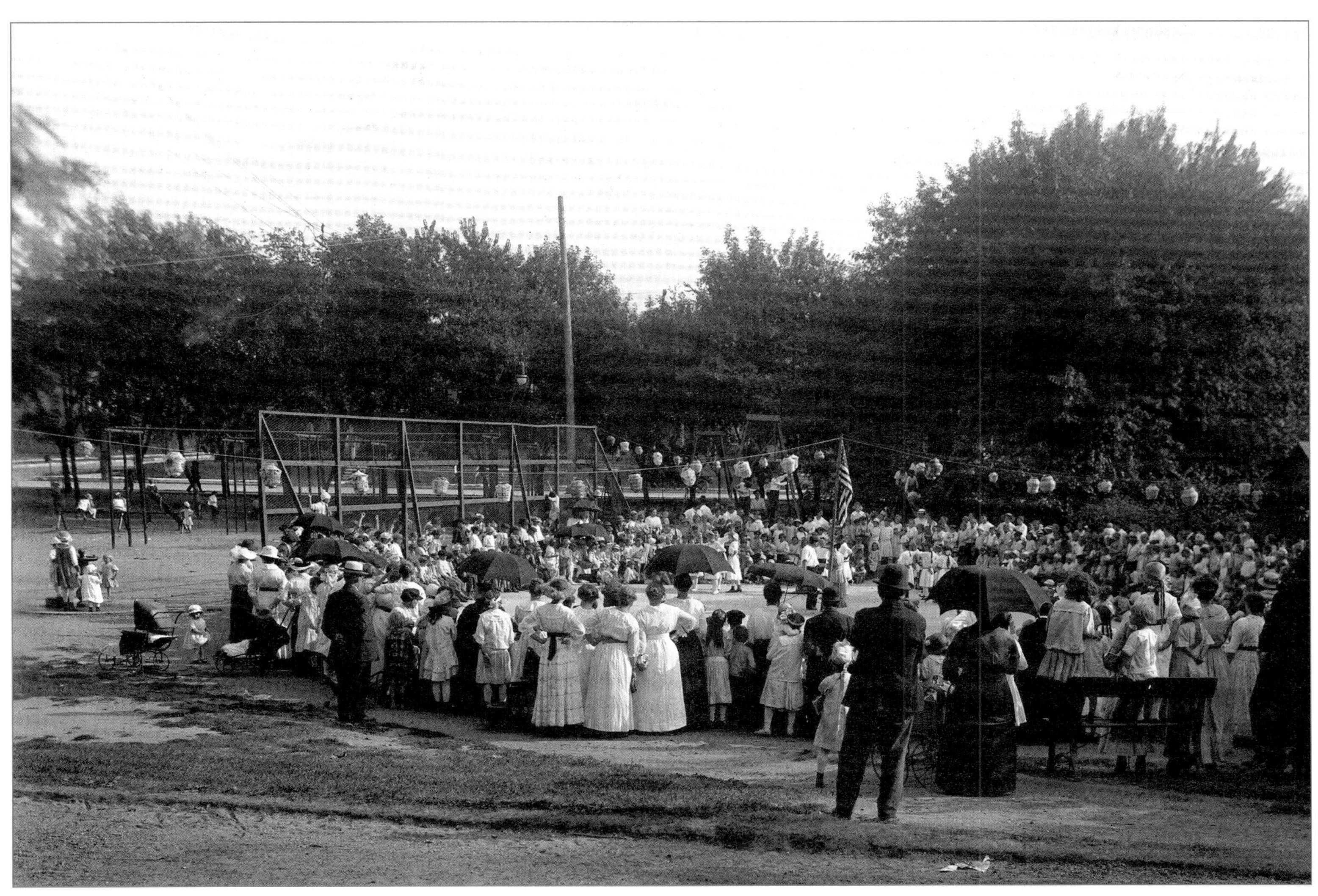

Milwaukee's parks have always been places to enjoy outdoor activities. While most of the people in this August 1915 photograph in Kosciuszko Park were watching several groups of young ladies dancing, some younger children were more interested in the park's playground equipment. ***Serial # A07101-2***

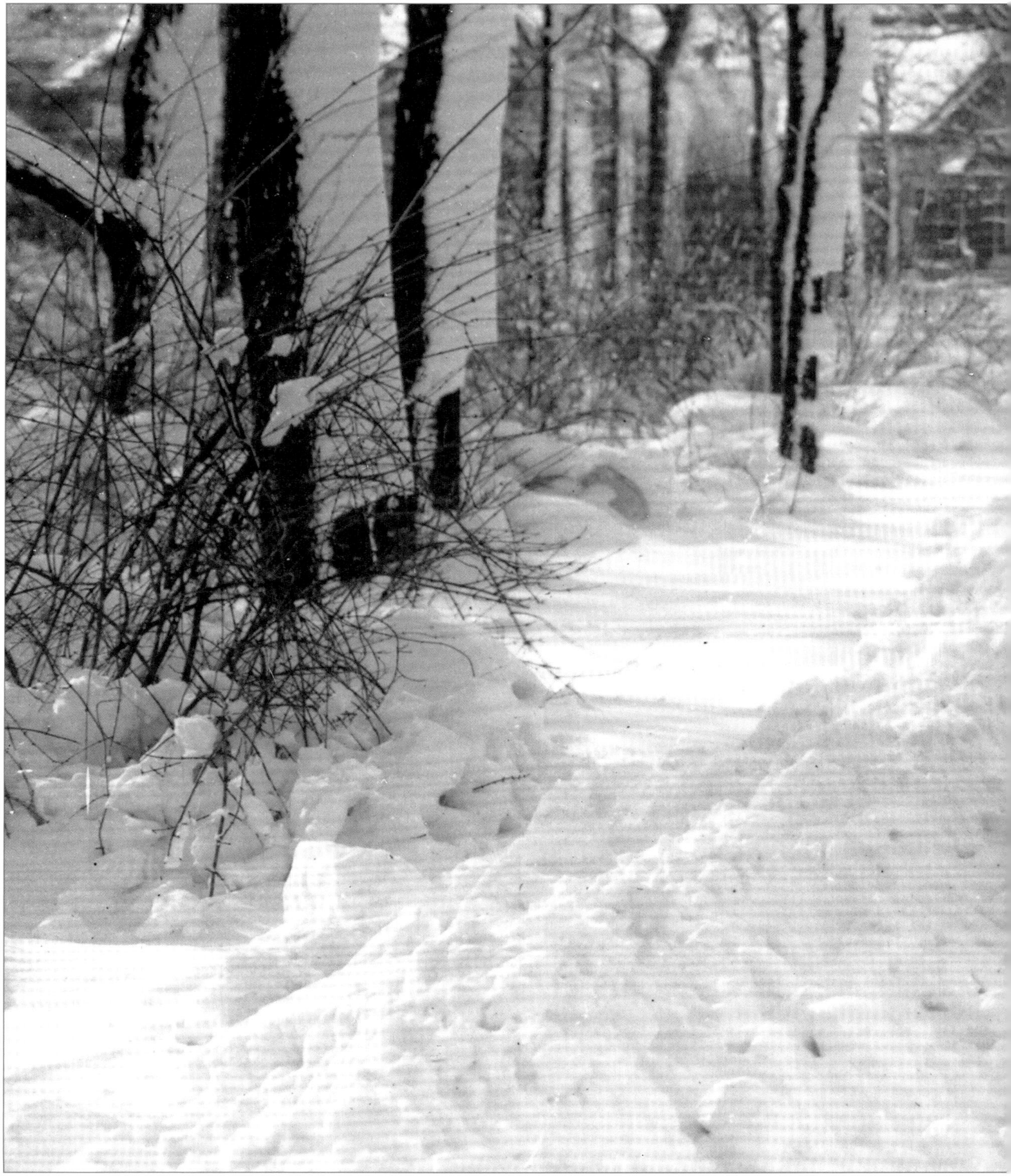

Perhaps some interesting gossip caused these young women to stop while on their walk through Kosciuszko Park after a storm left some fresh snow in March 1916.

Serial # A07202

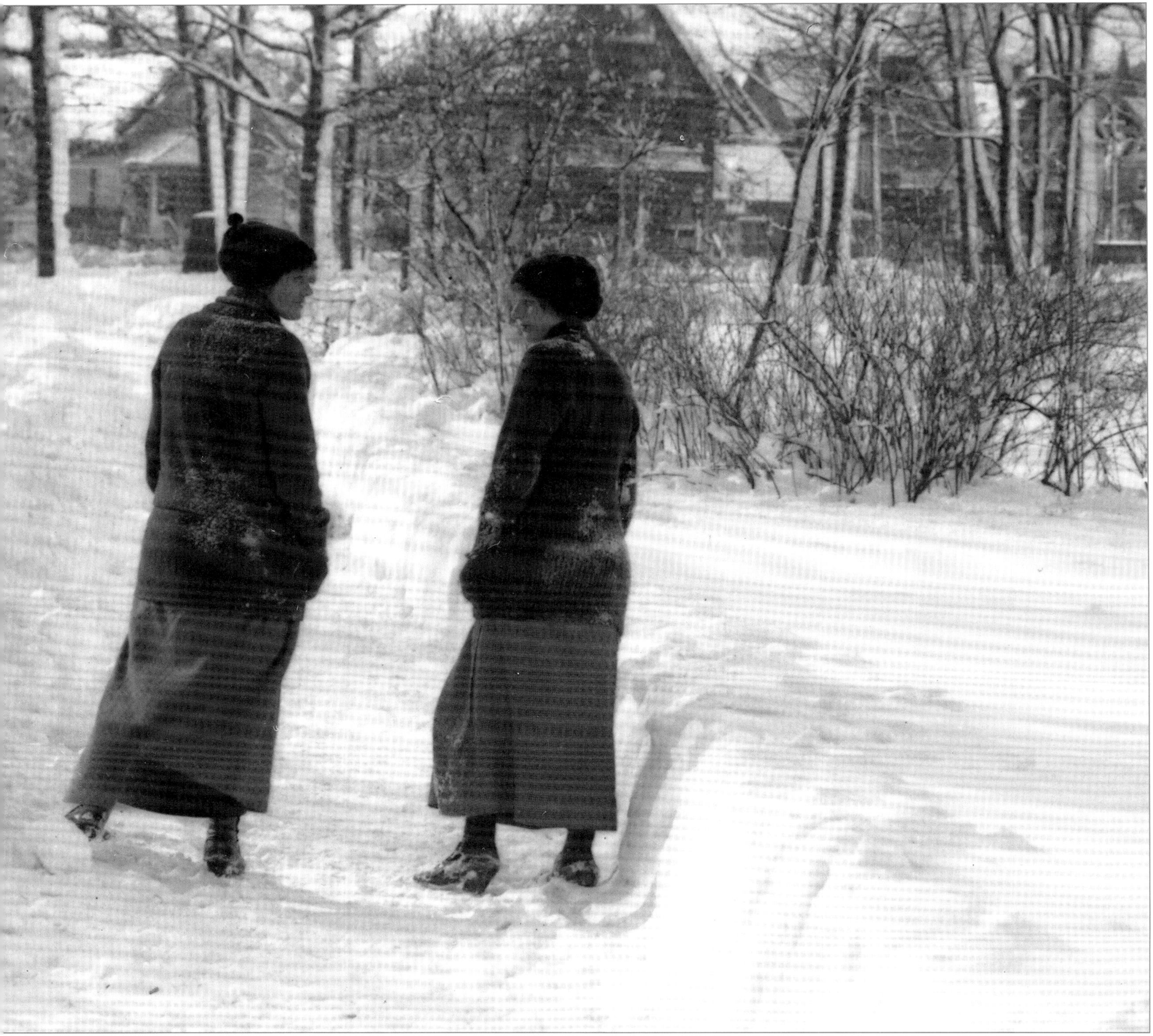

CHAPTER TWO

FAMILY

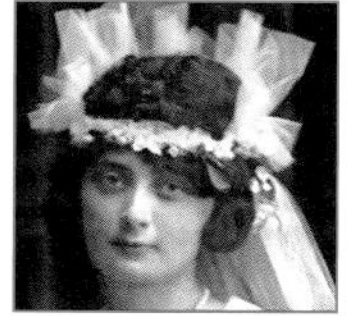
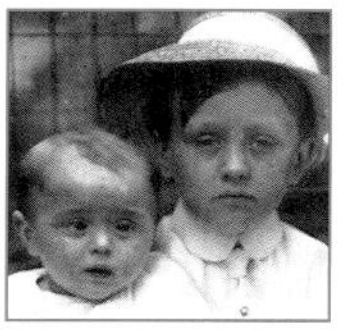
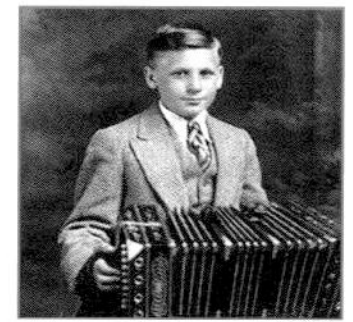
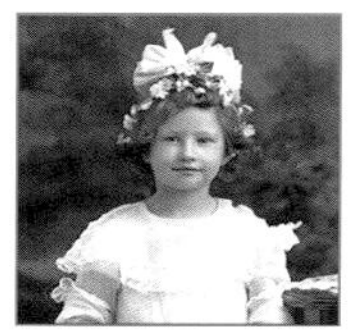
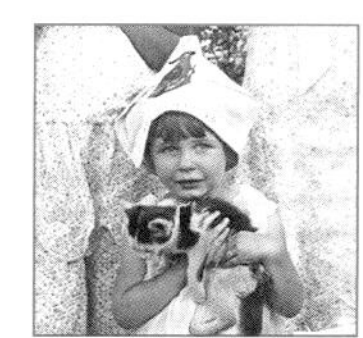

With the rise of the tintype in the late nineteenth century, even people of modest means had a chance at immortality, and later developments substantially enlarged the democratic possibilities of photography. No longer was it only the wealthy or well known who sat for their portraits; it could be anyone. Roman Kwasniewski's collection includes a generous sampling of photographs that embody the desire for a durable image on Milwaukee's Polish South Side.

His clients wanted likenesses, of course, but the likenesses they chose expressed characteristic values of the community. Kwasniewski's studio work is dominated by images of family. The portraits and party shots are to be expected, but clients also wanted records of family homesteads, be they ever so humble. The homes and gardens in the collection underscore the distinctive pride in property that blossomed on the South Side.

Even more important were family milestones, many of them religious. As the community's young people progressed from First Communion to confirmation and from graduation to marriage, Roman Kwasniewski preserved each step for posterity. The milestones included death. For those without a recent photograph, Kwasniewski took one in the coffin, and the resulting image was often shared with extended family members on the other side of the Atlantic.

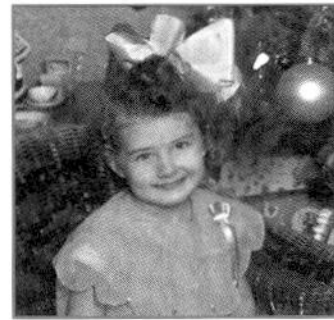
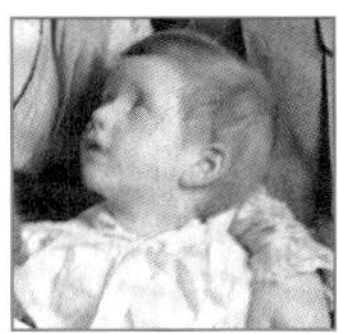
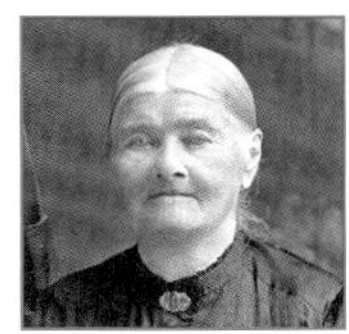
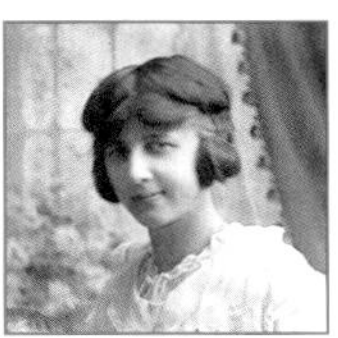
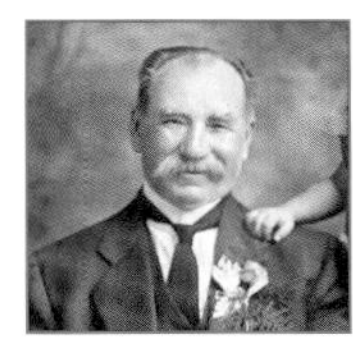

The Germans have a word for the South Side's characteristic outlook: *Gemütlichkeit*. It signifies a determinedly home-centered approach to life, an emphasis on comfort, harmony, and domestic tranquility. The term originated with Milwaukee's largest ethnic group, but it translates easily into Polish and the full range of other tongues that were heard in the community.

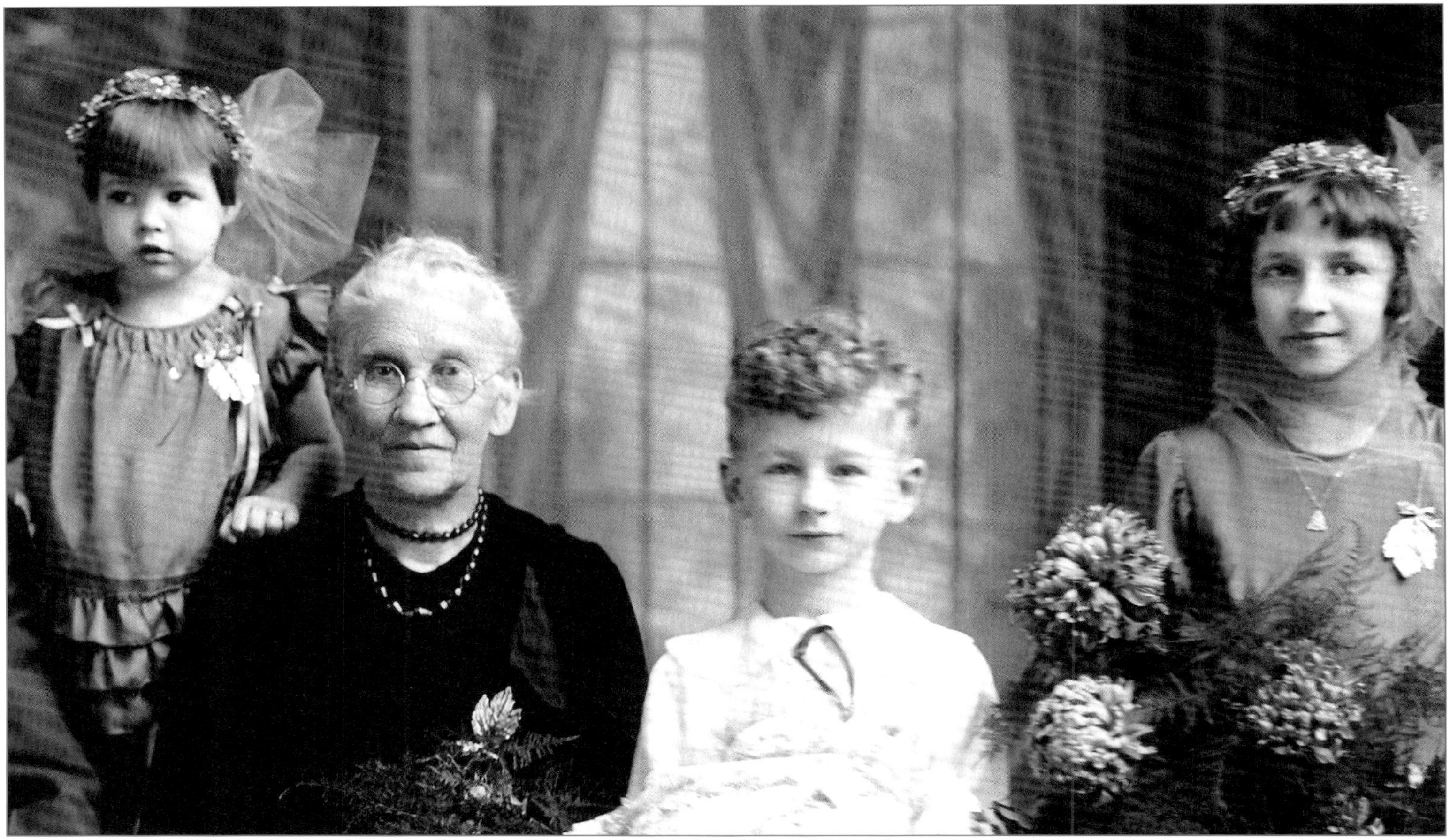

This young newlywed couple, members of the Frank J. Brown family, and their attendants visited Kwasniewski's Park Studio for a formal portrait on their special day in August 1921. The rather youthful looking naval servicemen felt it appropriate to wear their uniforms for the occasion. In Milwaukee County that year, the highest percentage of brides (43 percent) were between twenty and twenty-four years of age. Grooms were older, with the highest percentage (34 percent) between the ages of twenty-five and twenty-nine. Illustrating further that women married younger, 18 percent of the brides in 1921 were between fifteen and nineteen, whereas only 2 percent of the grooms fell into that age group. *Serial # 17952*

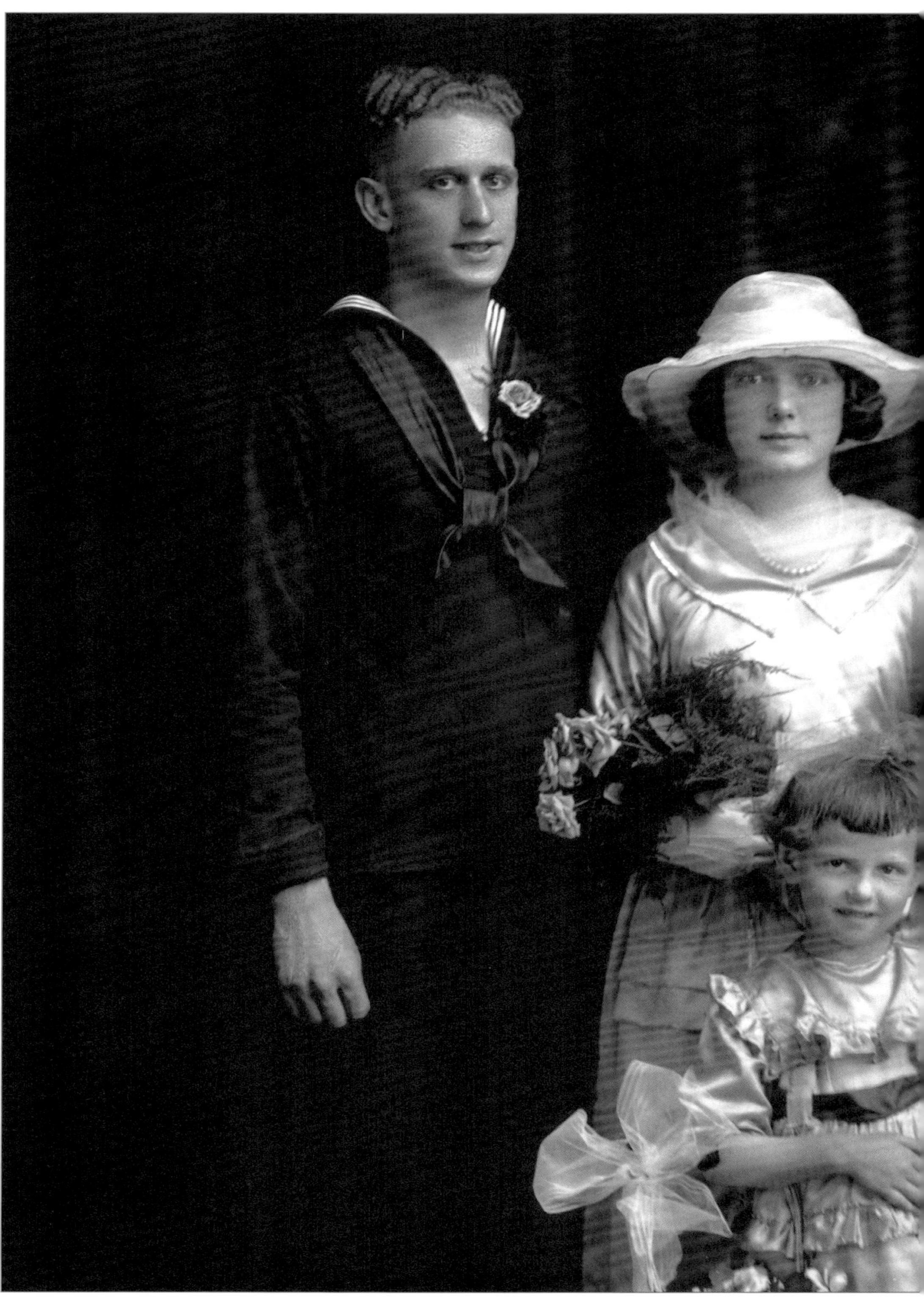

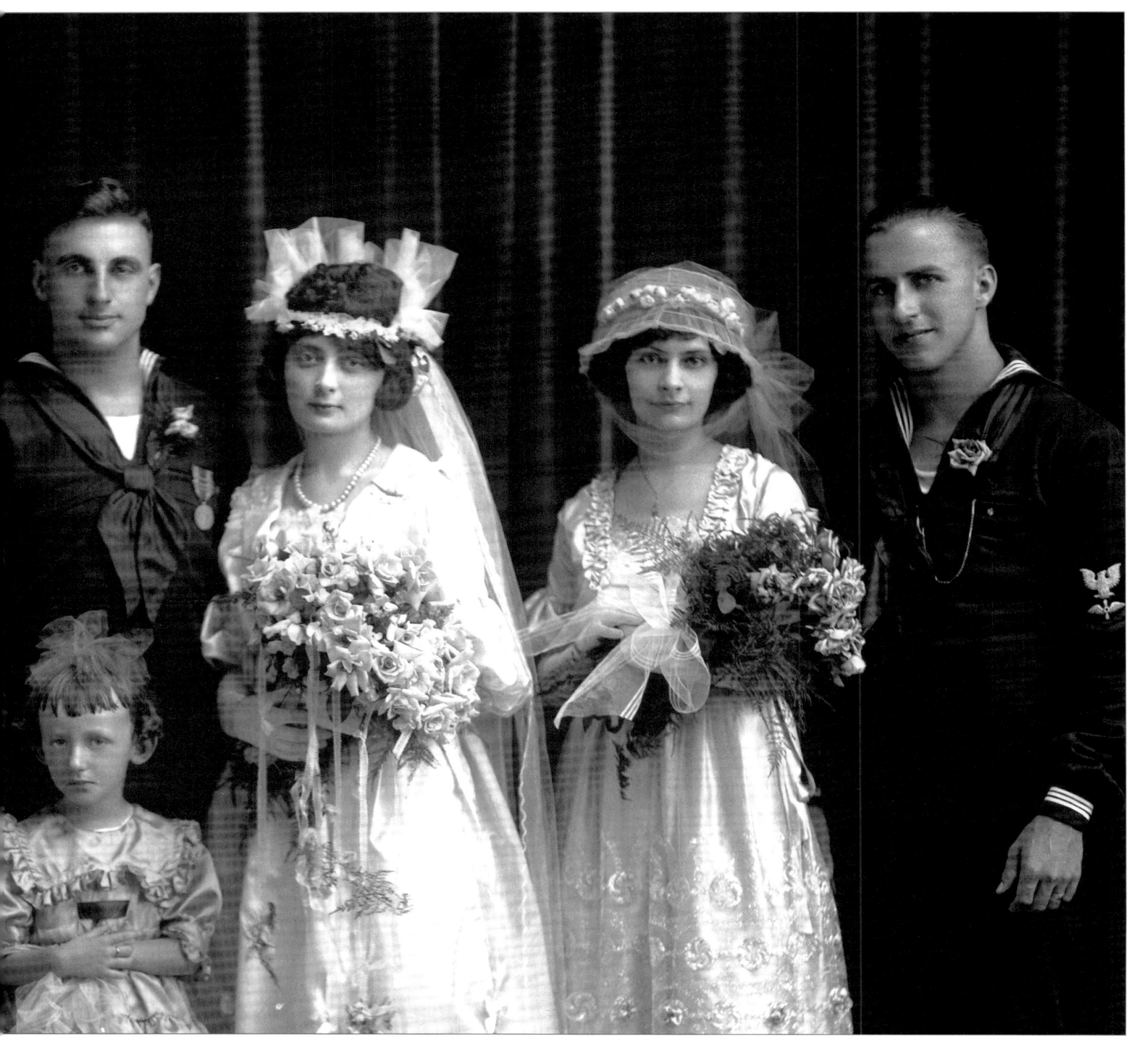

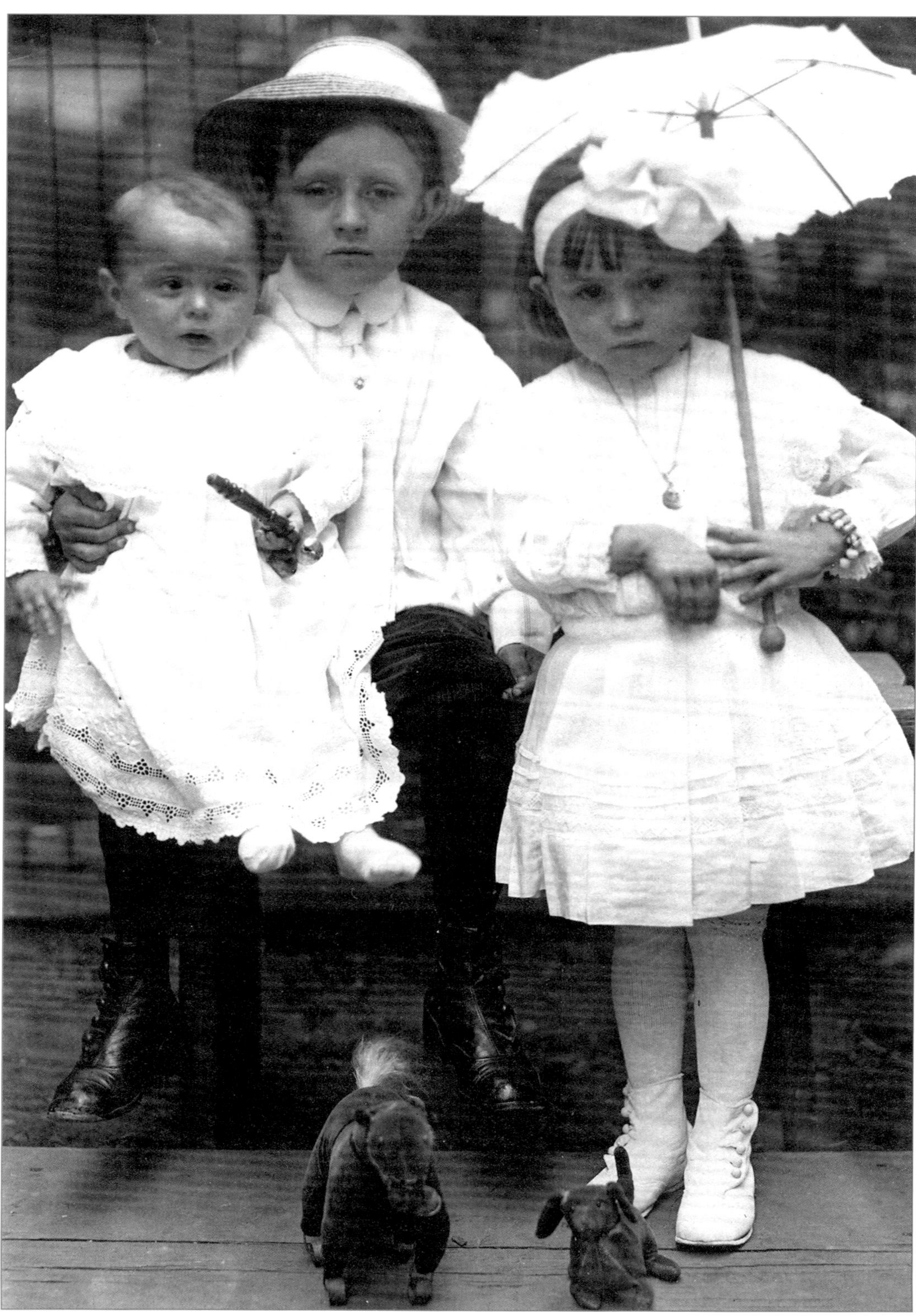

Kwasniewski captured these siblings, with their special stuffed animals at their feet, dressed in their Sunday best. Undated. *Serial # A11155*

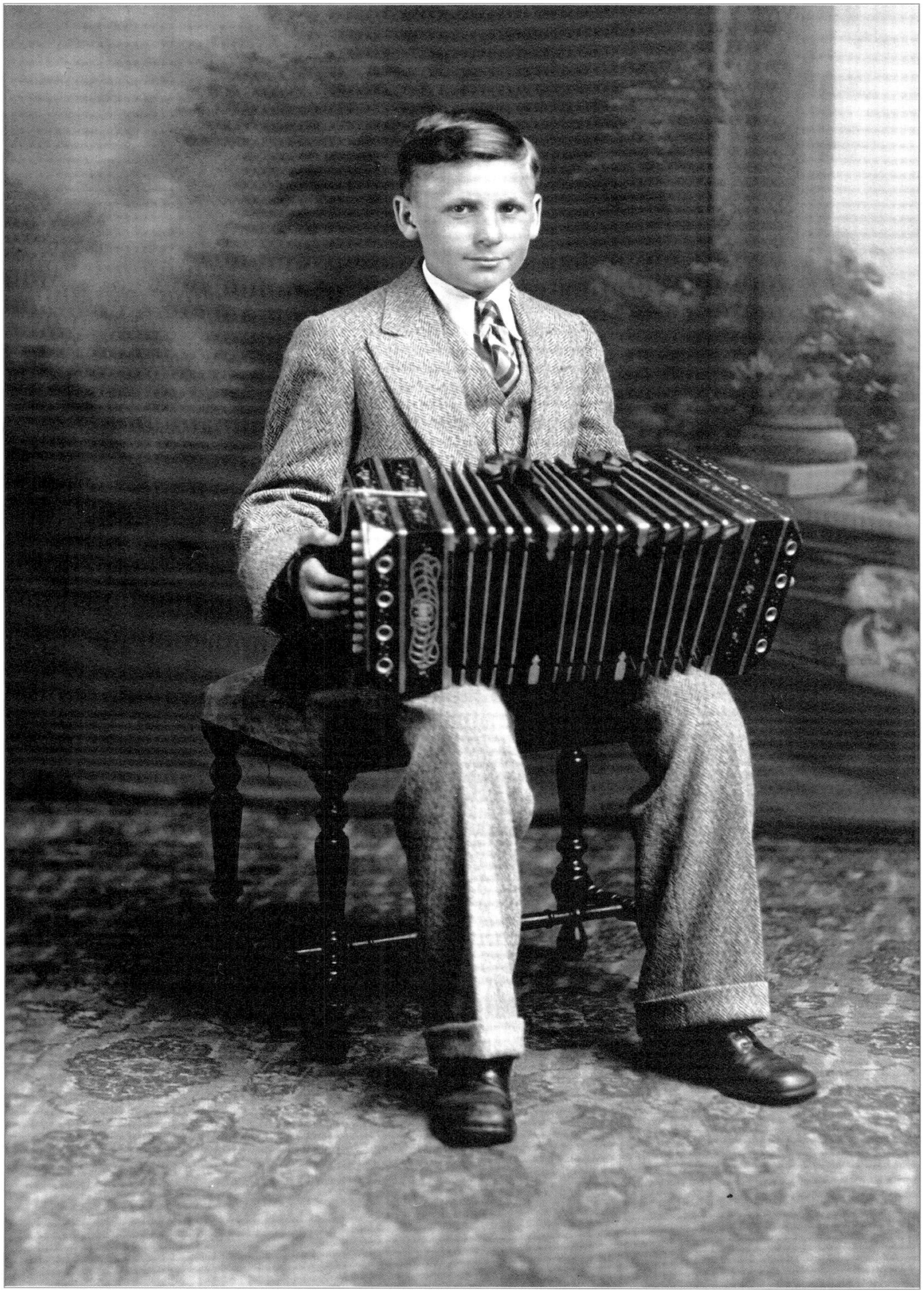

Kwasniewski probably took this young musician's photograph around 1930. ***Serial # A11127***

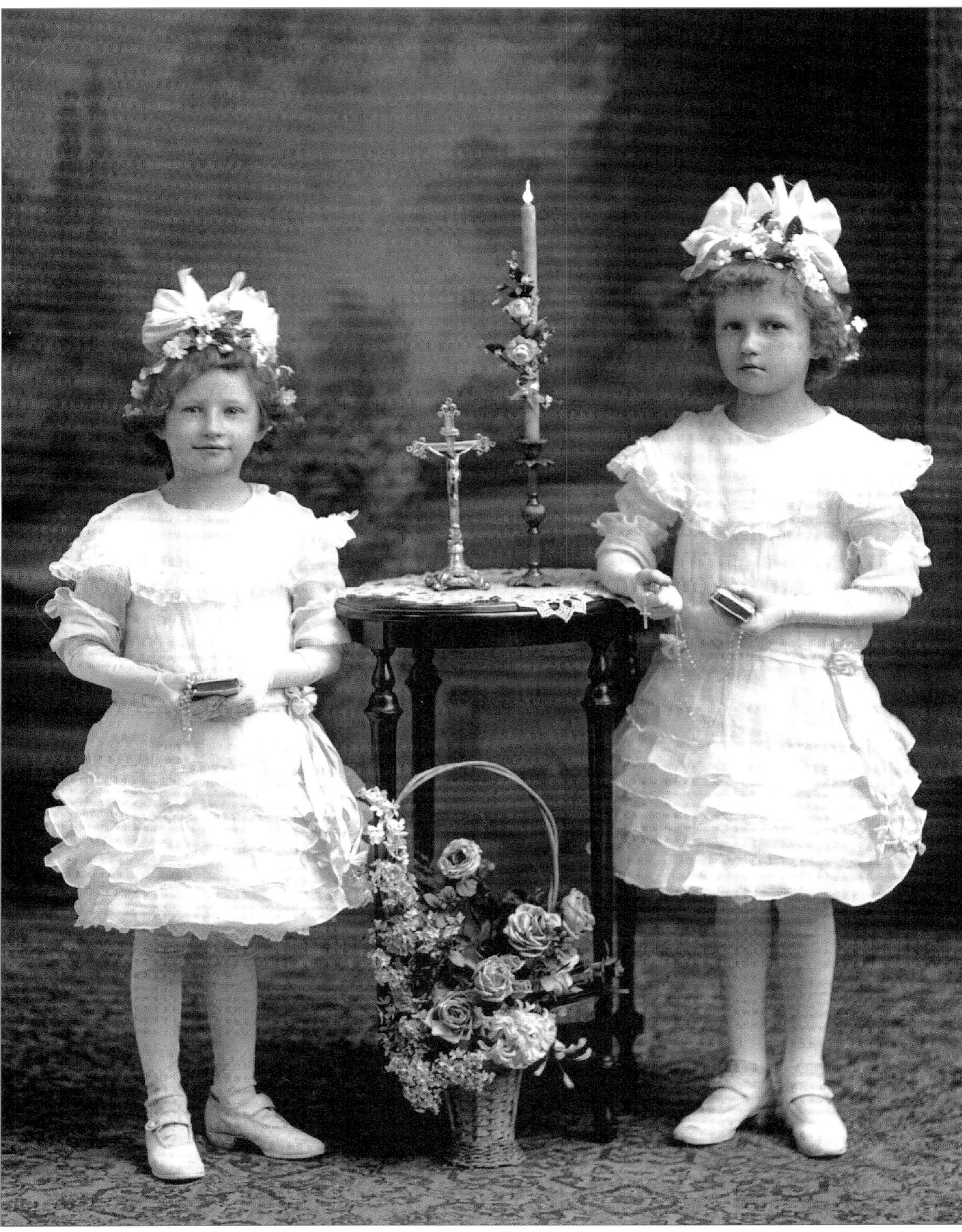

First Holy Communion photographs were a large part of Kwasniewski's business. He photographed these young ladies from the Josef Wozniak family in 1923. ***Serial # 21407***

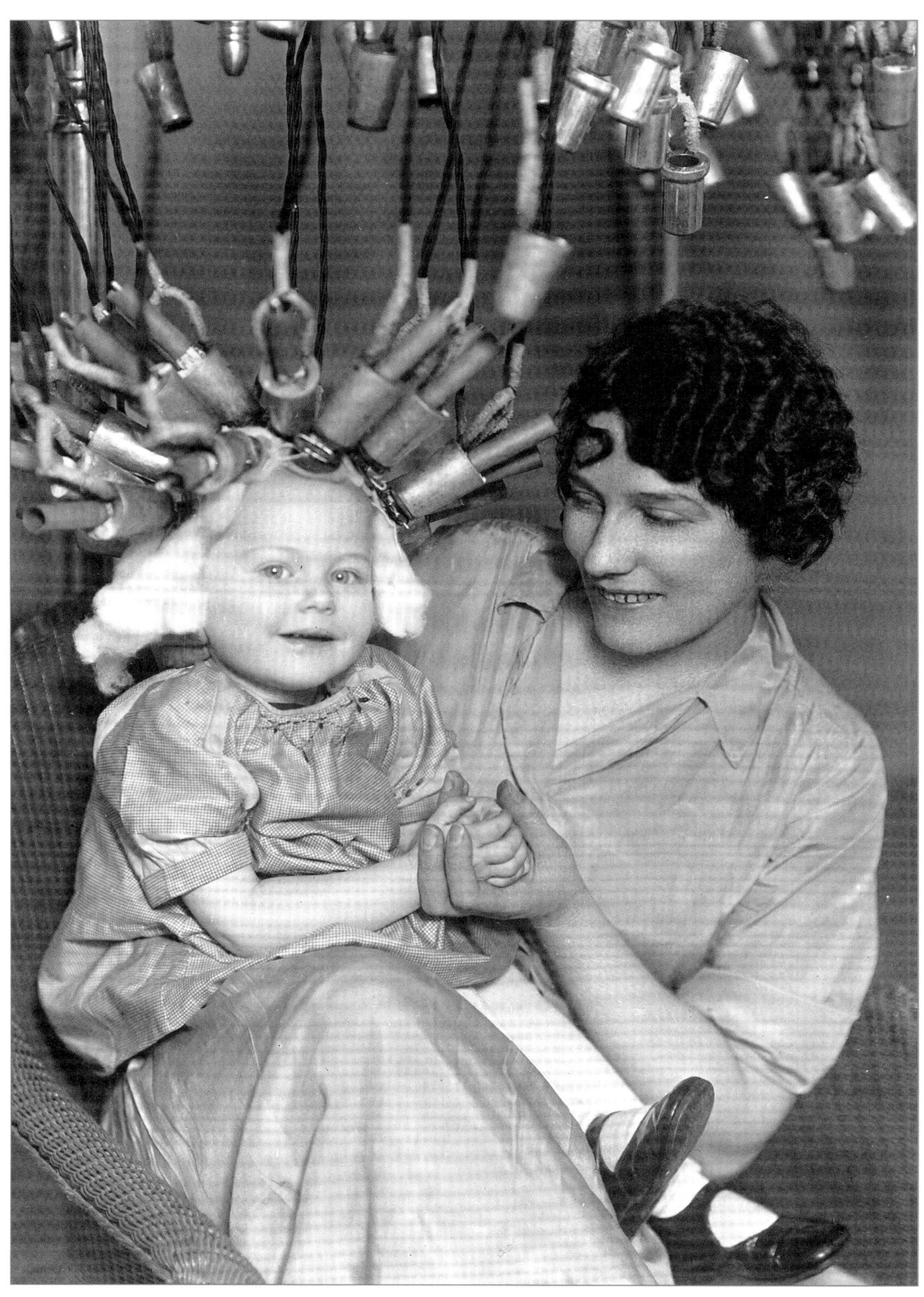

Mom eased the fears of this young girl, who managed to sit through the trauma of getting a "permanent wave," in 1927. ***Serial # 26249***

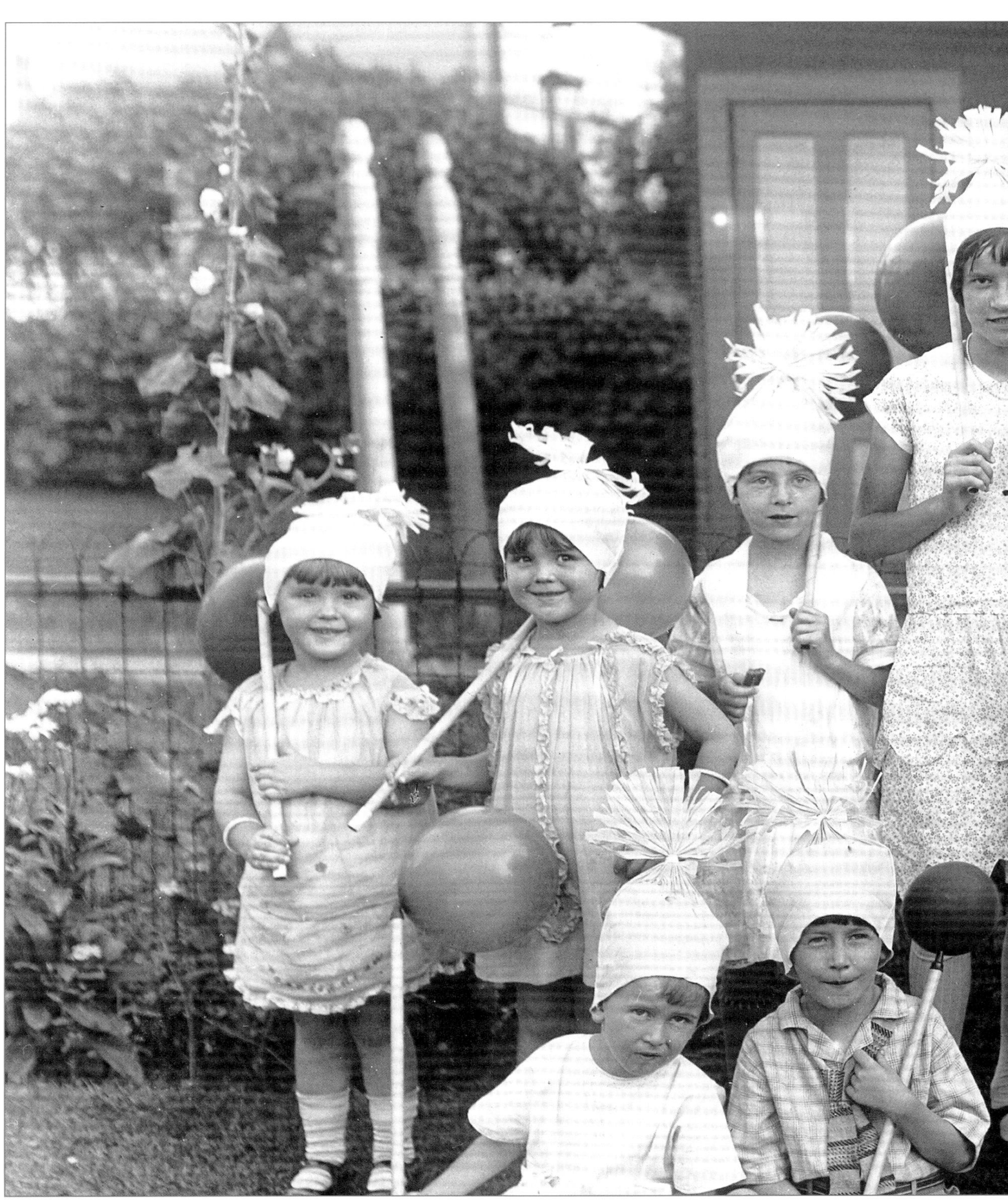

Children gathered outdoors for a birthday party on a summer day in 1928 were treated to hats and balloons. ***Serial # 28602***

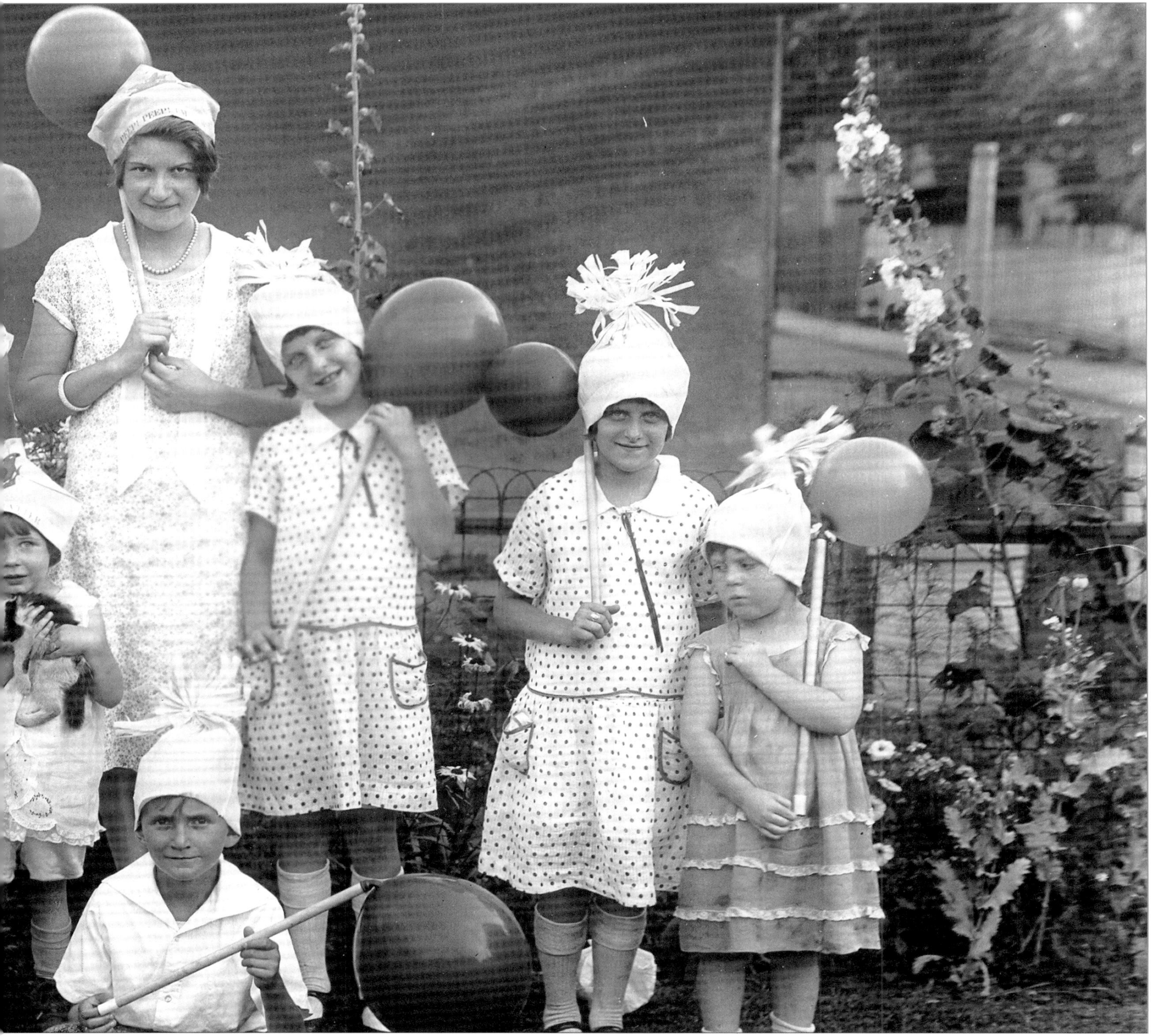

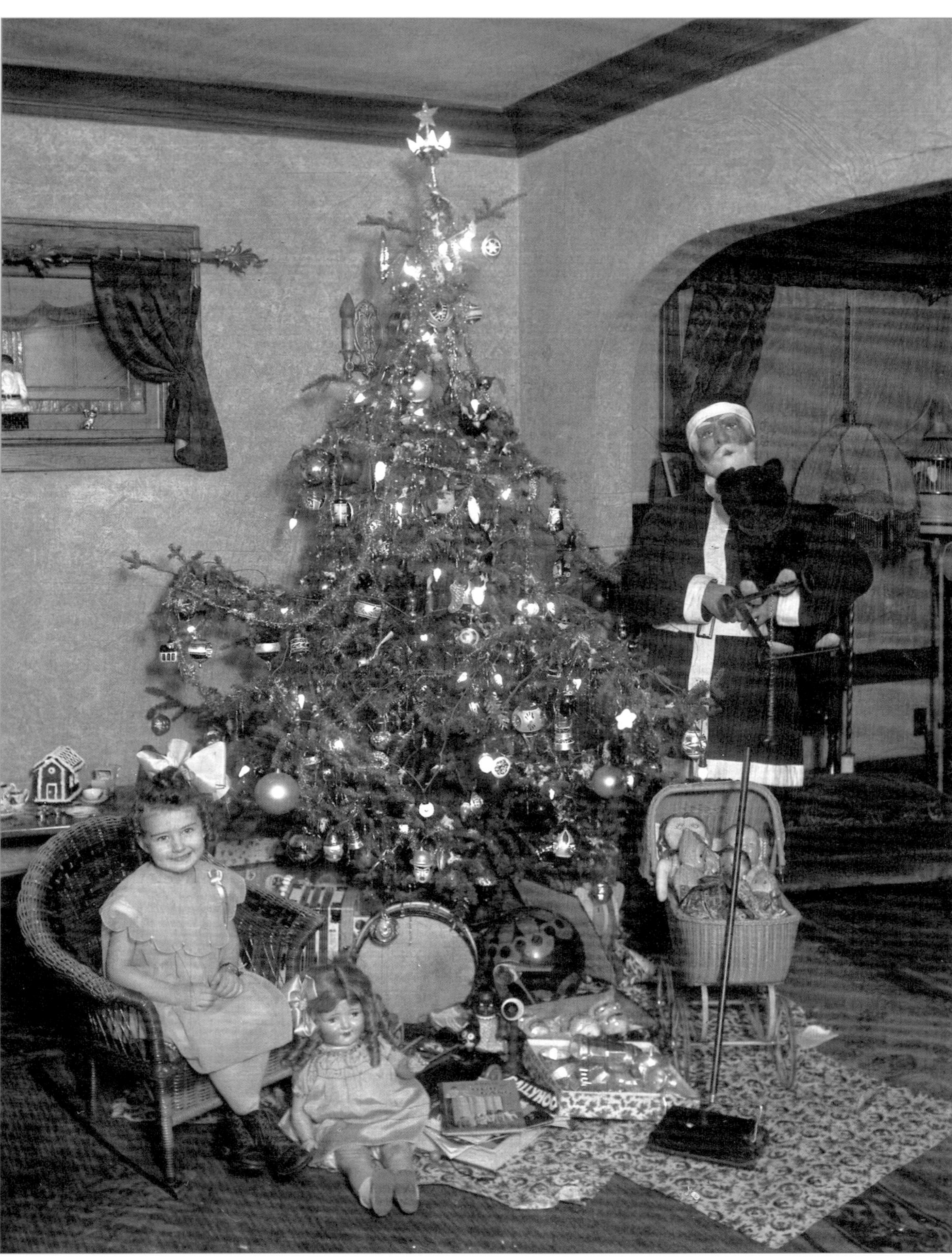

Judging from her sweet smile and the gifts under the tree, this little darling's 1932 Christmas wishes were fulfilled.
Serial # 32002

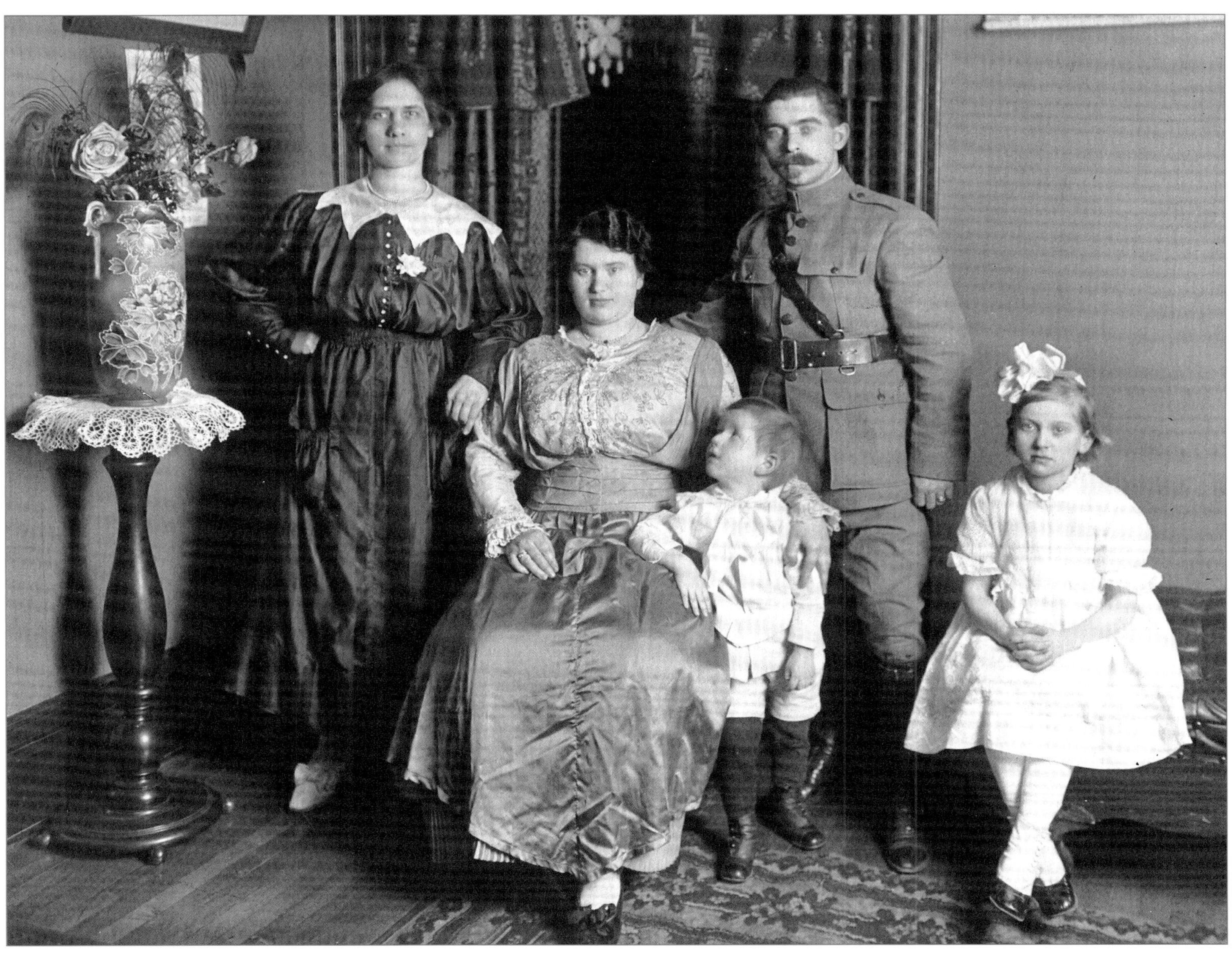

A Kosciuszko Guard member posed with his family around the time of World War I. The military unit was organized in June 1874 after a call for volunteers from the pulpit of St. Stanislaus Church. A group of Milwaukee Poles who had met earlier that month suggested forming a military organization. Largely made up of Polish Americans, the company fought valiantly in both world wars. *Serial # A10092*

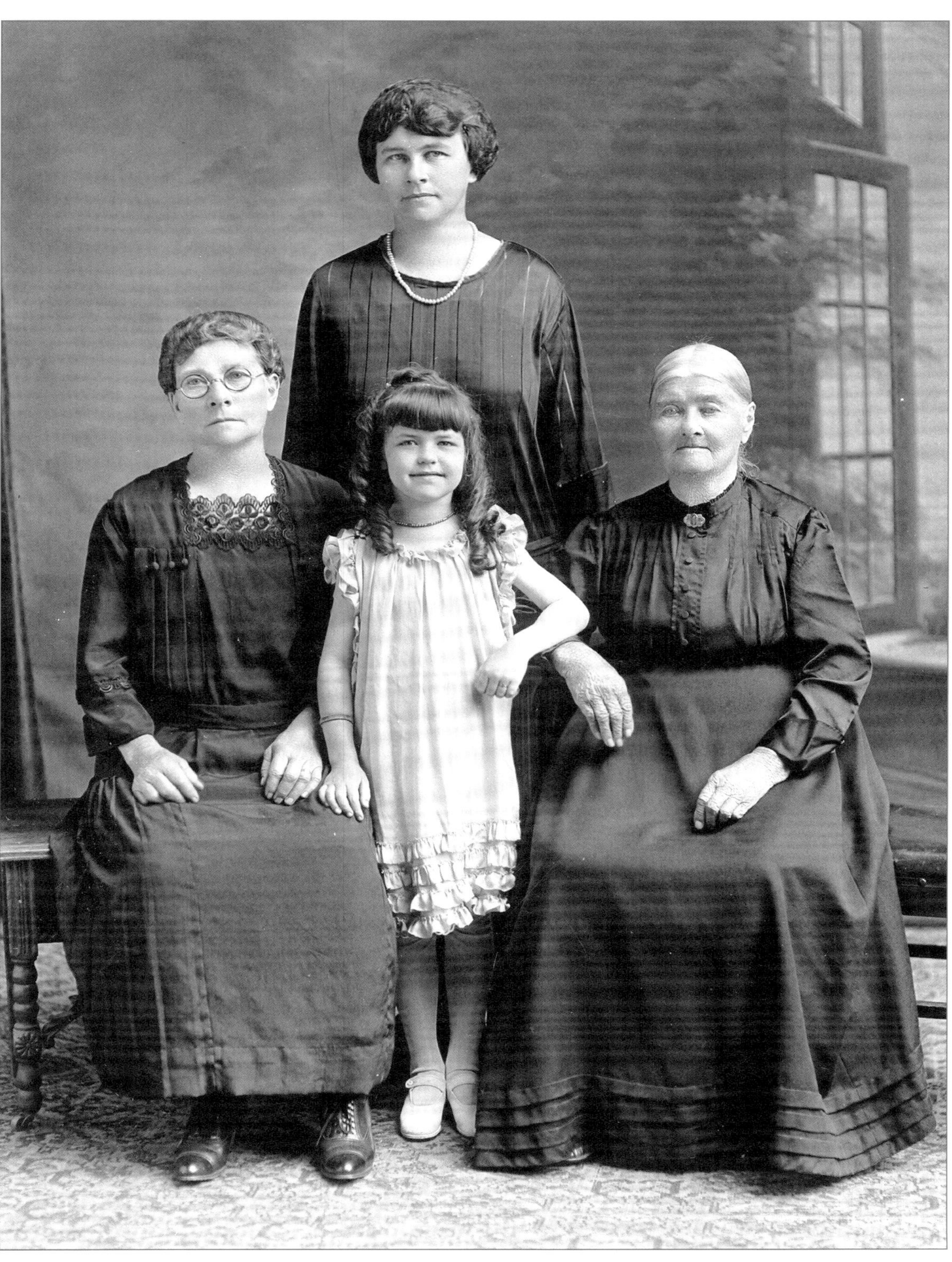

Four generations of the Bollender family visited Kwasniewski's studio for this 1924 portrait. *Serial # 23773*

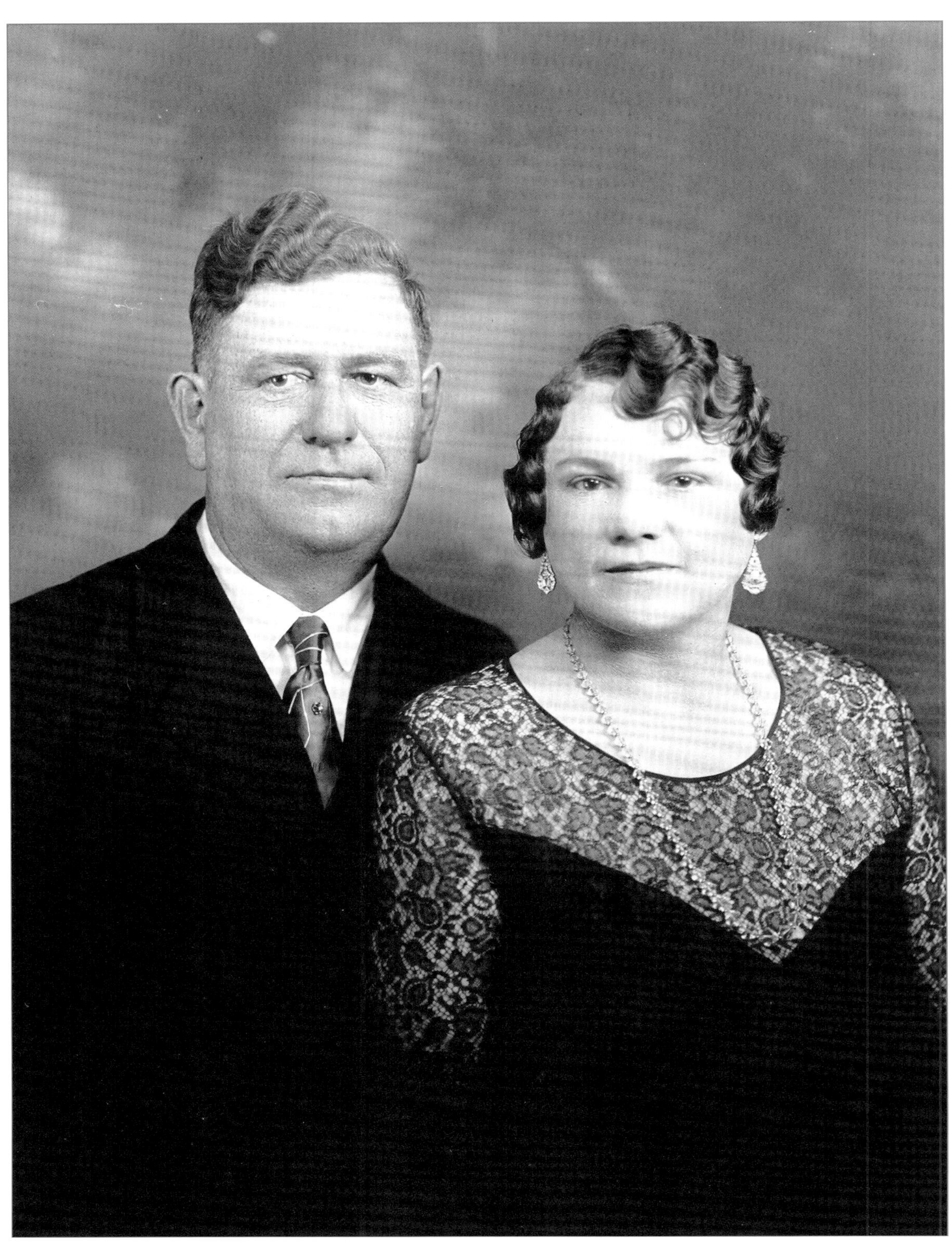

Wisconsin State Senator Walter Polakowski and his wife posed for this portrait in November 1930. Polakowski, a Socialist, served as a member of the Wisconsin Senate for the 1923 through 1933 sessions. An upholsterer by trade, he was first elected to public office in 1920 as a member of the State Assembly. ***Serial # 30578***

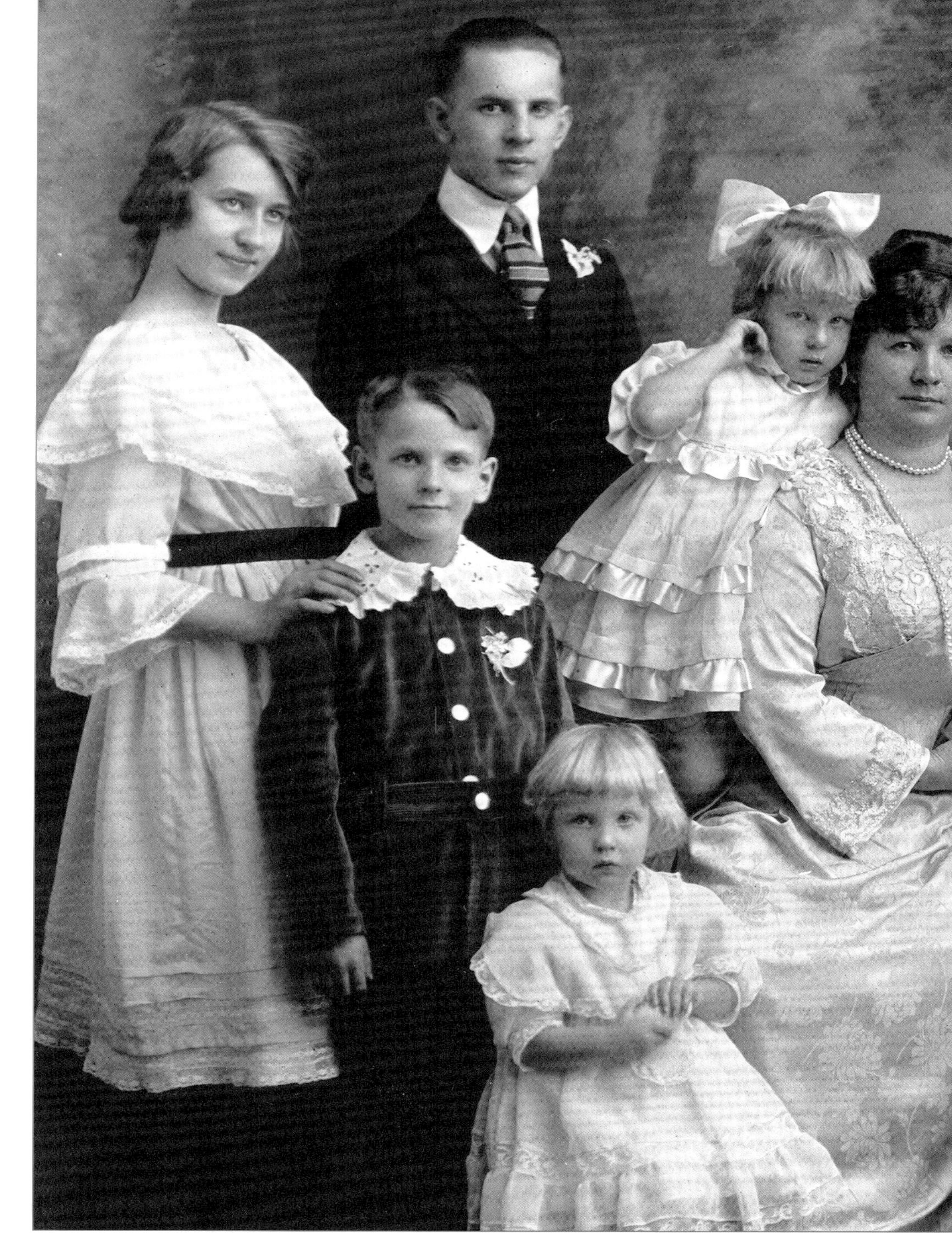

Polish Catholic families, like this one, often were large. This family dressed in their best for this photograph taken around 1920. ***Serial # A11248***

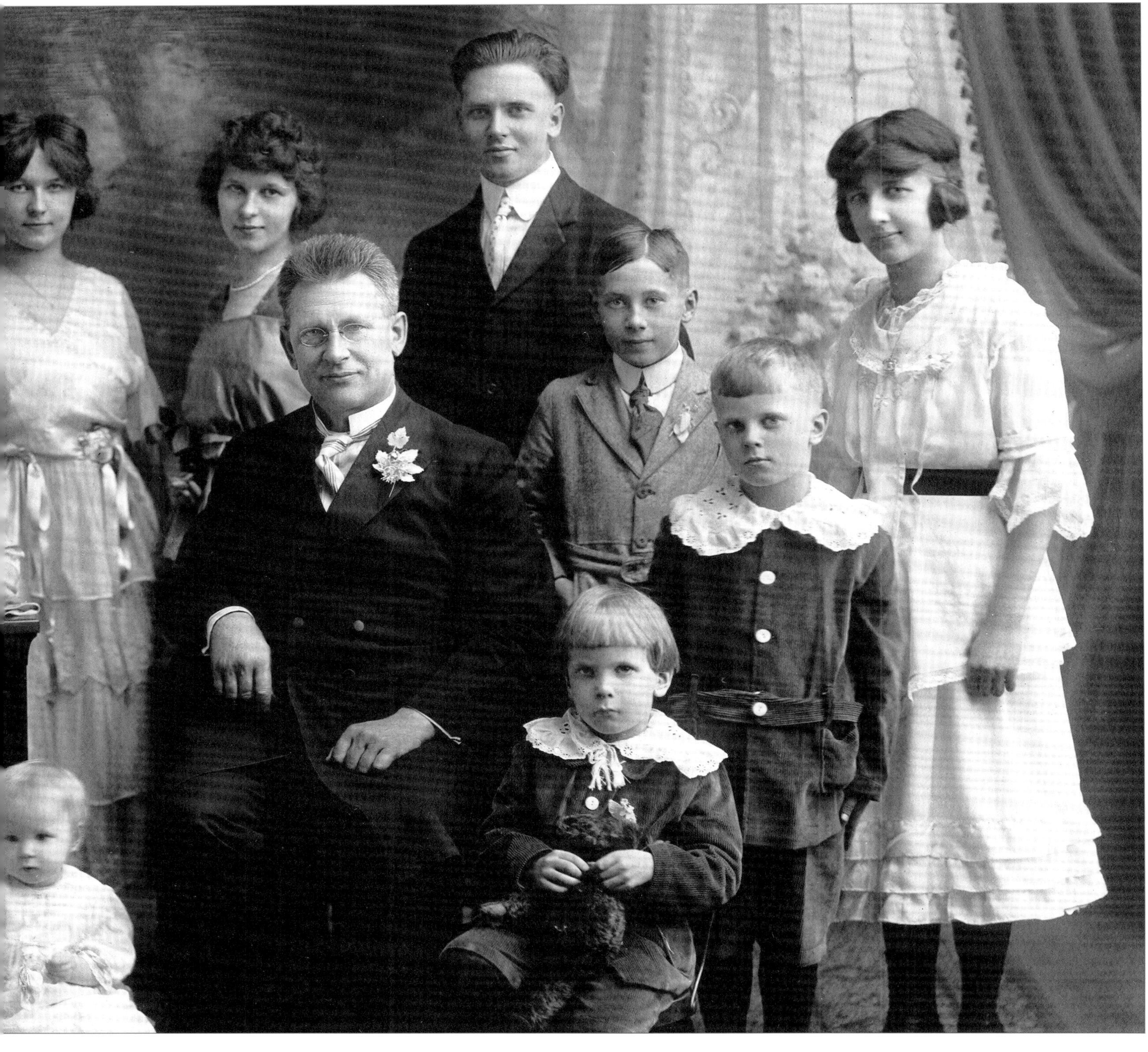

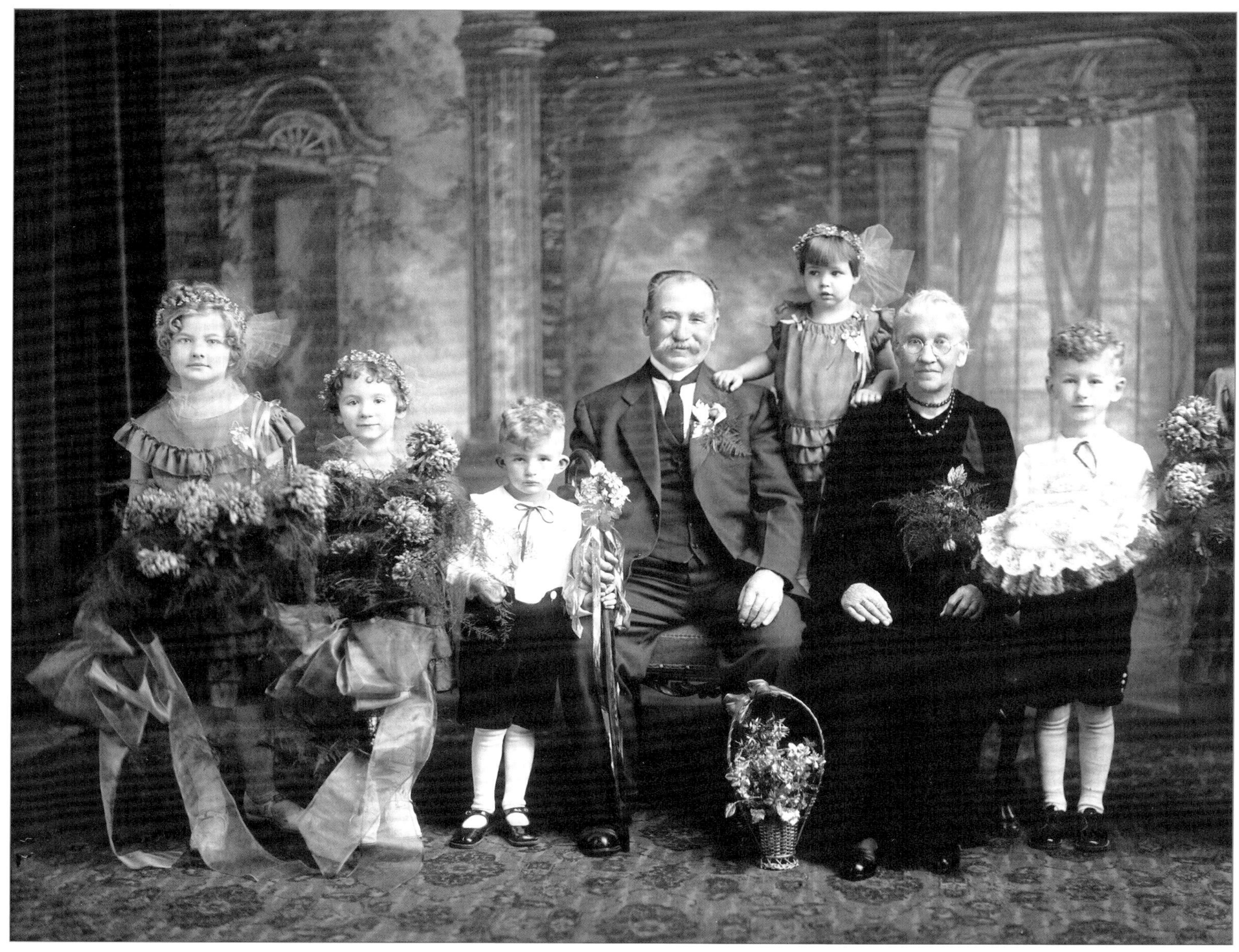

Joseph and Antoinette Grajek, joined by family youngsters in this photograph, celebrated a special wedding anniversary in 1931. ***Serial # 31429-2***

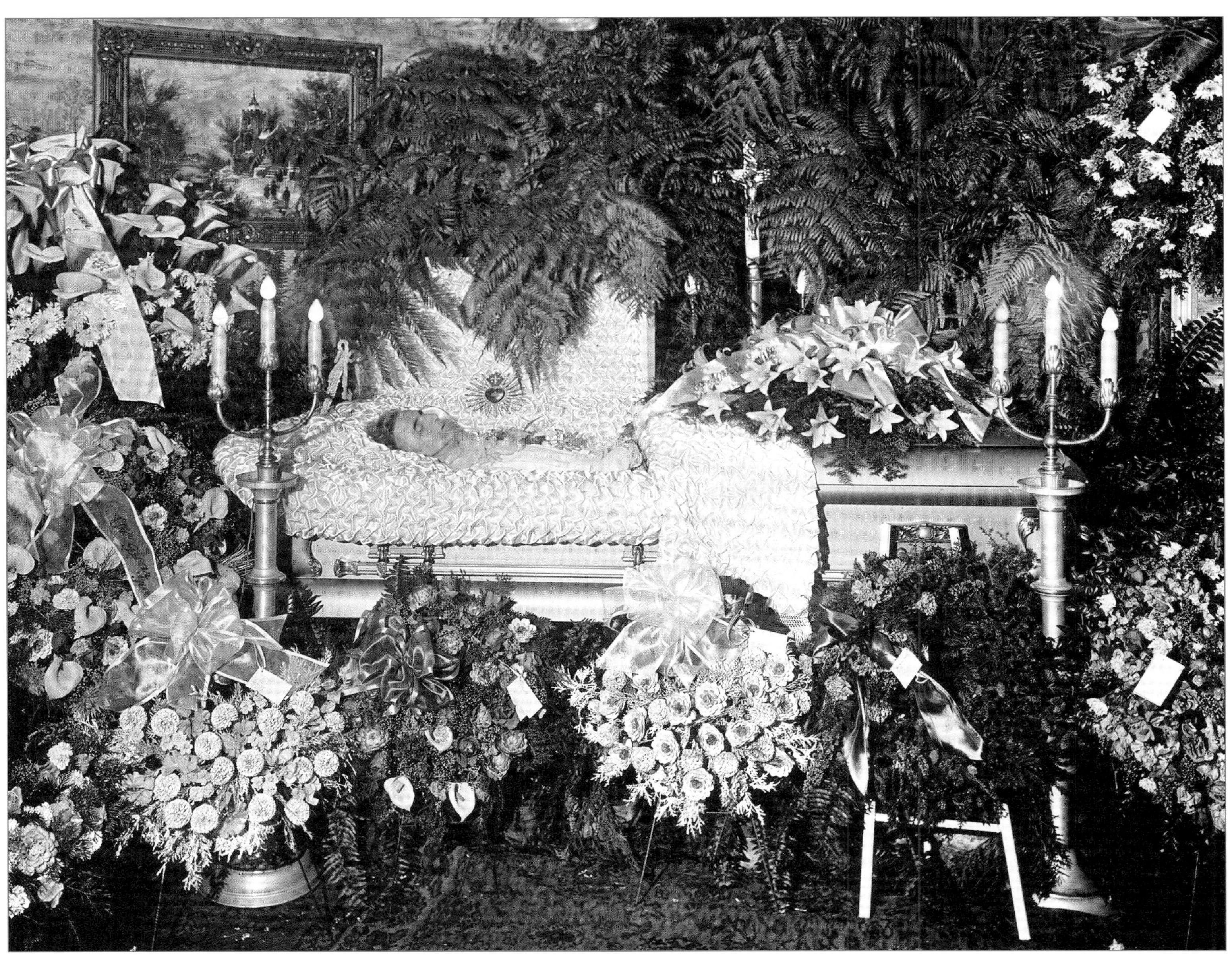

Postmortem photography was a common practice in the late nineteenth and early twentieth centuries. The earliest of these types of photographs, particularly those of children, preserved images of individuals who often had not been photographed while they were living. By 1936, when this photograph was taken, the funeral parlor had nearly completely replaced the home as the place for holding wakes. ***Serial # A03510***

CHAPTER THREE

Church and School

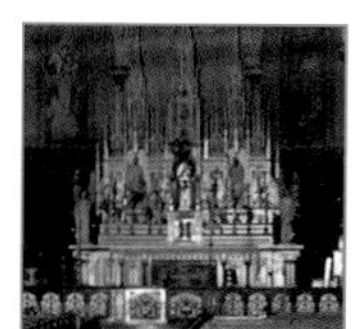

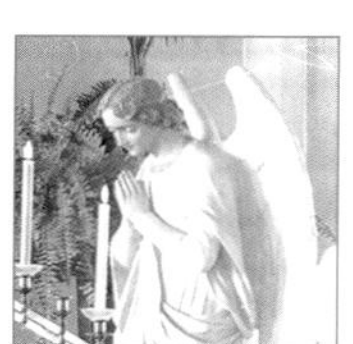

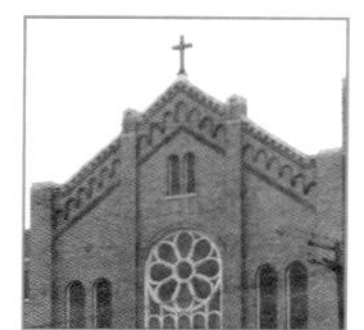

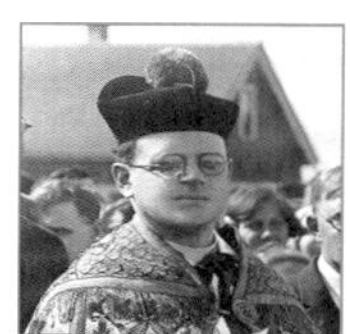

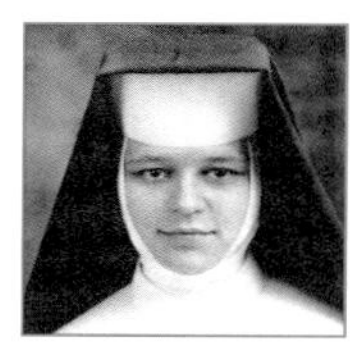

The skyline of Milwaukee's South Side has always been a thicket of steeples. The neighborhood's churches stand as monuments of faith and anchors of identity, each with its own architectural amenities and its own roster of communicants. A handful were built for German Catholics (St. Anthony, St. Lawrence) and German Lutherans (St. Jacobi, St. Martini), but the vast majority developed as strongholds of Polish Catholicism—so strong, in fact, that they virtually defined the living areas of Roman Kwasniewski's time. The South Side, a neighborhood in its own right, was further subdivided into communities that coincided with the borders of Catholic parishes. When older residents are asked where they grew up, many will unhesitatingly reply not with a subdivision name or a street address but with the name of their first parish: St. Hyacinth's, St. Vincent's, St. John Kanty, or any one of a dozen others.

Each parish was, in modern terms, a full-service institution. Worship was the primary activity, of course, but the church was a busy social center as well. Dozens of groups—sodalities, fraternals, guilds, fellowships—met in the parish halls of the South Side, often sporting their own ban-

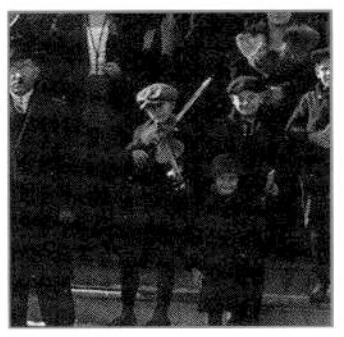 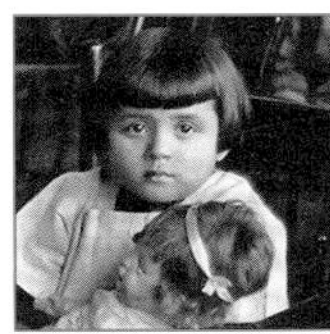 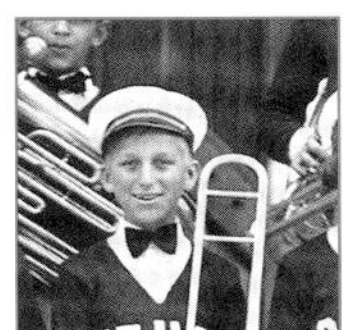 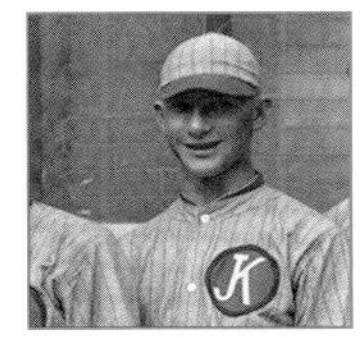 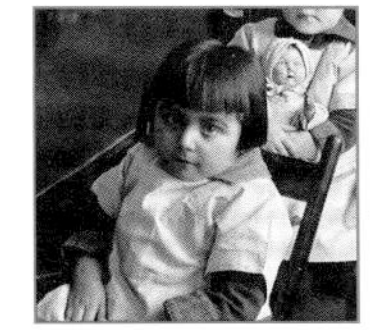

ners and uniforms. Thousands of young people took part in parish-sponsored athletic leagues. The church even played a role in the economic and political life of its members. Employers regularly recruited workers through parish priests, and it was not unheard-of for pastors to offer political advice from the pulpit.

No Catholic parish was considered complete without a school. Although public education was available without charge, nearly 80 percent of the neighborhood's schoolchildren attended parochial institutions in 1910—the highest proportion in the city. Typically administered by nuns, the schools offered lessons in faith and heritage as well as academics; they were considered the cornerstones of the Polish Catholic community's future. Every parish had a grade school, and two—St. Stanislaus and St. Josaphat—operated their own high schools, preparing students for success in the world of work.

Both church and school were oriented to the family, but Catholic efforts to build community did not end there. Long before tax-supported agencies provided a social "safety net," religious institutions, particularly orphanages, stepped in when families were sundered by death, disease, or poverty. The largest, St. Joseph's, was a frequent Kwasniewski subject. The orphanage served generations of South Side youngsters, and its successor institution—the Child Development Center of St. Joseph—continues to serve children and families in the same neighborhood.

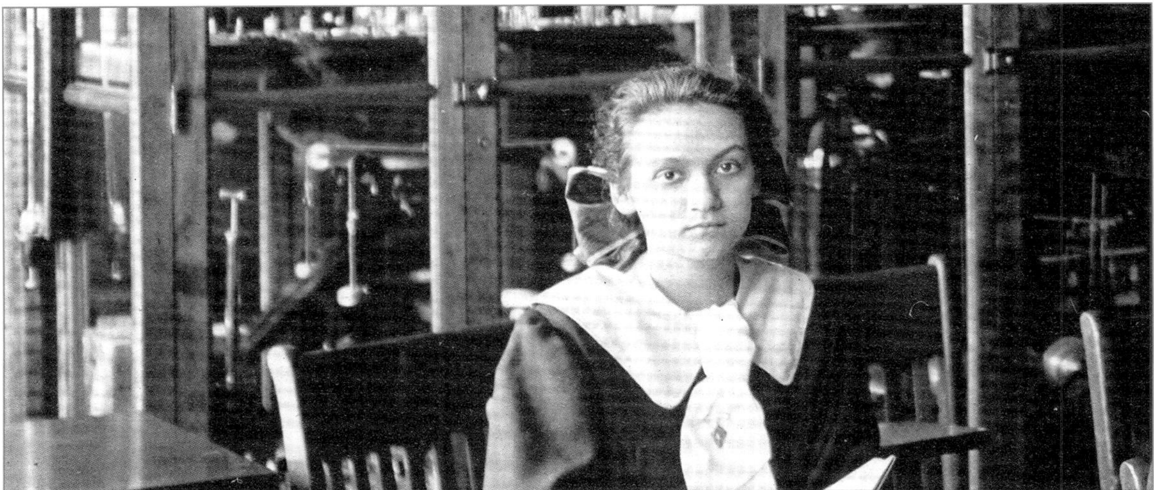

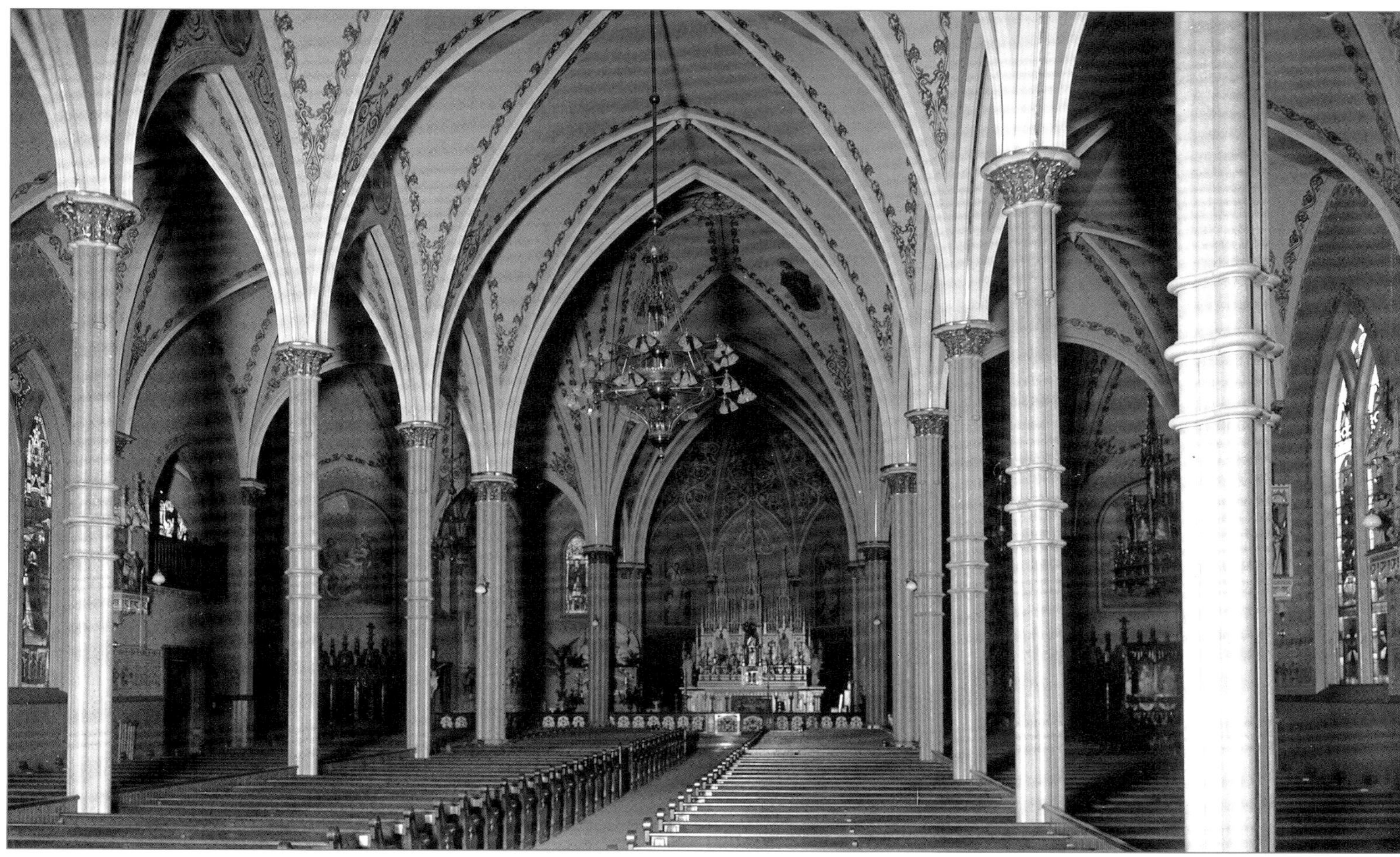

Natural light streaming into SS. Cyril and Methodius Catholic Church added to the ambience of grandeur at the time that this undated photograph was taken. The vast interior is evidence that the church, located at what is now Hayes Avenue and South Fifteenth Street, had a large congregation. *Serial # A06116*

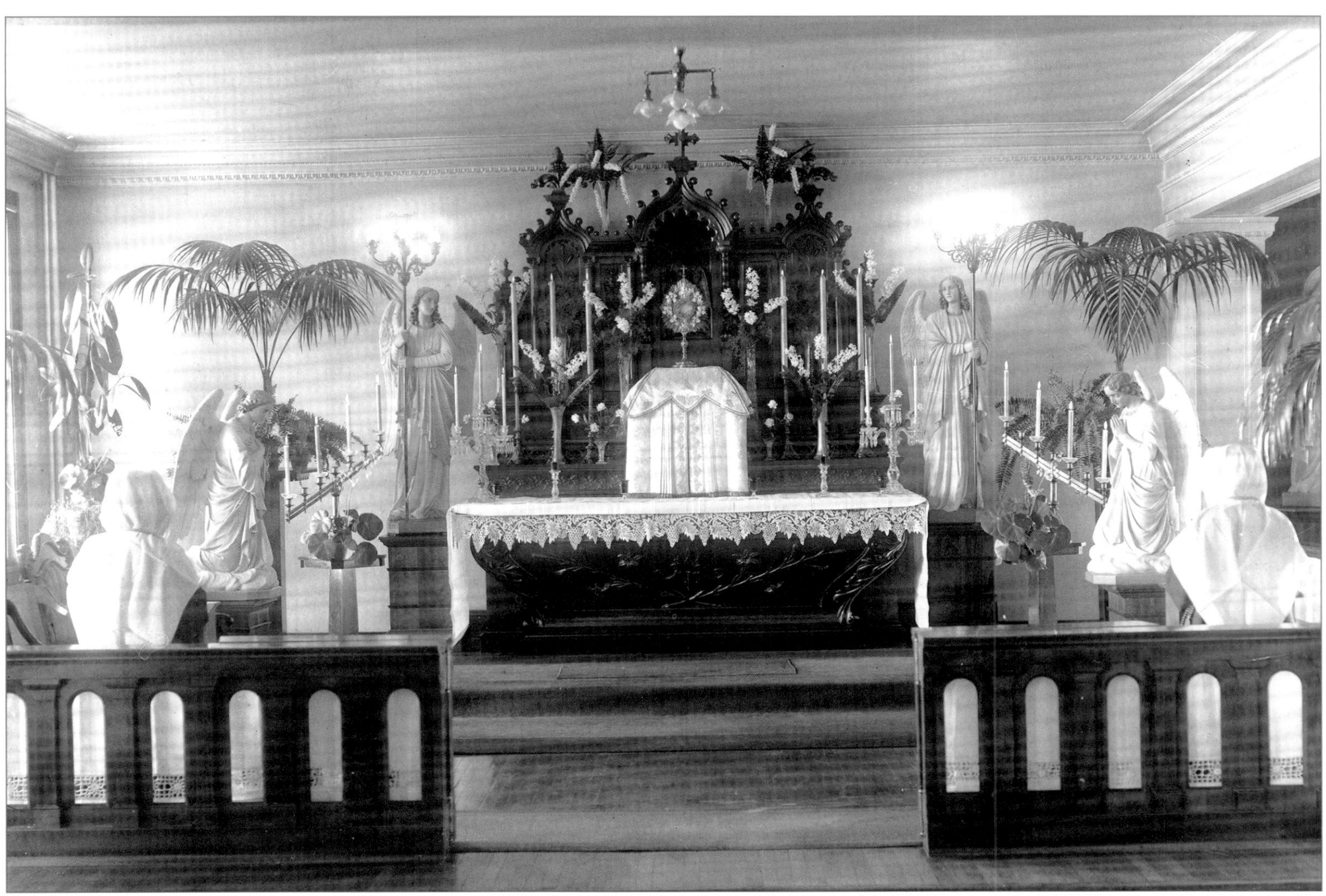

The presence of the two nuns worshiping in solitude is barely distinguishable in this ethereal photograph of the altar of St. Joseph's orphanage chapel. Undated. ***Serial # A06184-1***

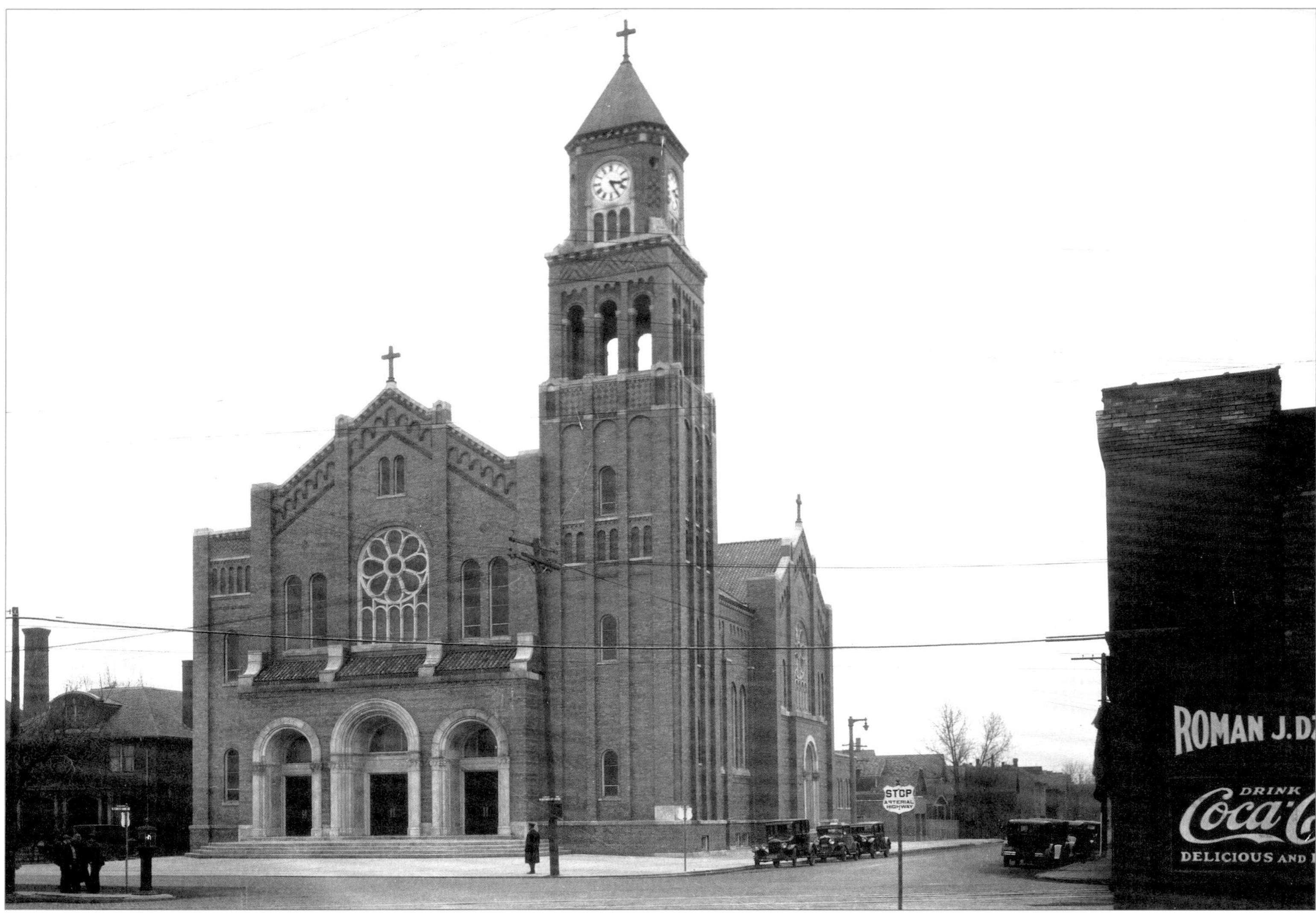

Milwaukee architect Francis S. Gurda designed and supervised the construction of a new church for St. Adalbert's congregation, begun in 1930. This photograph of the church, located at the busy thoroughfares of Twentieth and Becher Streets, was taken shortly after the completion of the $250,000 structure. *Serial # A06230*

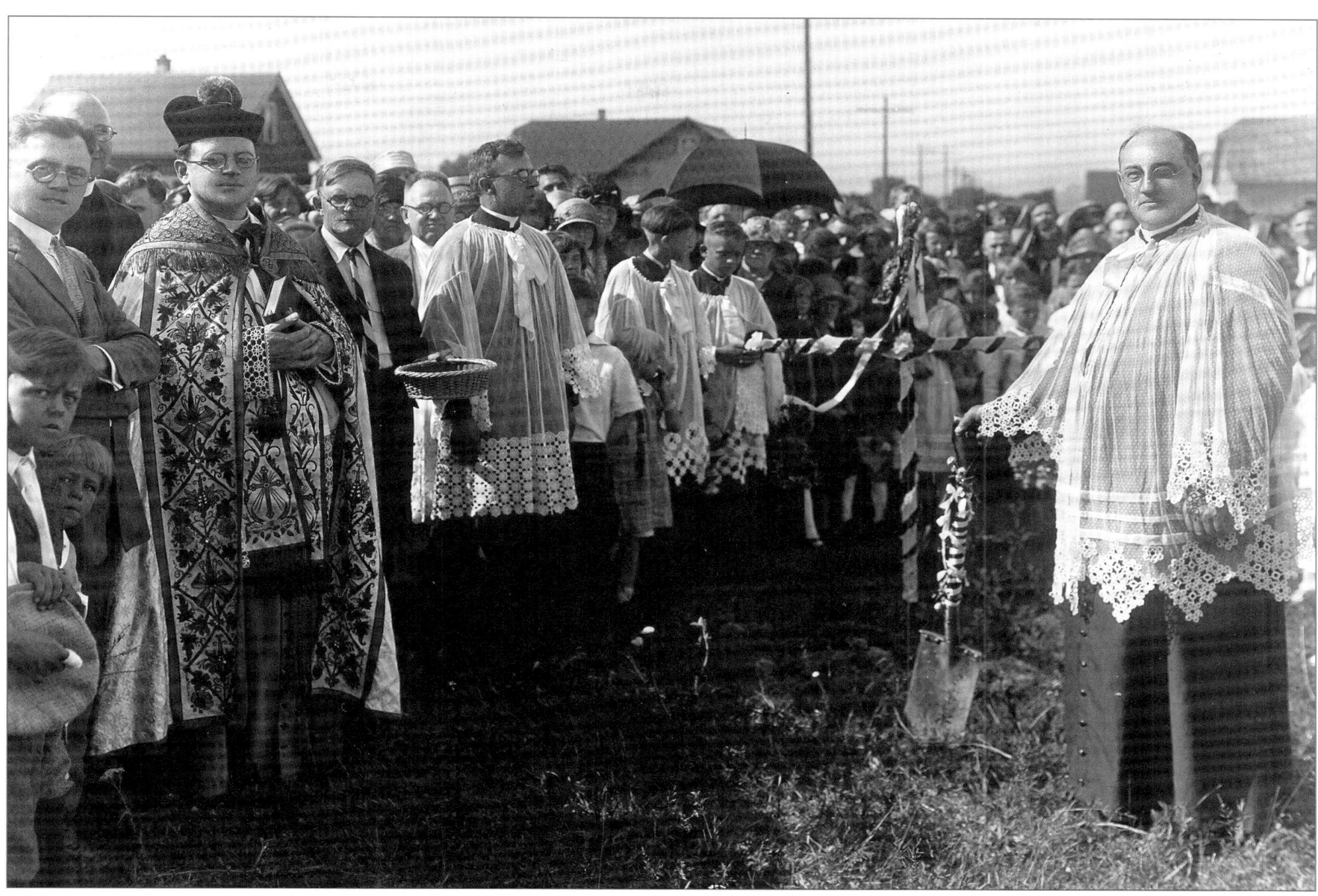

The groundbreaking ceremony for St. Alexander Church took place on July 26, 1925. Present to bless the occasion were (from left) Monsignor B. E. Goral; the Reverend Alexander Kosobucki, the parish's new pastor; and the Reverend Paul Chrzan, pastor of St. John Kanty, who delivered the sermon. The new parish, which was located on Eleventh Avenue (today South Sixteenth Street) between Ohio and Holt, was named Alexander after its first pastor. *Serial # 24682-2*

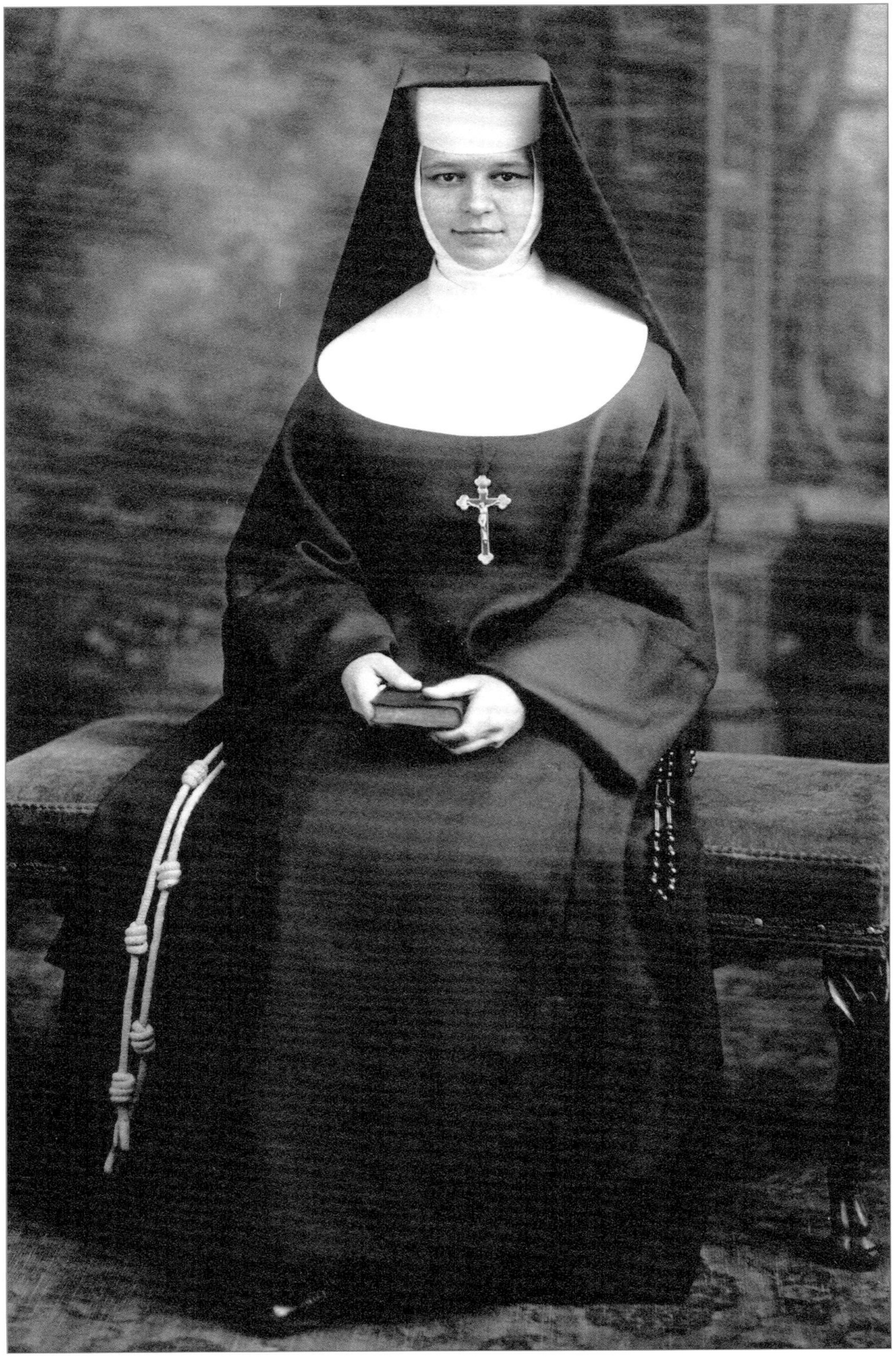

Sister Mary Rozalita of St. Adalbert's visited photographer Roman Kwasniewski for this studio portrait in November 1936. ***Serial # 36185***

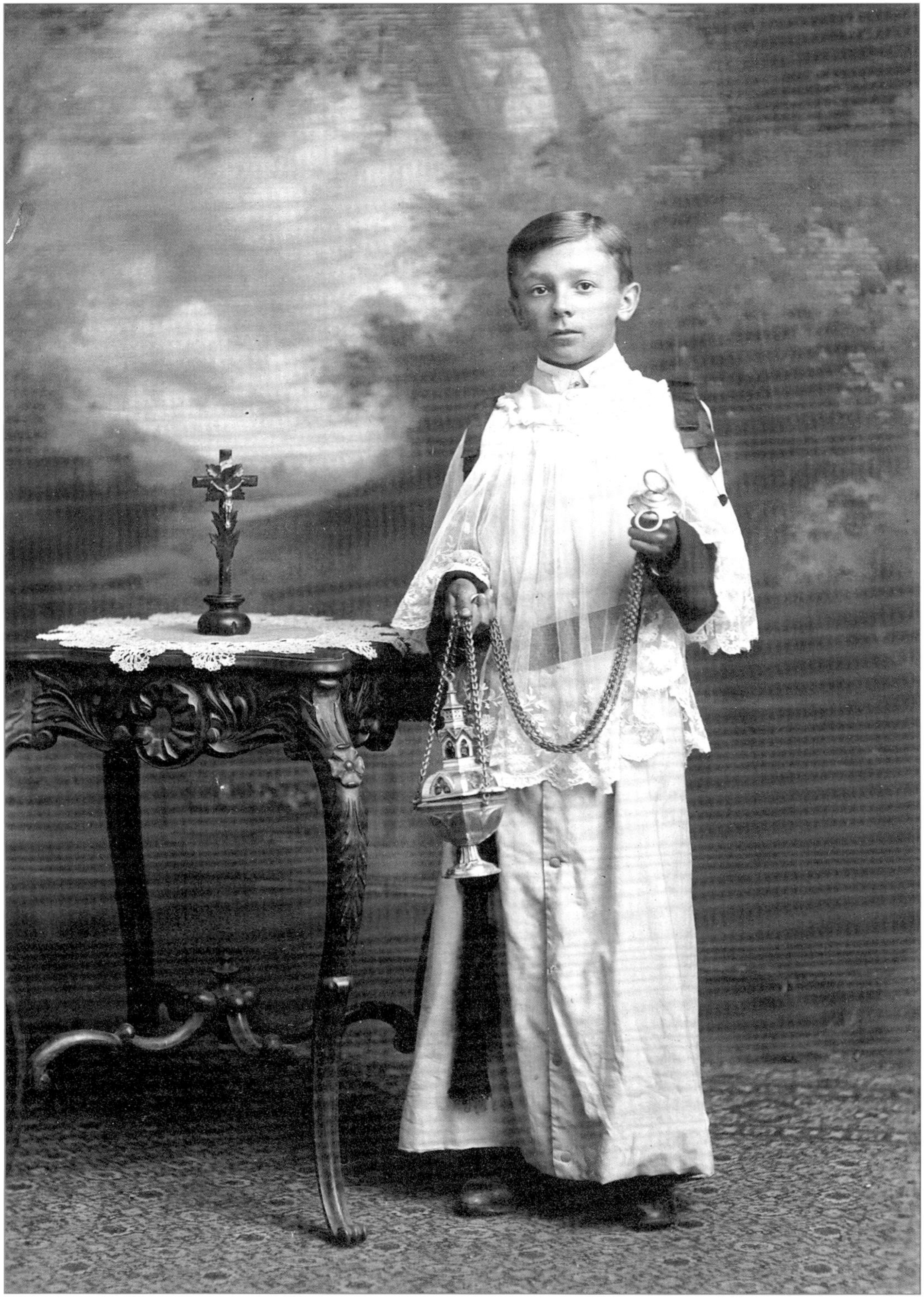

This undated photograph of an unidentified altar boy, holding an elaborate incense burner, depicts a strong Catholic upbringing.
Serial # A00688

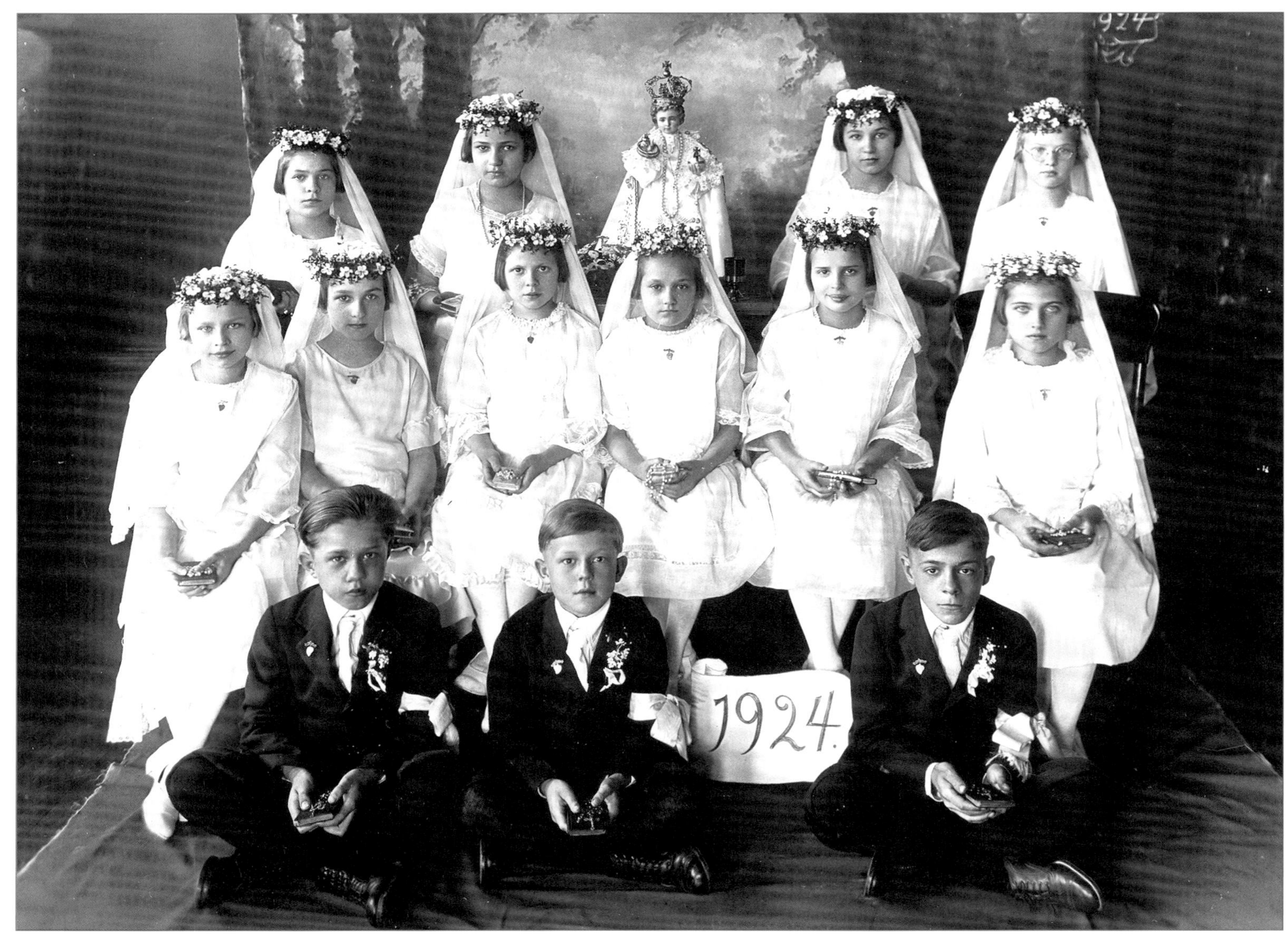

This 1924 photograph captured an important day in the religious life of these St. Joseph orphanage communicants. The orphanage, operated by the Felician Sisters and once located at what is now South Eighteenth Street and Euclid Avenue, provided food, shelter, clothing, schooling, and religious instruction to thousands of children. ***Serial # 23683***

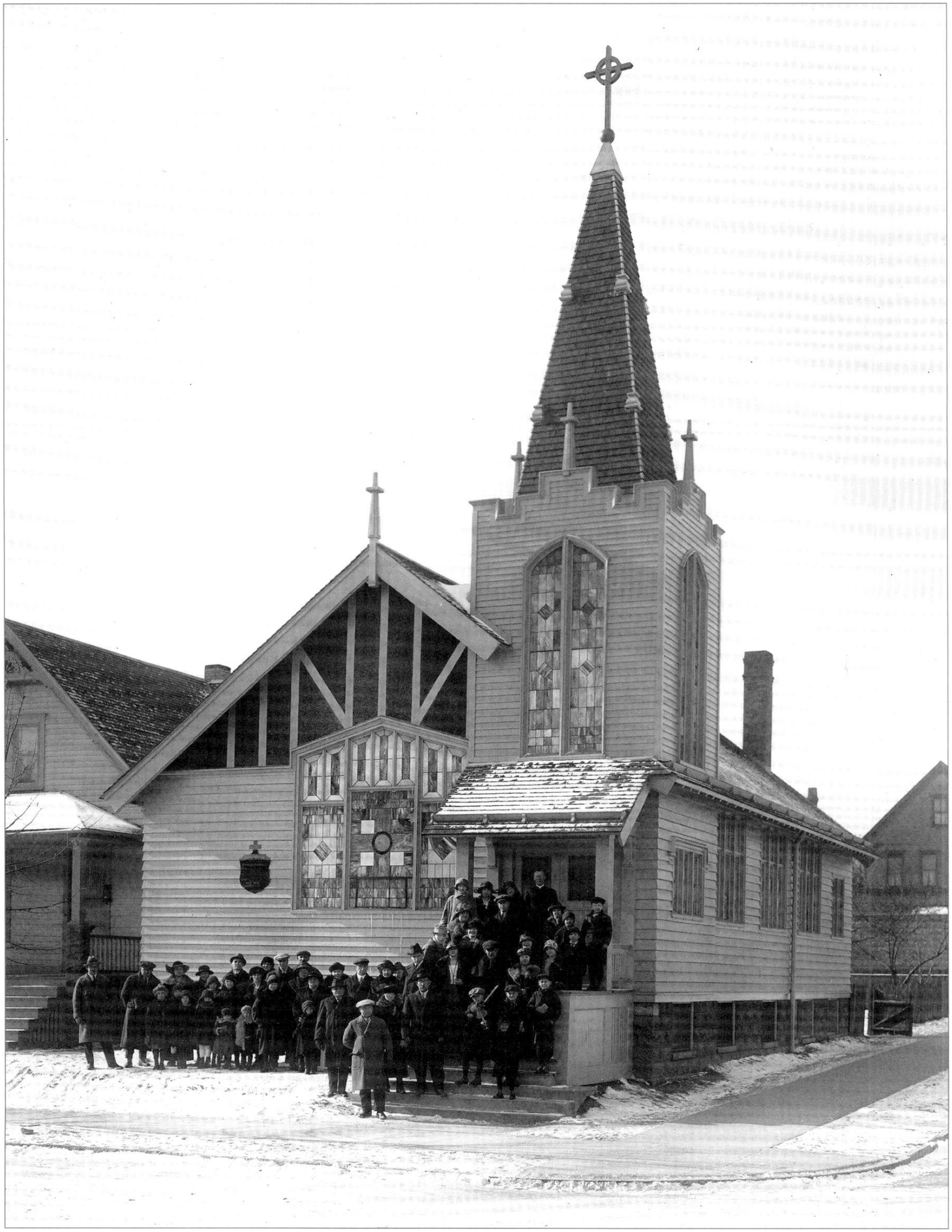

Pastor Stanley Maslowski and his congregants, including a young violin player, posed outside St. Peter's Polish Methodist Episcopal Church, located at Seventh (today South Twelfth Street) and Hayes Avenues, in January 1923. Although Catholicism was the predominant religion among Poles, not all of Milwaukee's Poles were Catholic. ***Serial # 23013A***

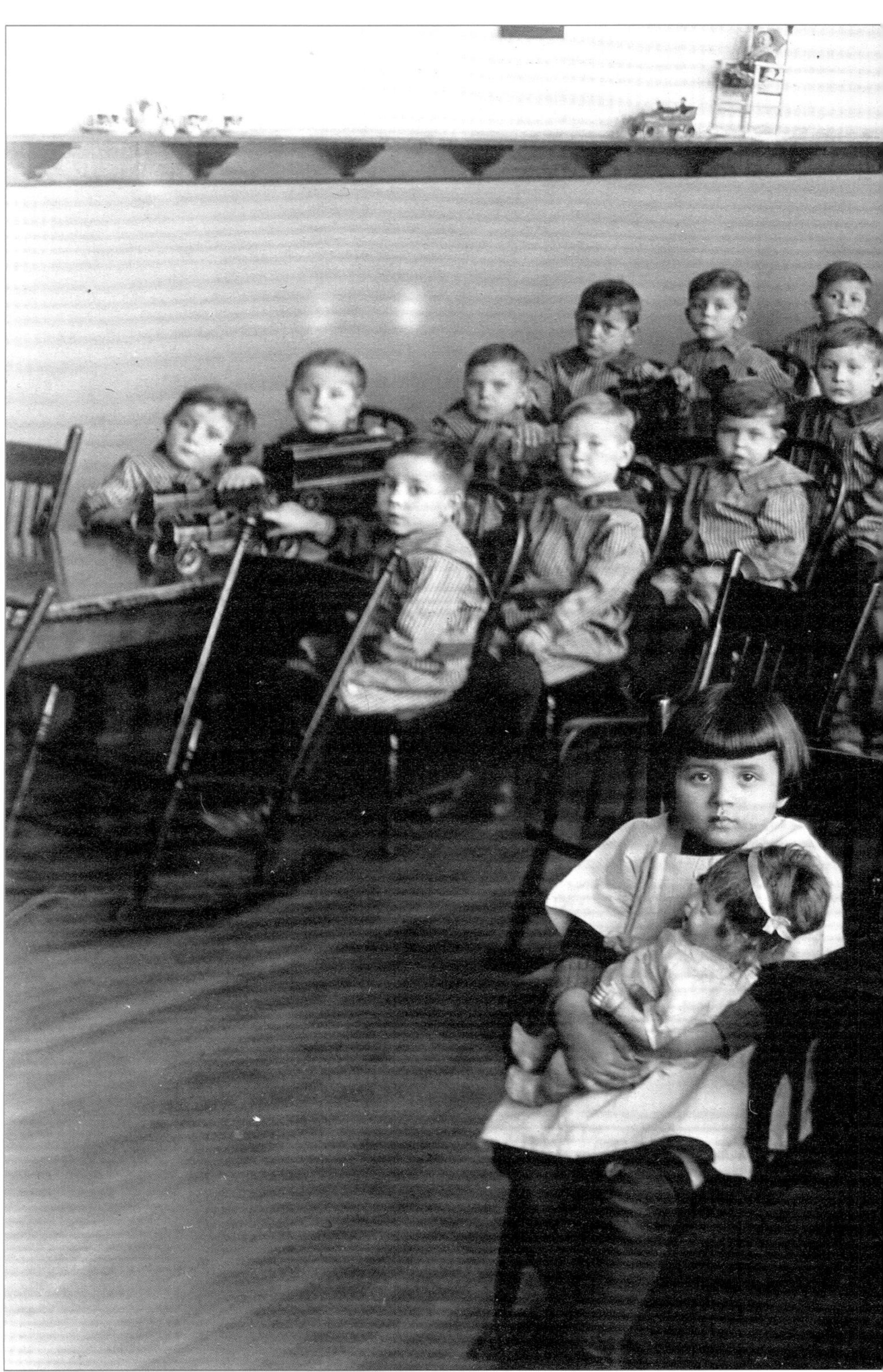

Gathered separately in a room at St. Joseph's orphanage, the girls had dolls and miniature pianos to play with, while the boys had toy vehicles and soldiers to keep them occupied. This photograph may have been taken in 1924. Orphanages helped poor families through difficult times by temporarily caring for children. Most of these children had at least one parent and likely returned home after a few years. ***Serial # A00501-2***

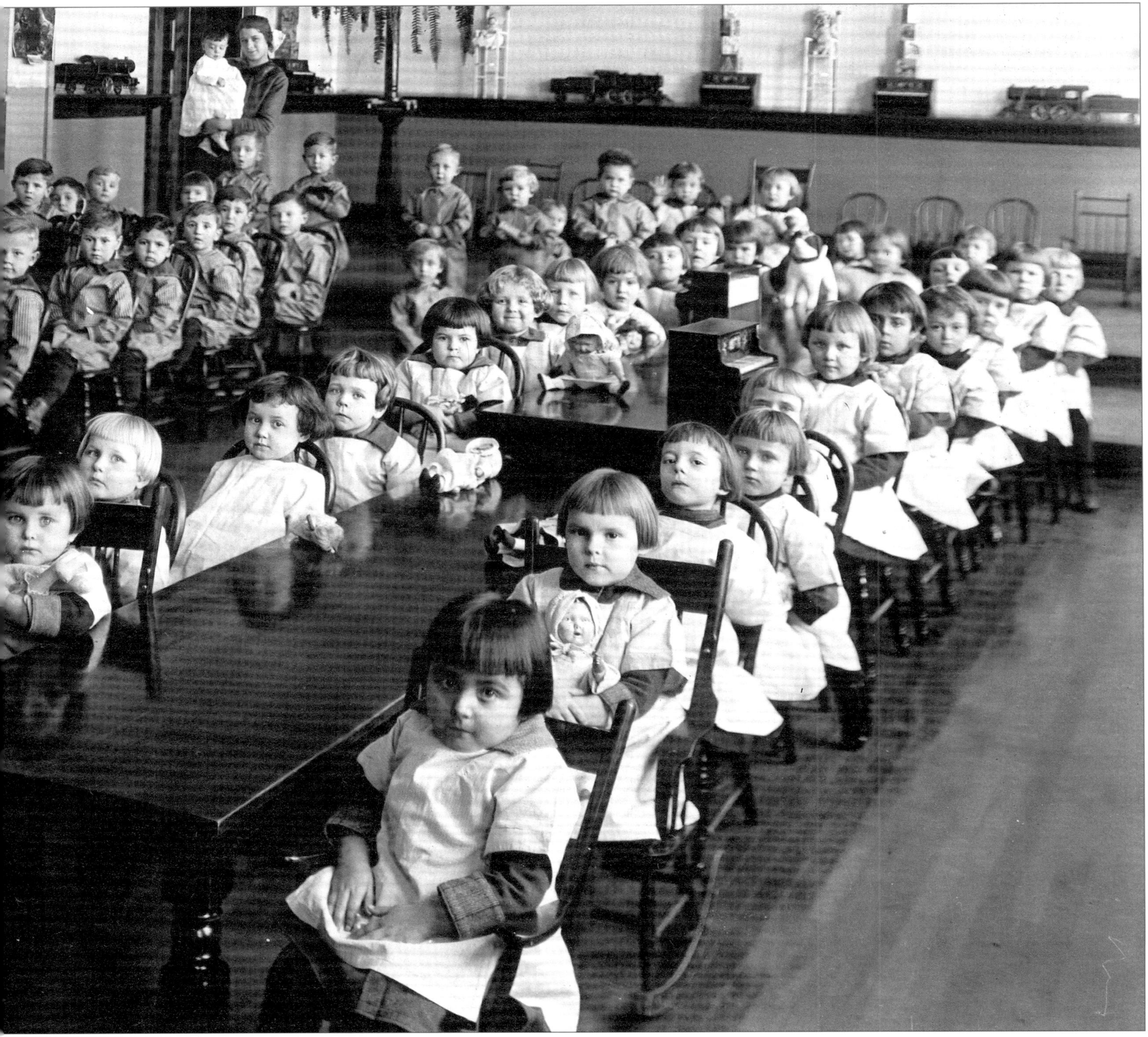

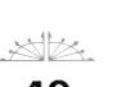

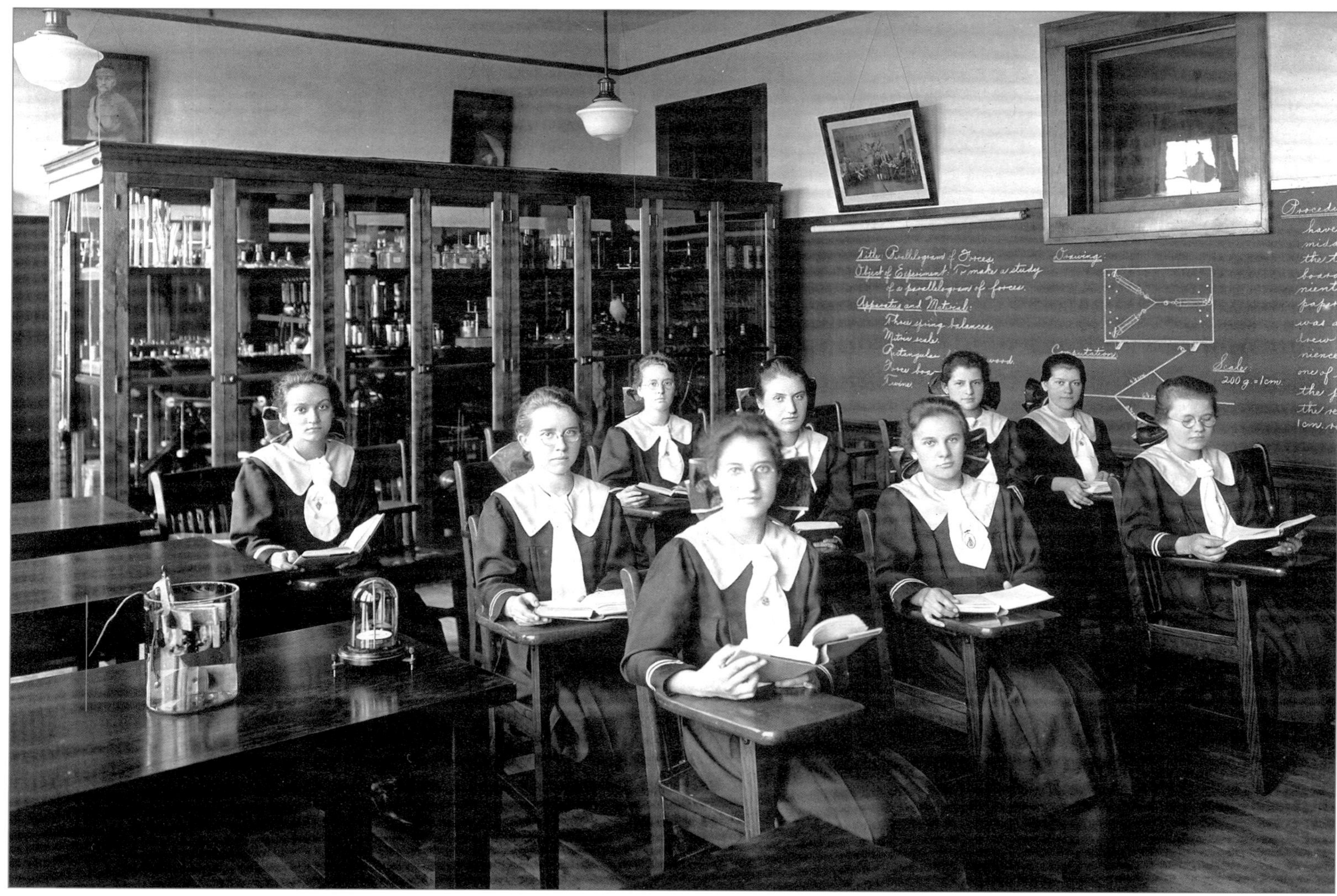

Appearing to pause from their studies, these young ladies posed in their science classroom at the St. Joseph Orphan Asylum in 1924. ***Serial # 23684***

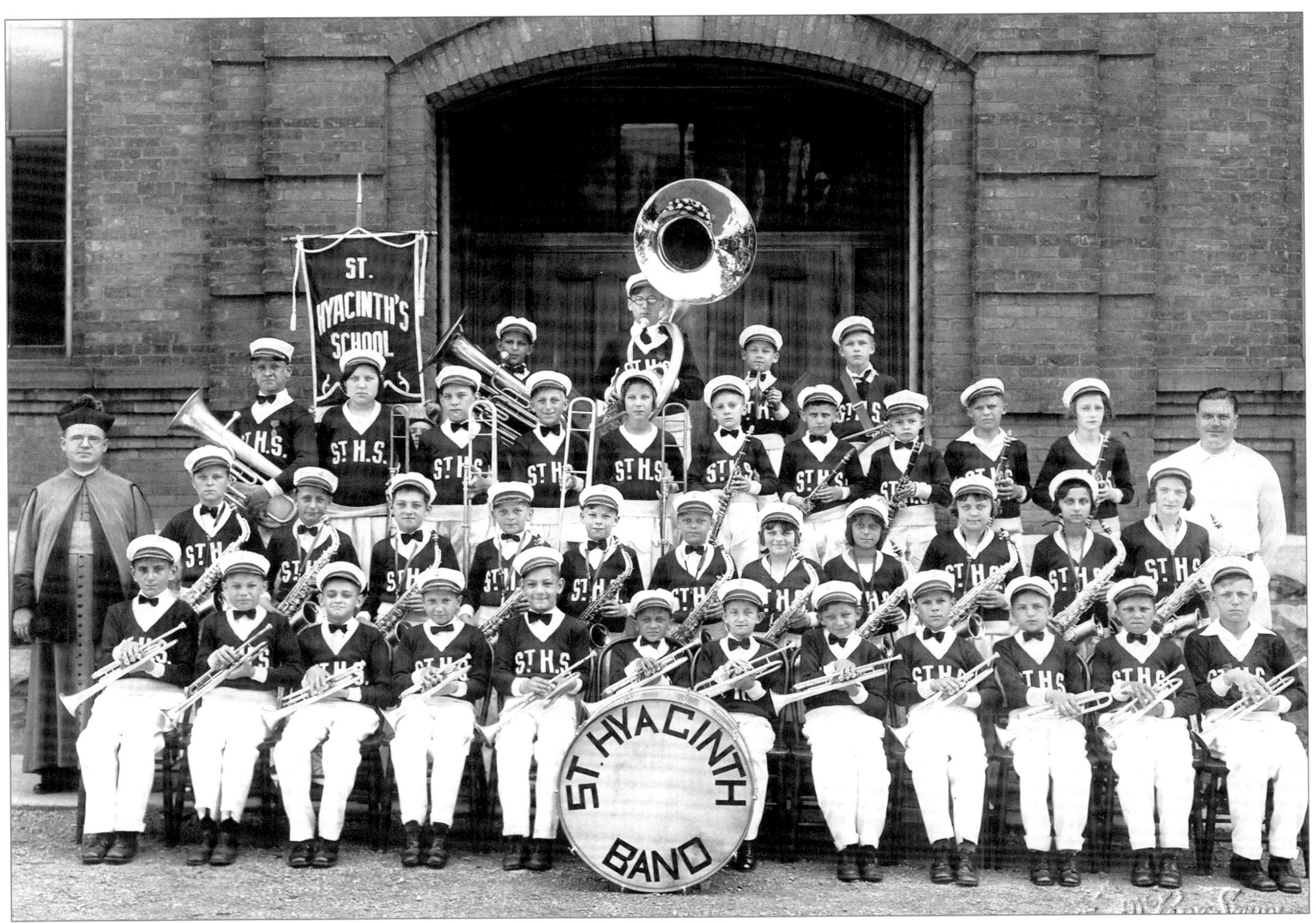

These St. Hyacinth's School students may have developed an appreciation for music by playing an instrument in their school's band in 1931. ***Serial # A03442***

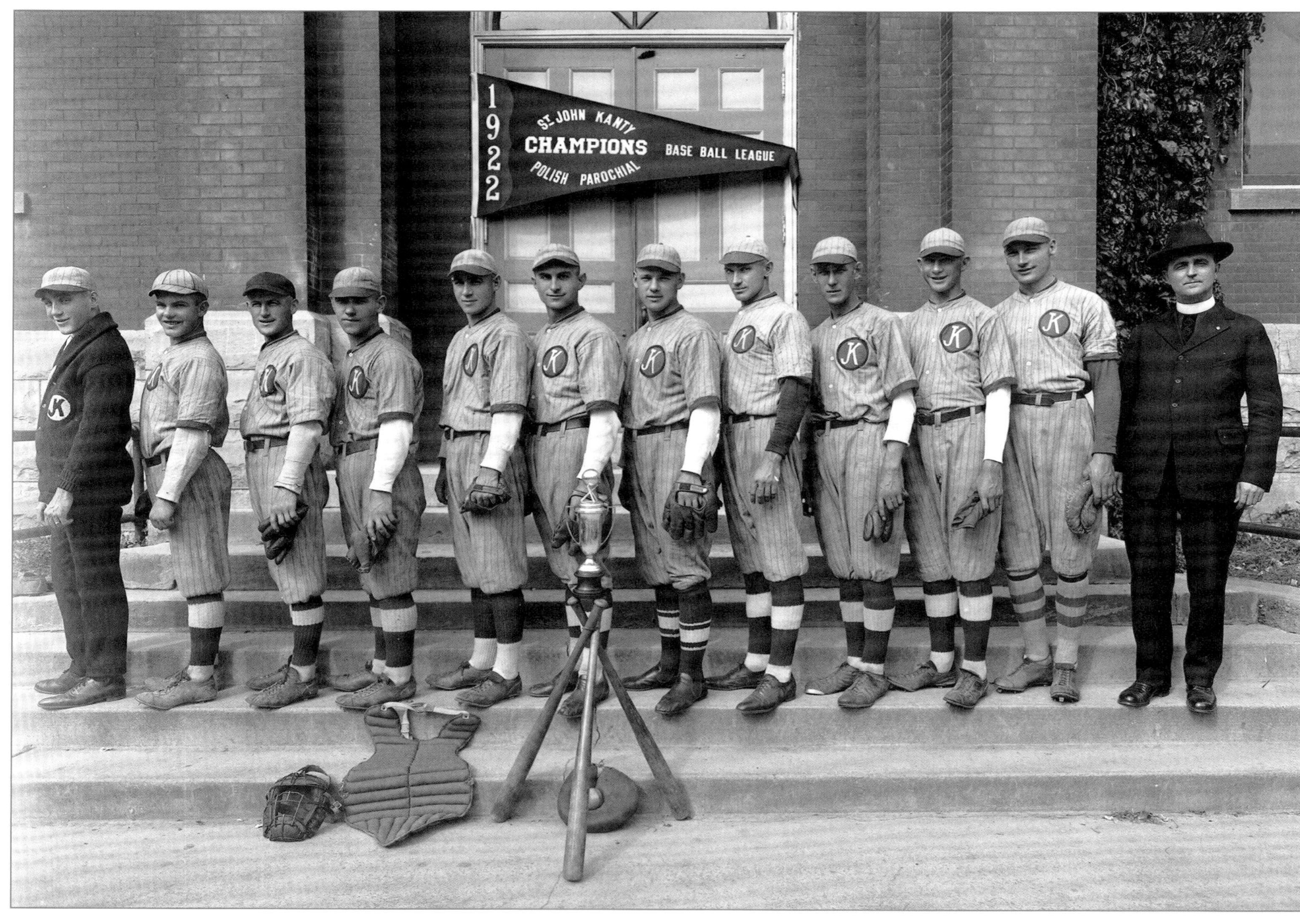

Glowing with pride, the championship 1922 St. John Kanty School baseball team lined up for a victory photograph.

Serial # 20064-3

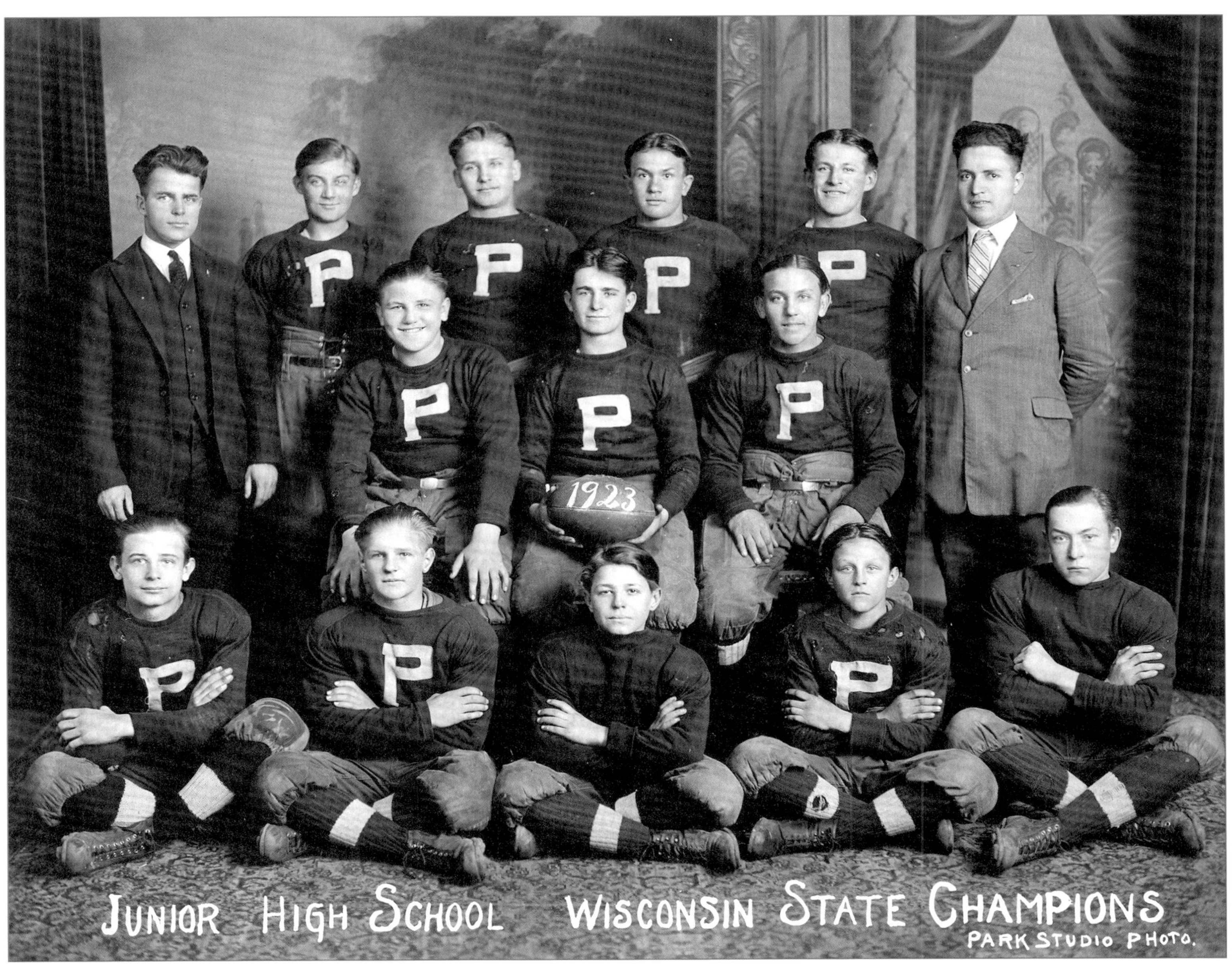

The condition of their uniforms indicates that grit and determination led the 1923 Kosciuszko Pre-Vocational Junior High School football team to a state victory. The P on their uniforms stands for "prevocational." ***Serial # 22213***

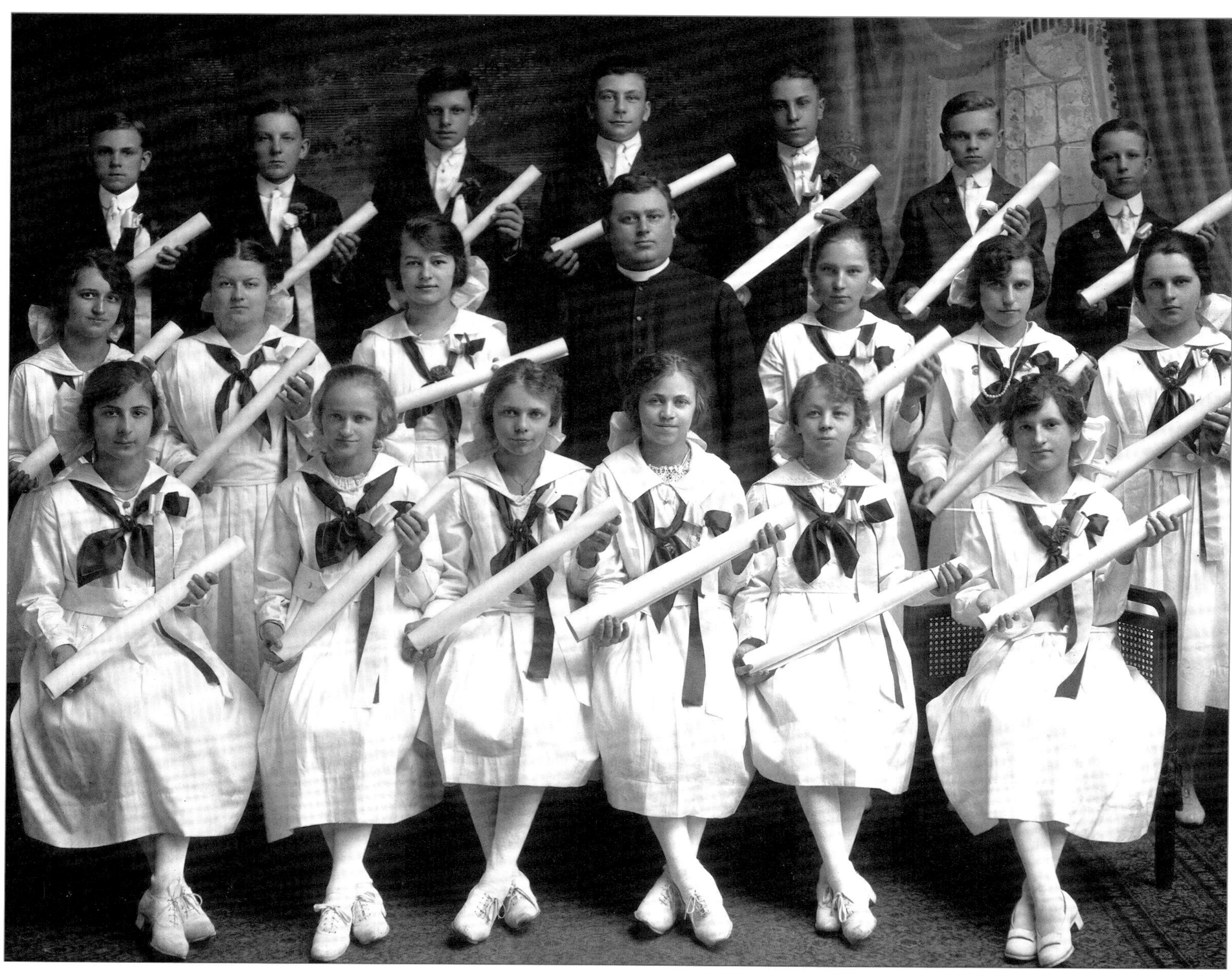

The graduates of St. Stanislaus School proudly held their diplomas for this photograph taken circa 1919. *Serial # 11912*

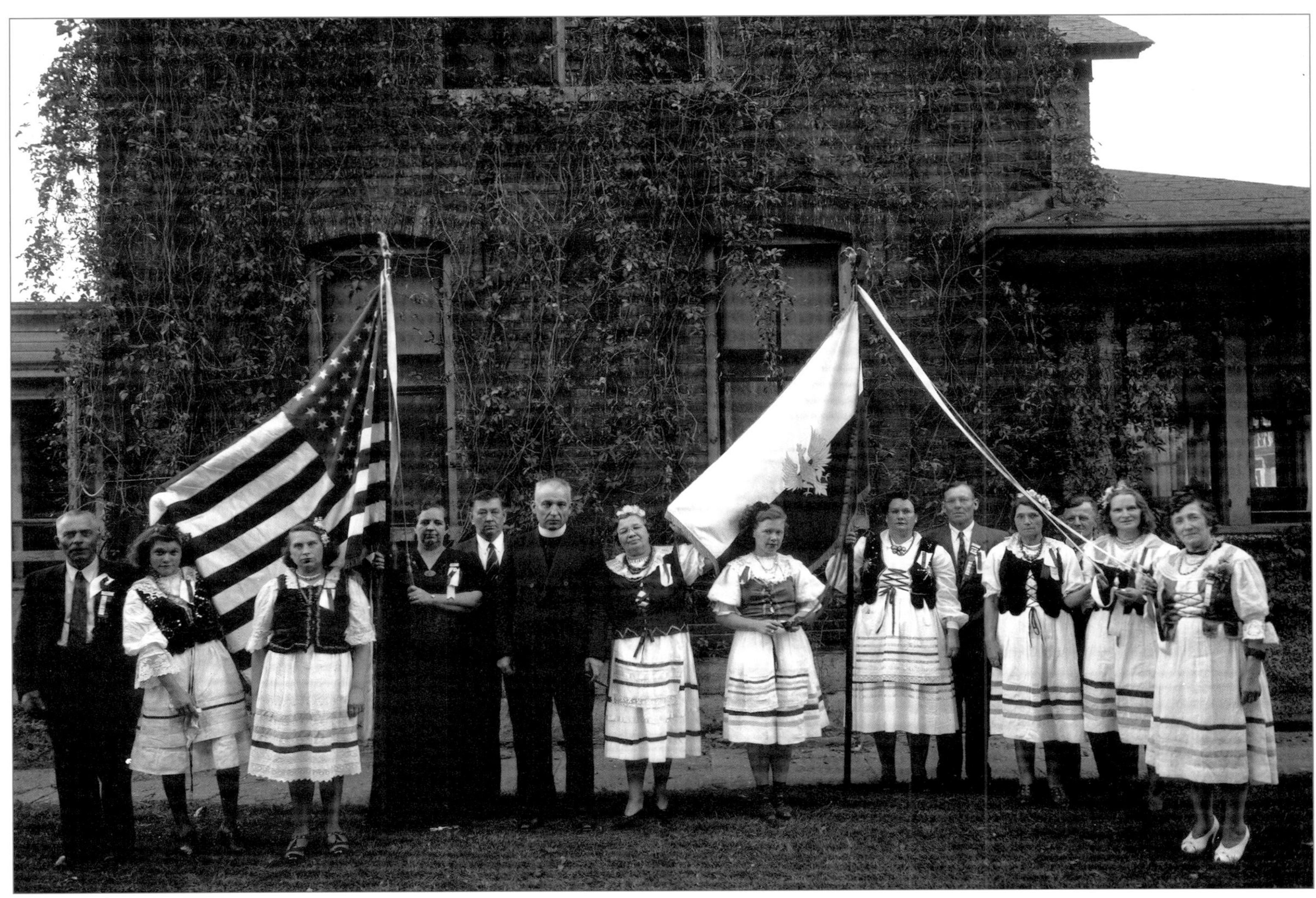

In 1941 the Sacred Heart of Jesus Roman Catholic Church, at 1037 South Eleventh Street, held a ceremony dedicating the U.S. and Polish flags. Poland's national flag is bicolored, a band of white over an equal-sized band of red. The flag in this photograph also incorporated Poland's national emblem, the white eagle.

Serial # A06194-2

CHAPTER FOUR

SOCIAL LIFE

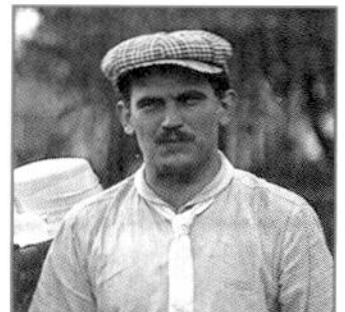

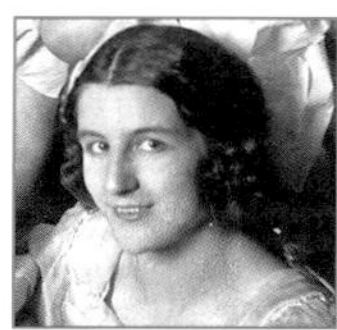

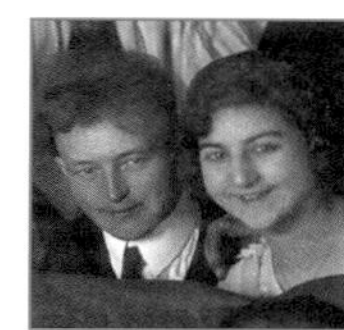

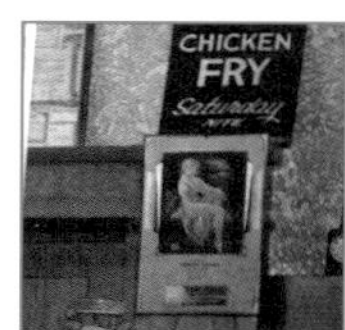

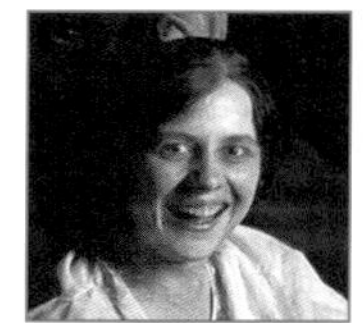

After church, school, and family, Polish South Siders valued the voluntary associations that cropped up by the hundreds as the community evolved. Some were ethnic in nature: dance groups, dramatic troupes, and military organizations that preserved a conscious connection with the homeland. Others satisfied a passion for sports. Sandlot baseball was enormously popular on the South Side, and thousands participated in bowling leagues, shooting clubs, cycling organizations, and other athletic pursuits. Still other associations were simply groupings of friends who came together for special occasions.

The most visible agents of community weren't associations at all but places where South Siders gathered in their free time: bars, pool halls, and barber shops for the men; soda fountains for the younger set. In the early twentieth century, movie theaters joined the list; mass entertainment was steadily supplanting purely local leisure-time pursuits. There was a corresponding shift in modes of pleasure driving. Kwasniewski's most active years coincided with the period when Sunday drivers were transferring their allegiance from horse-drawn carriages to cars and from bicycles to motorcycles.

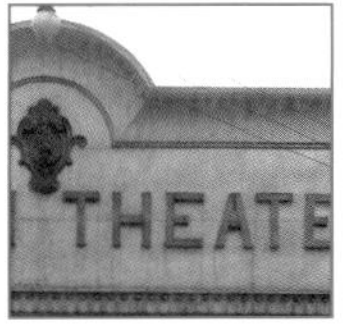

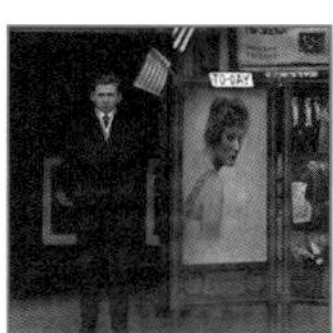

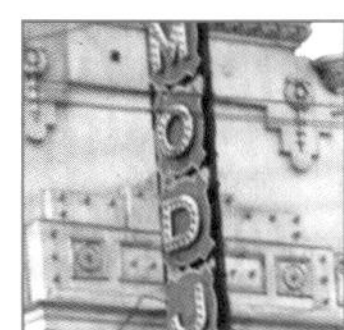

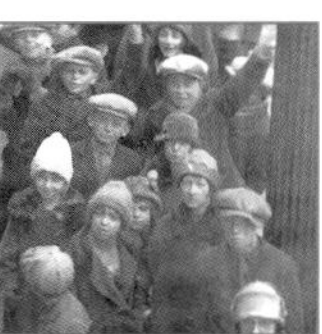

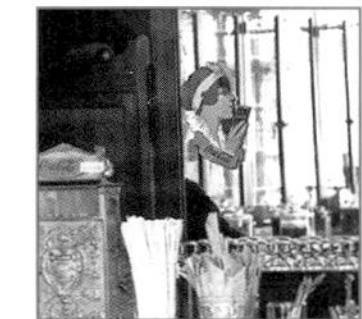

The very existence of leisure time was a great step forward for the community. Recreation was a foreign concept in the early years of the South Side's Polonia; the emphasis then was largely on survival. But there is a larger lesson in this suite of images. Recorded here is the daily round of life on Milwaukee's South Side, a round different from but in every way equivalent to our own. Kwasniewski's photographs demonstrate that epochs and eras exist only in hindsight; they are boxes historians invent to hold what they judge to be the unifying themes. But no one lives inside a theme. For the people of every epoch, our own included, life simply goes on—adjusted as circumstances change but flowing through time in a seamless, ceaseless sequence of days, months, and years.

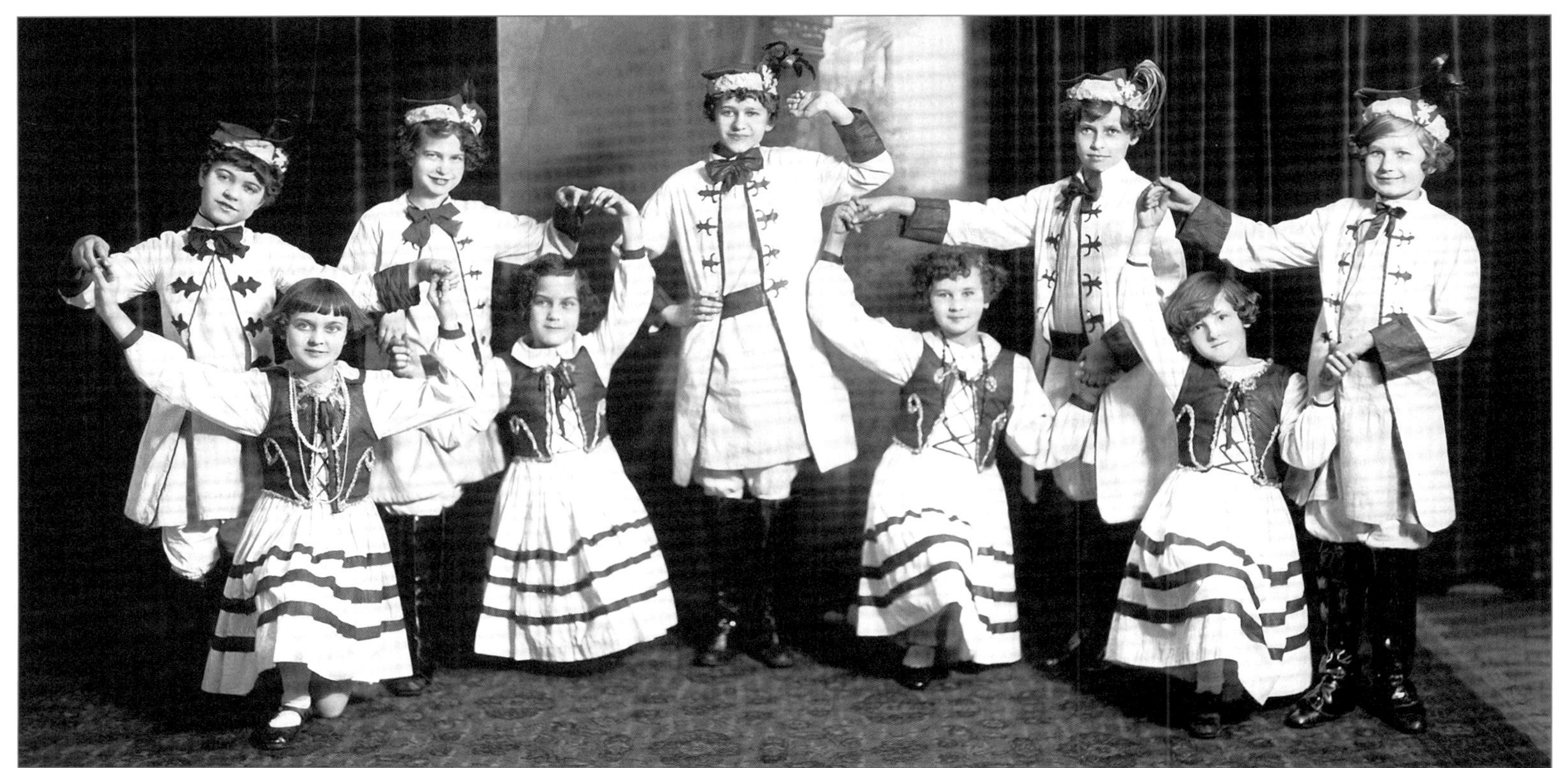

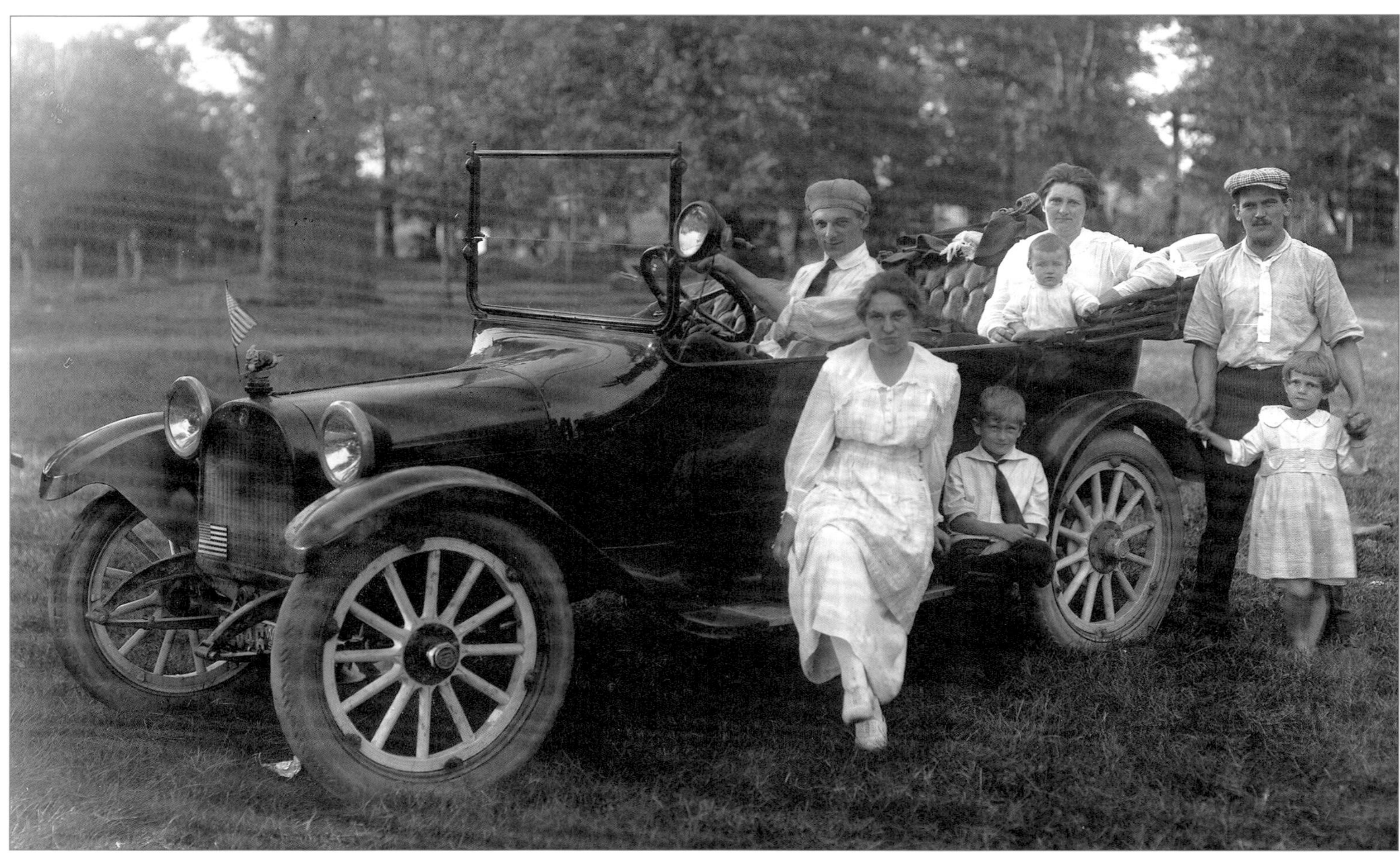

Roman Kwasniewski (standing) stepped out from behind the camera to have himself photographed with his family and another couple in 1917. The two families spent the day at a South Side Hunting and Fishing Club picnic. ***Serial # A00101***

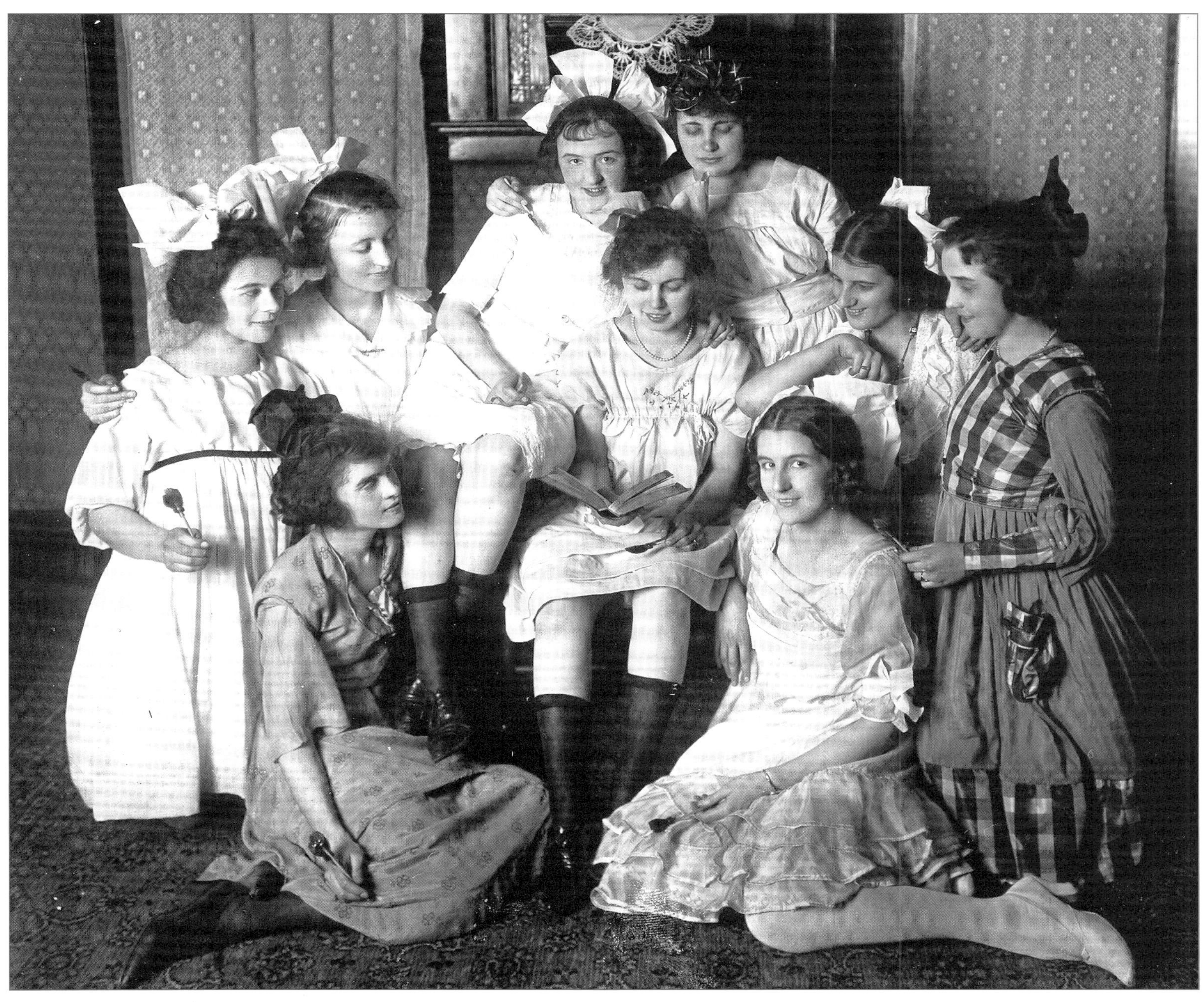

A hint of mischief surrounds these young ladies who gathered for this photograph in 1920. ***Serial # 14480***

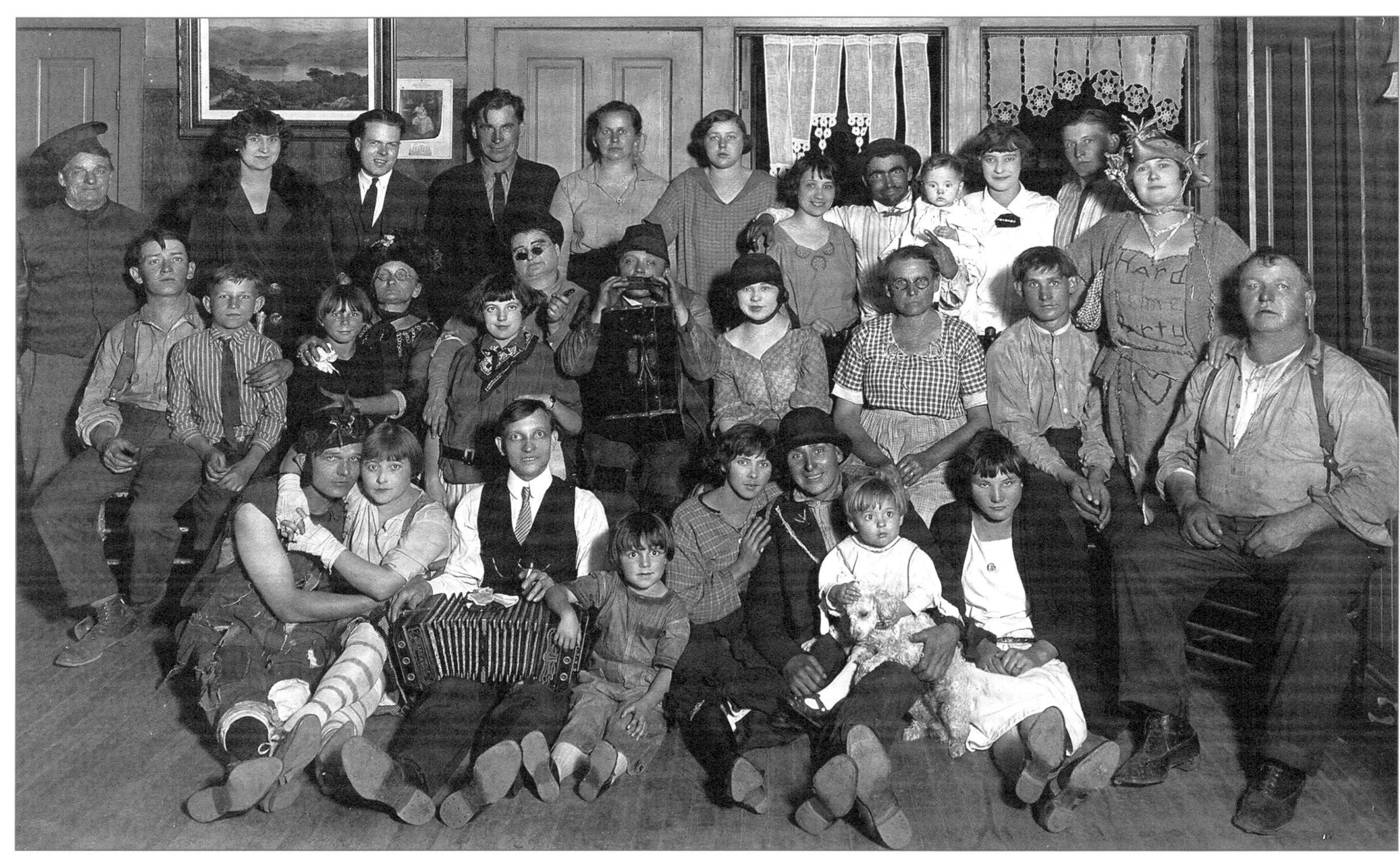

Friends gathered for a "Hard Time Party" in 1924. Theme parties of this type were common during this period.

Serial # 23870

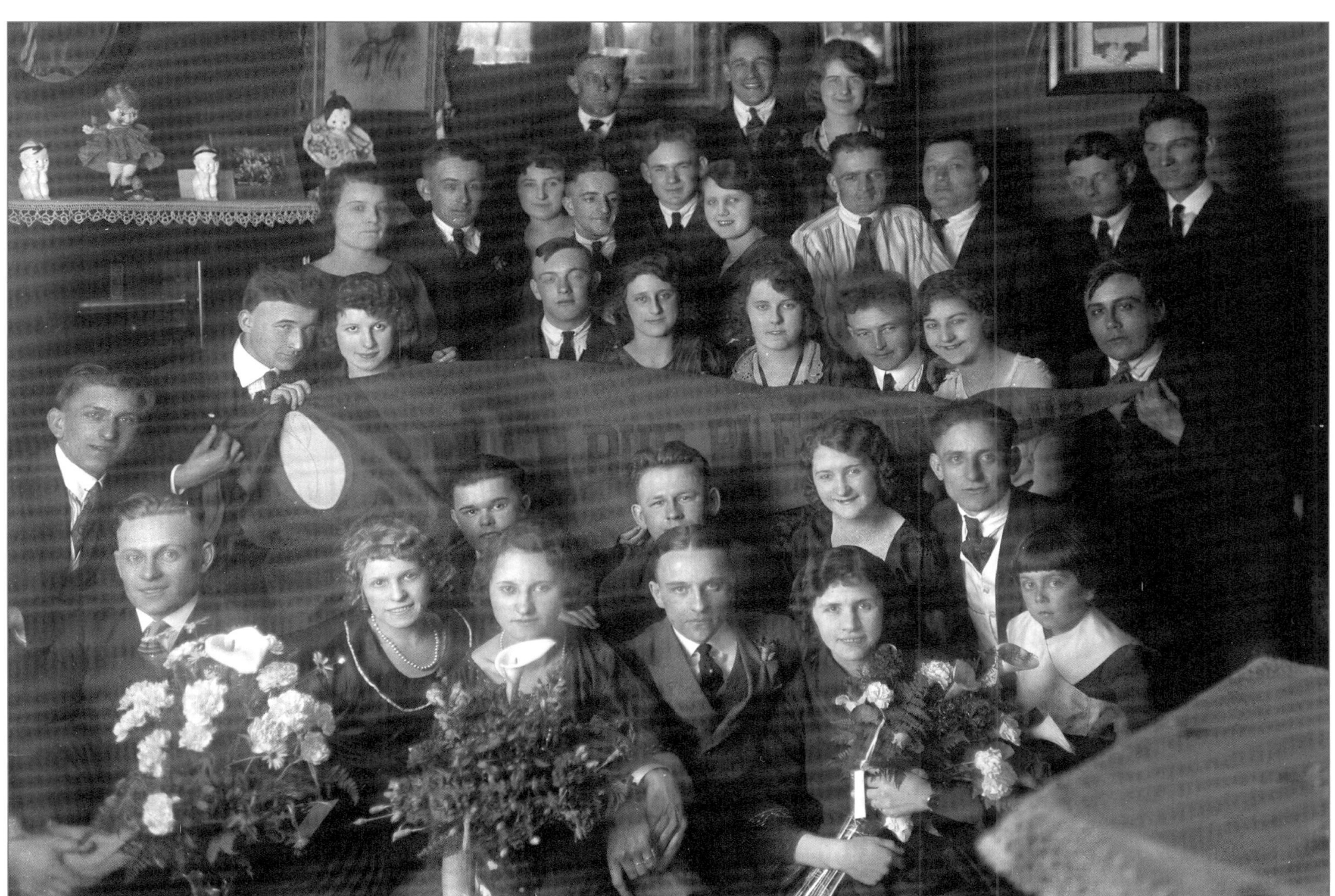

"Pleasure clubs" such as the Rose Bud Pleasure Club sponsored various types of social activities, including dinners, theme parties, and dances. This 1921 photograph was taken on a mid-April day when the club met for a dinner party at the Kurczewski residence on Arthur Avenue. *Serial # 17292*

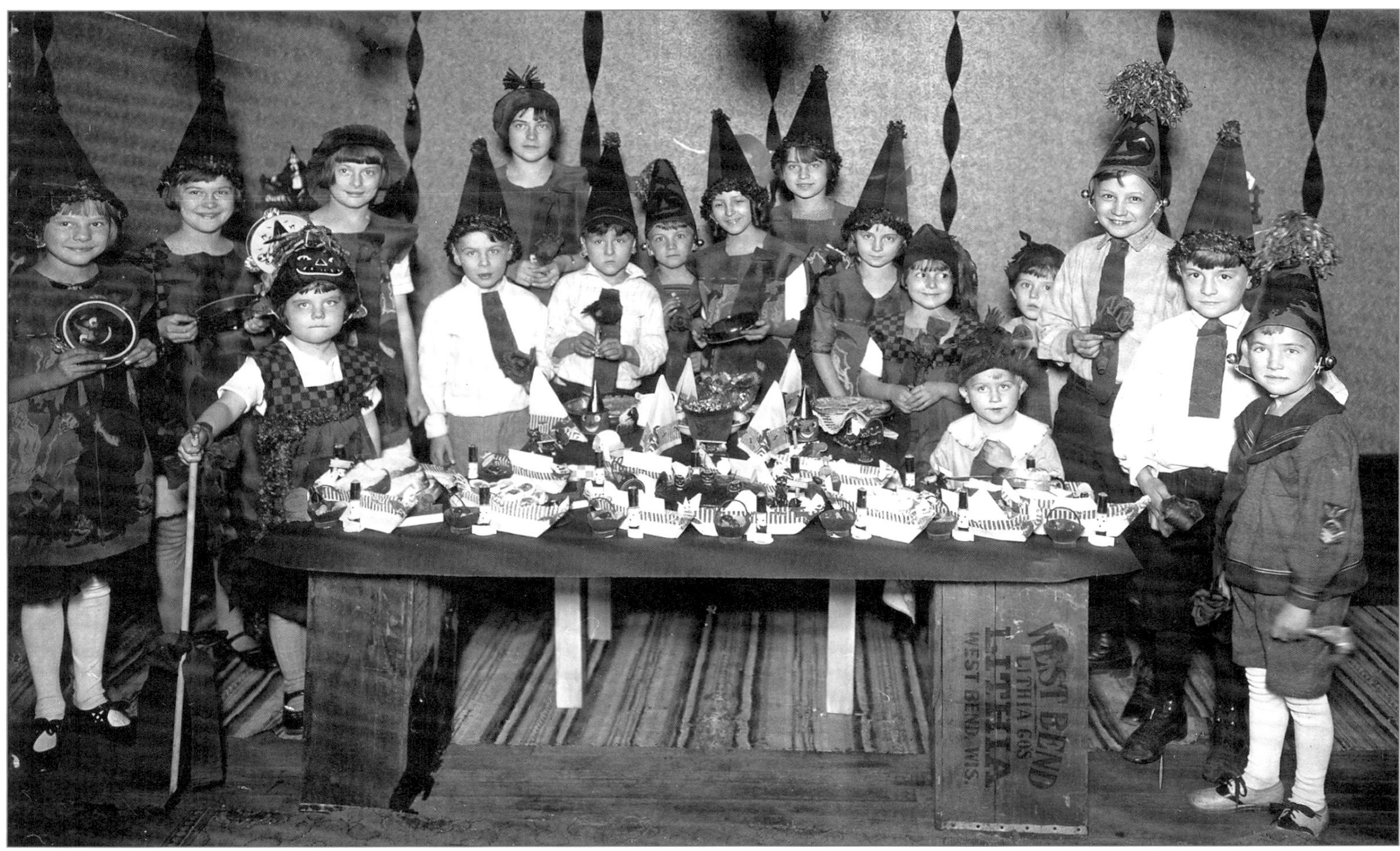

These merrymakers at a Halloween party in 1925 were all smiles knowing that the makeshift table full of treats awaited them.

Serial # 24874

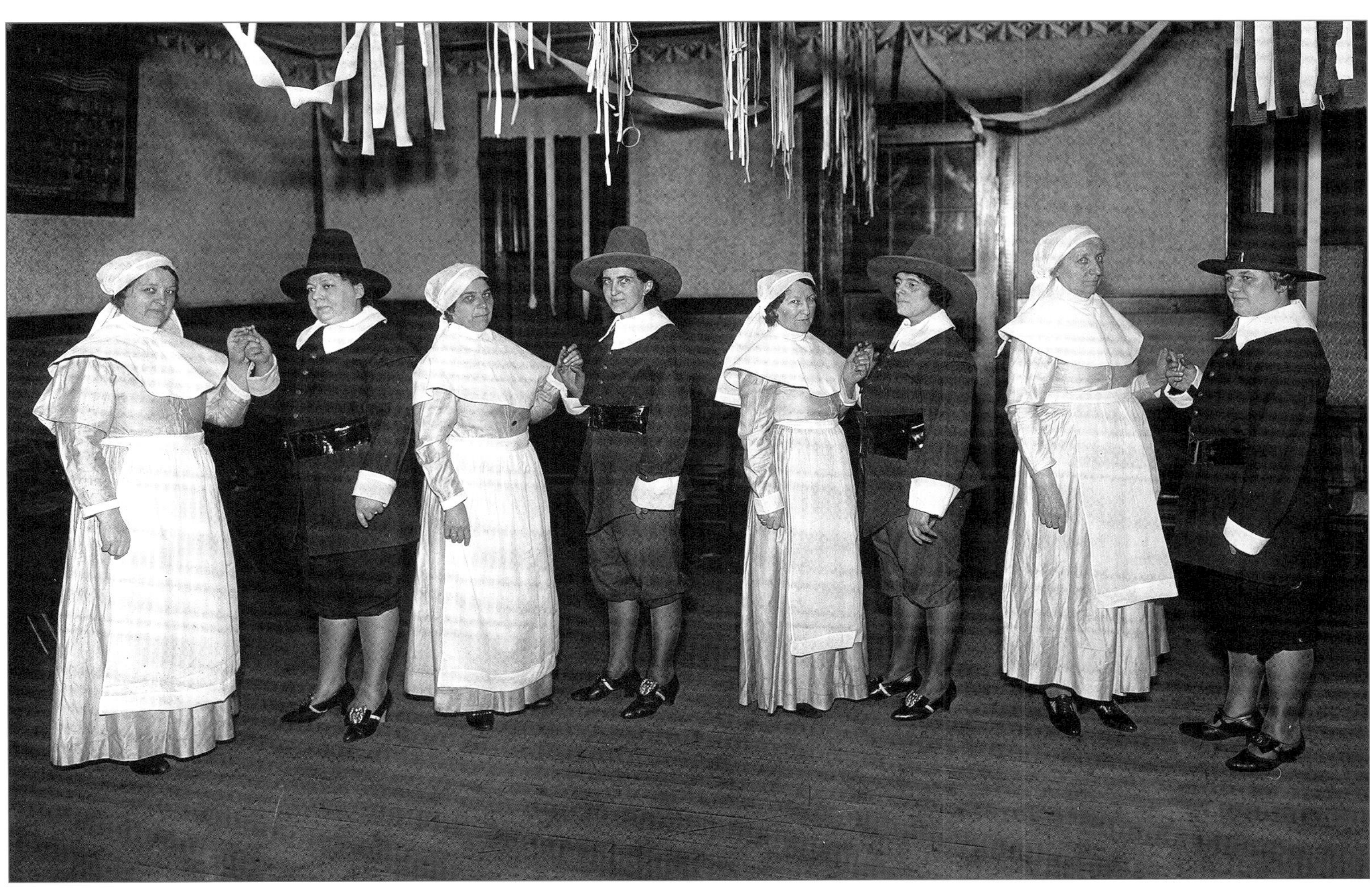

Attired for a 1933 Thanksgiving celebration, these individuals, all women, appeared ready for some dancing.

Serial # A00059

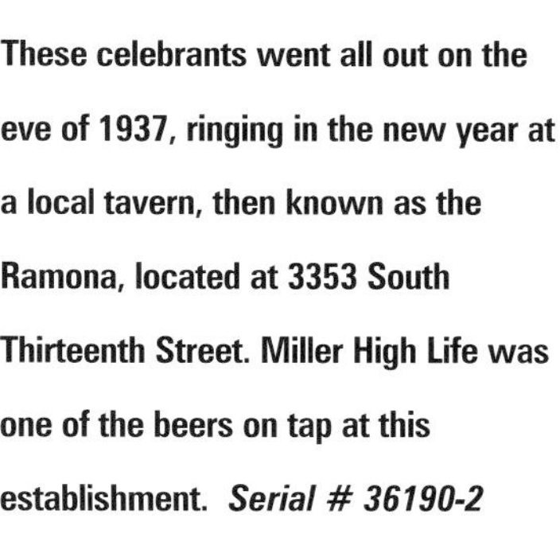

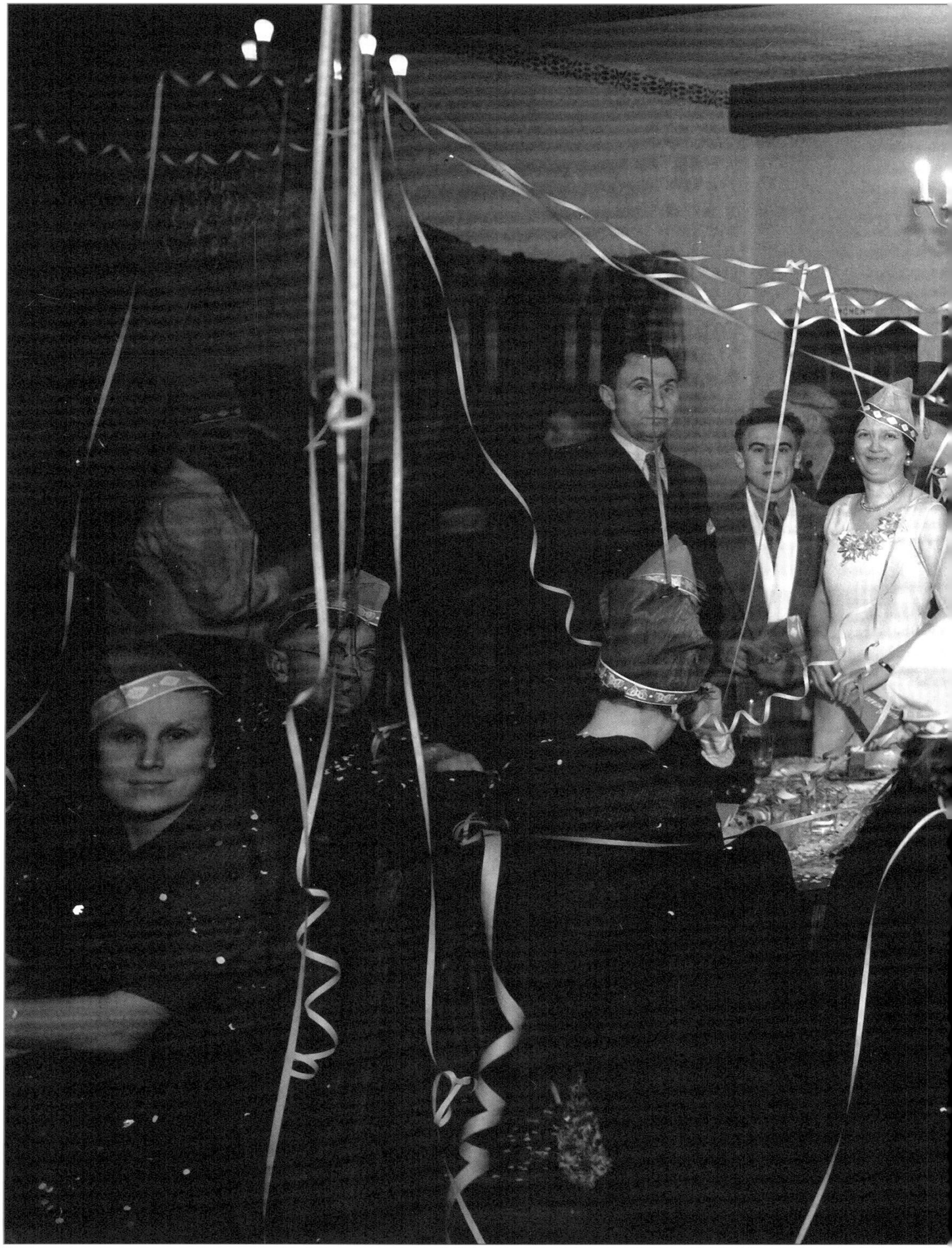

These celebrants went all out on the eve of 1937, ringing in the new year at a local tavern, then known as the Ramona, located at 3353 South Thirteenth Street. Miller High Life was one of the beers on tap at this establishment. ***Serial # 36190-2***

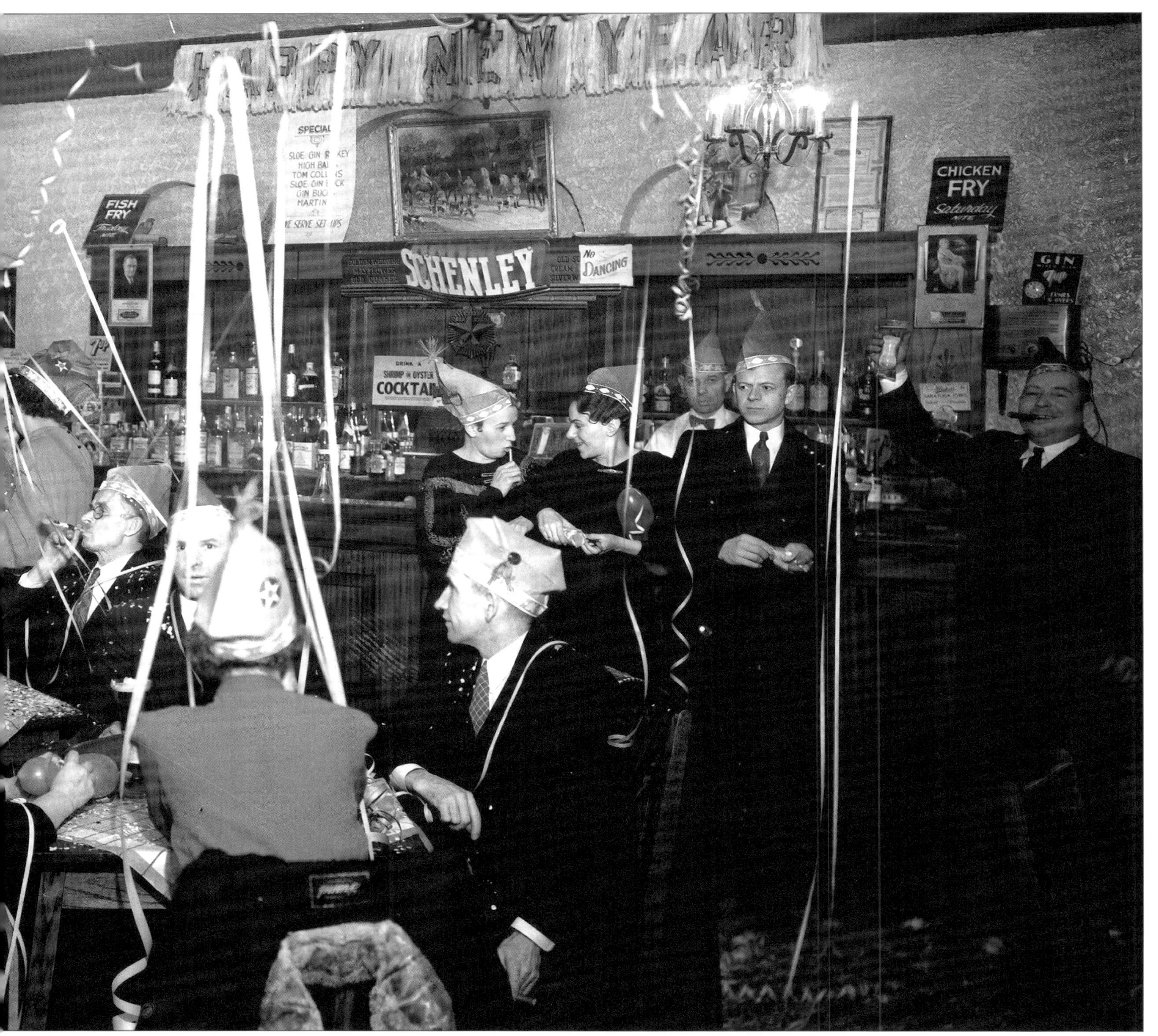
SPECIAL
FISH FRY
SCHENLEY
No DANCING
CHICKEN FRY
Saturday NITE
DRINK A
COCKTAI
GIN

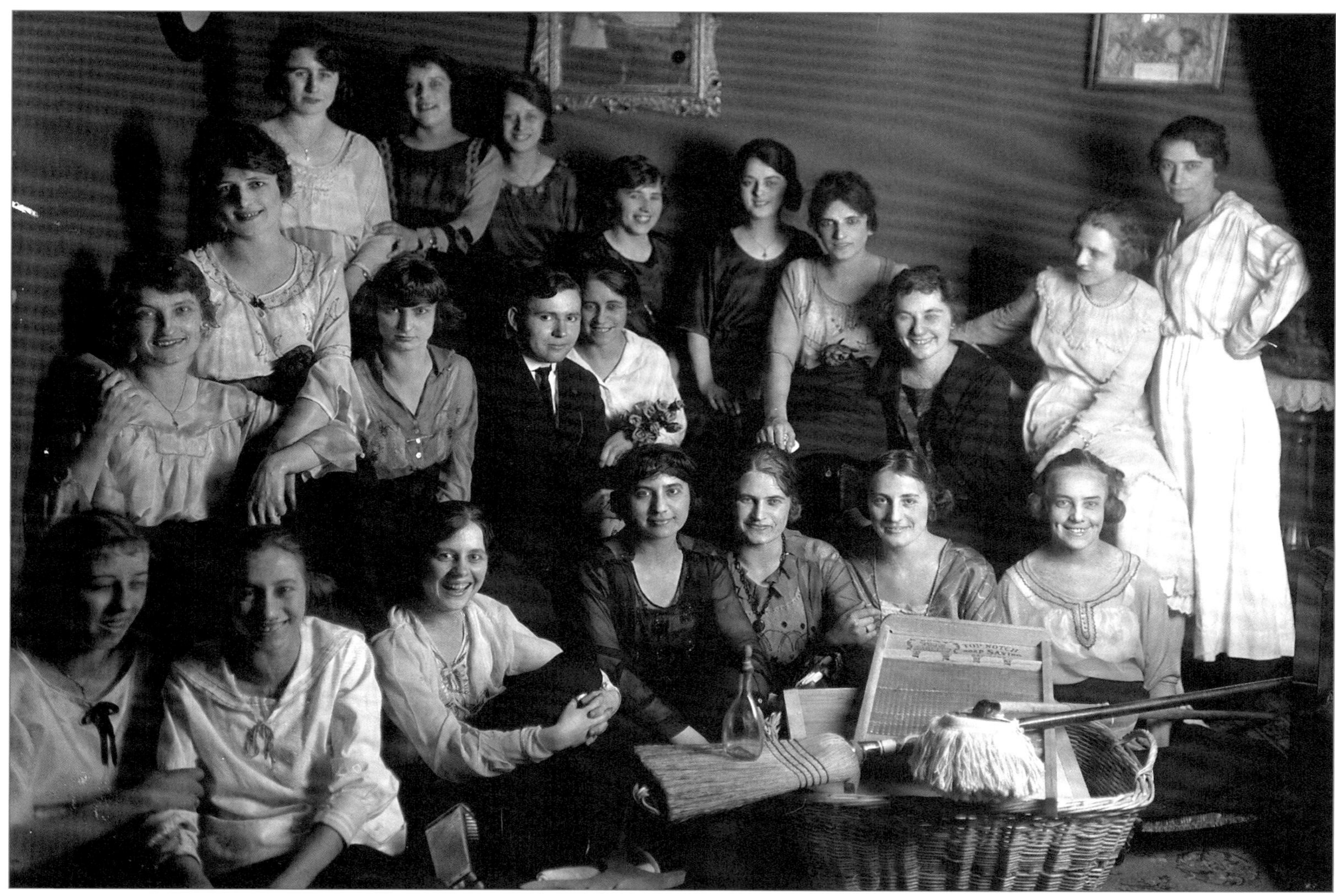

Family and girl friends appear to have thrown a special party, identified as a "washboard party," possibly a wedding shower, for the young couple in the center of the photograph. The photograph was taken in July 1920 for a member of the Ciezki family. ***Serial # 15127***

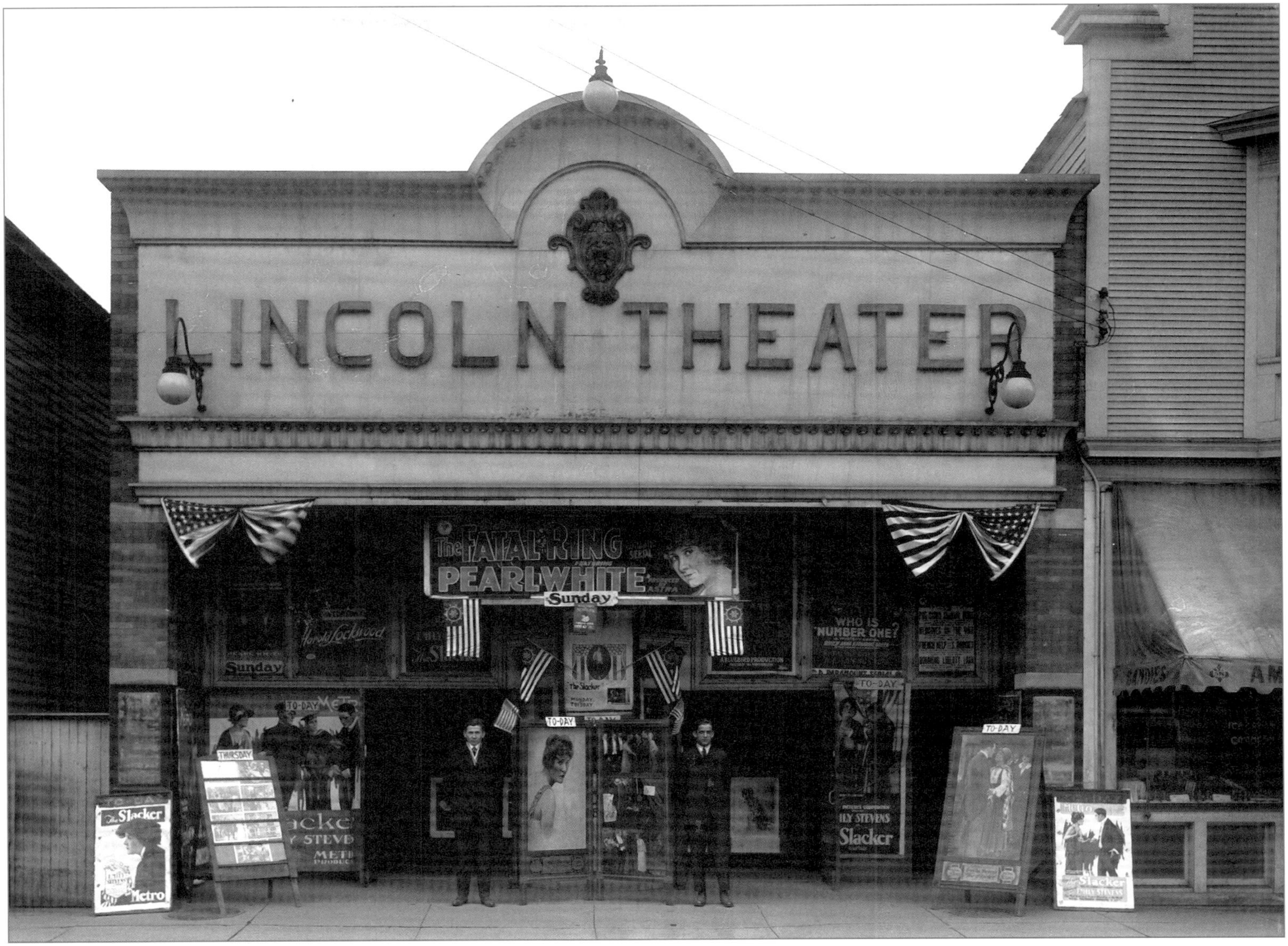

The Lincoln Theater, located on Lincoln Avenue, was built in 1910, around the time when movie theaters were gaining in popularity. By 1910 Milwaukee had sixty-four operating movie theaters. In the 1950s, with the advent and affordability of television, the golden age of the movie theater began to draw to a close. The Lincoln Theater closed in 1955. This photograph is from around 1918. ***Serial # A07329***

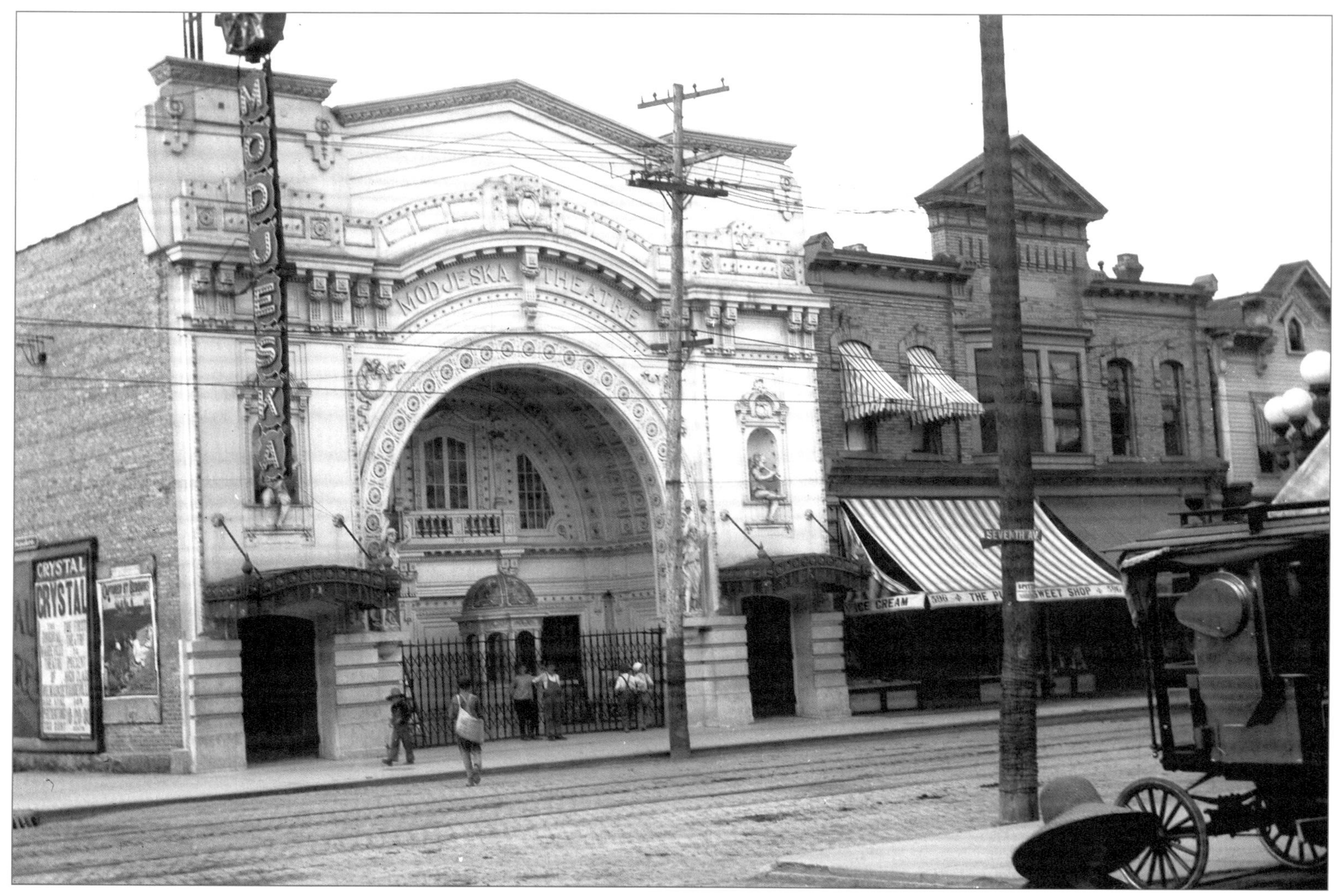

The ornate Modjeska Theatre, pictured in this undated photograph, was built in 1910 at what was then the corner of Seventh Avenue (today South Twelfth Street) and Mitchell Street. In the mid-1920s the owners demolished the original nine-hundred-seat theater and replaced it with a larger structure at the same location, more than doubling the theater's seating capacity.

Serial # A07255

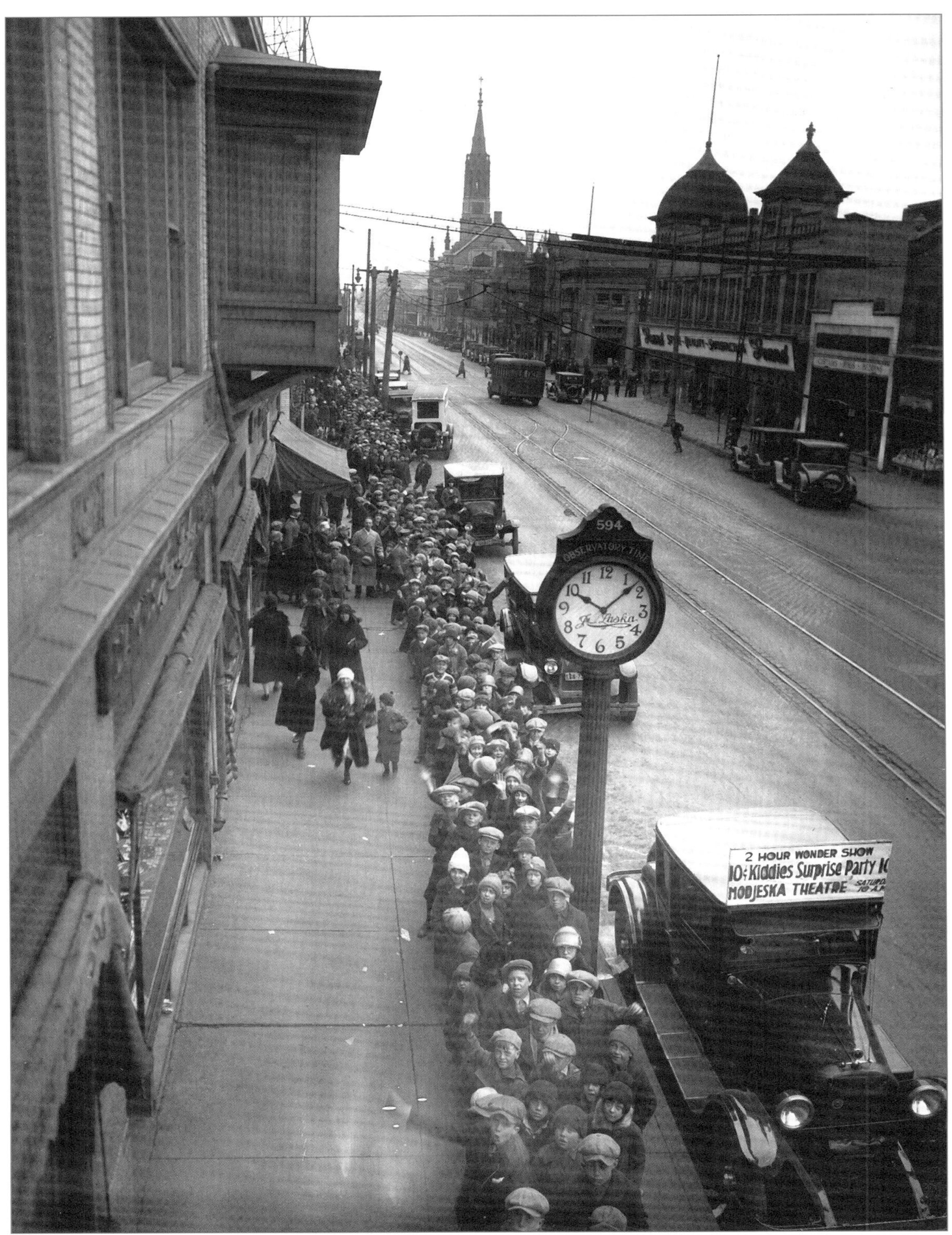

This crowd lining Mitchell Street attests to the popularity of the movie theater as a form of entertainment. These moviegoers were waiting to be admitted into the new two-thousand-seat Modjeska Theatre in 1926, for what appears to be a special show for kids. ***Serial # 25127***

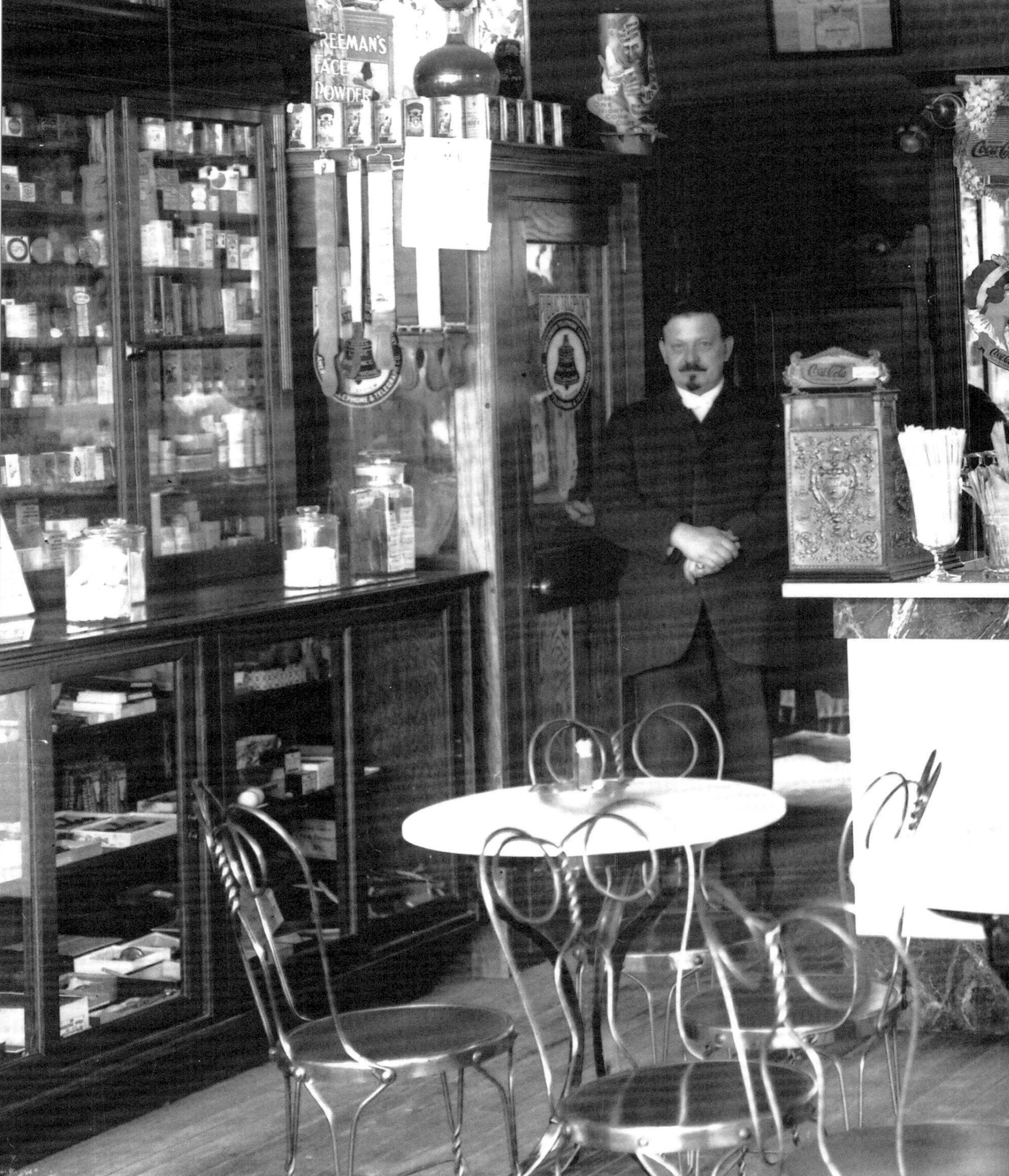

At one time soda fountains, located in neighborhood pharmacies, were popular social gathering places. Customers visiting this establishment in the early twentieth century could indulge in ice cream, sundaes, and soft drinks such as Coca-Cola.
Serial # A07058

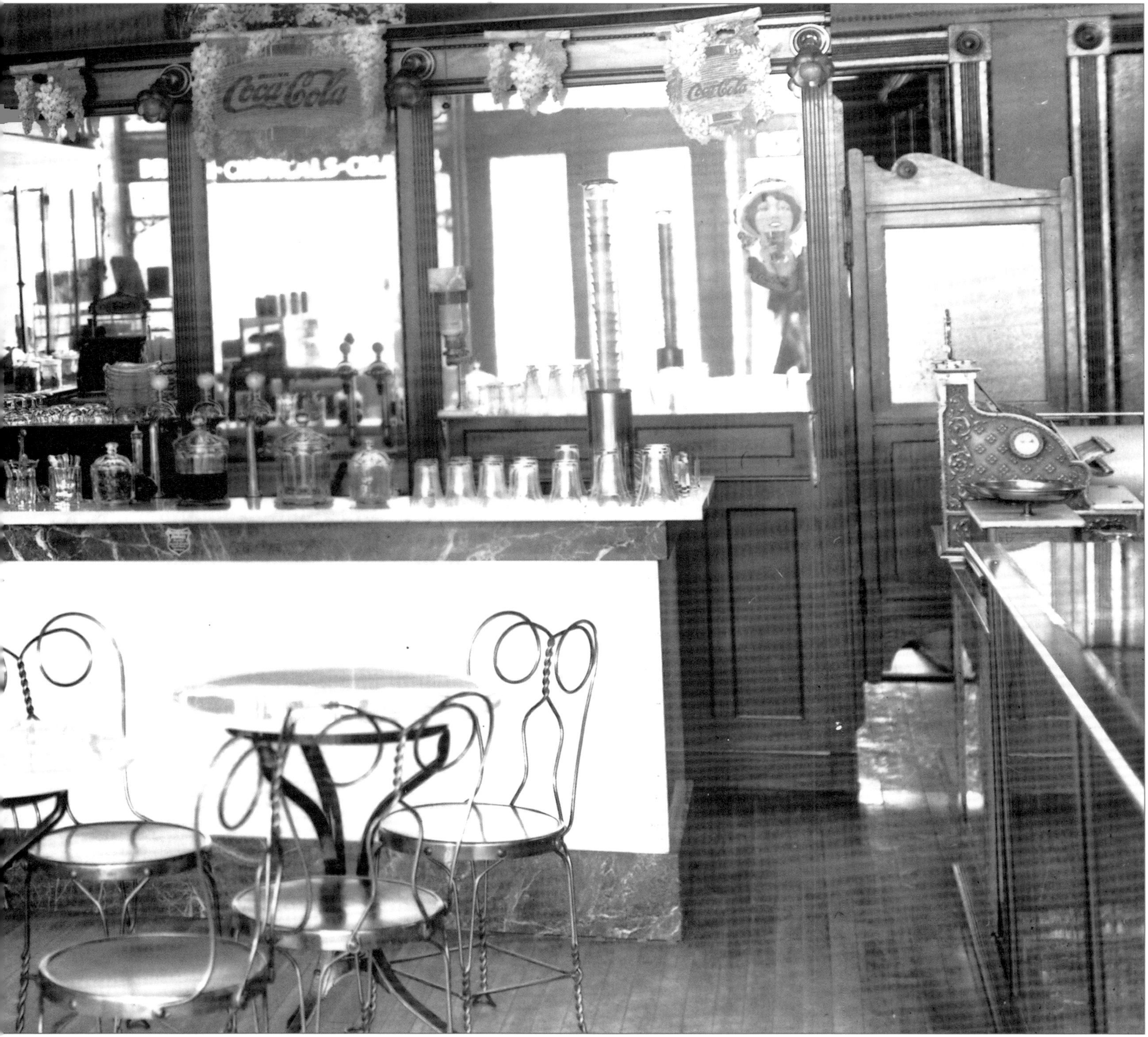

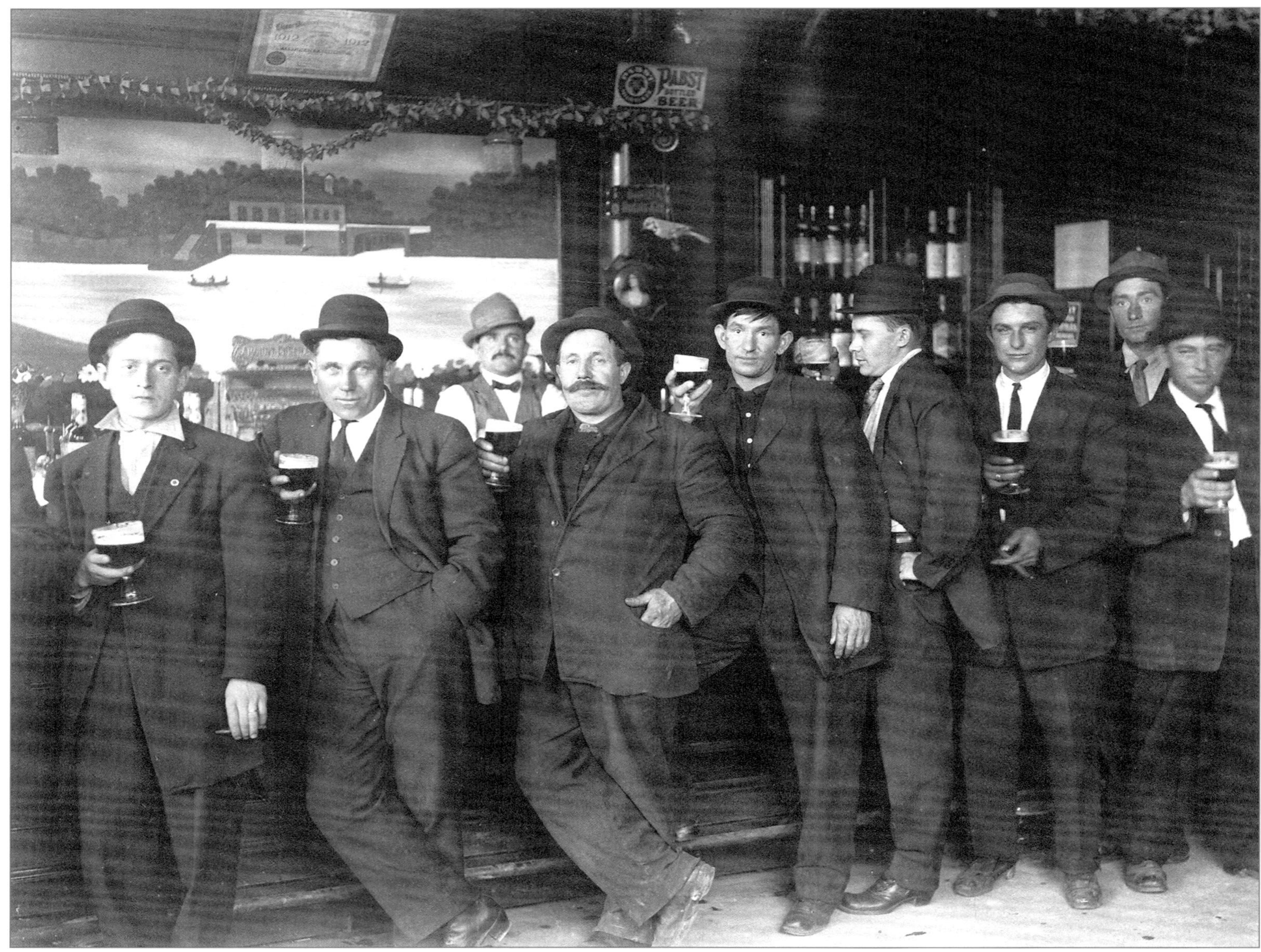

These men belly up to an unidentified bar in 1912. This saloon, like many in those days, used sawdust on the floor in front of the bar to blot up spilled beer. The sign above the bar indicates that the tavern sold Pabst. ***Serial # A15186***

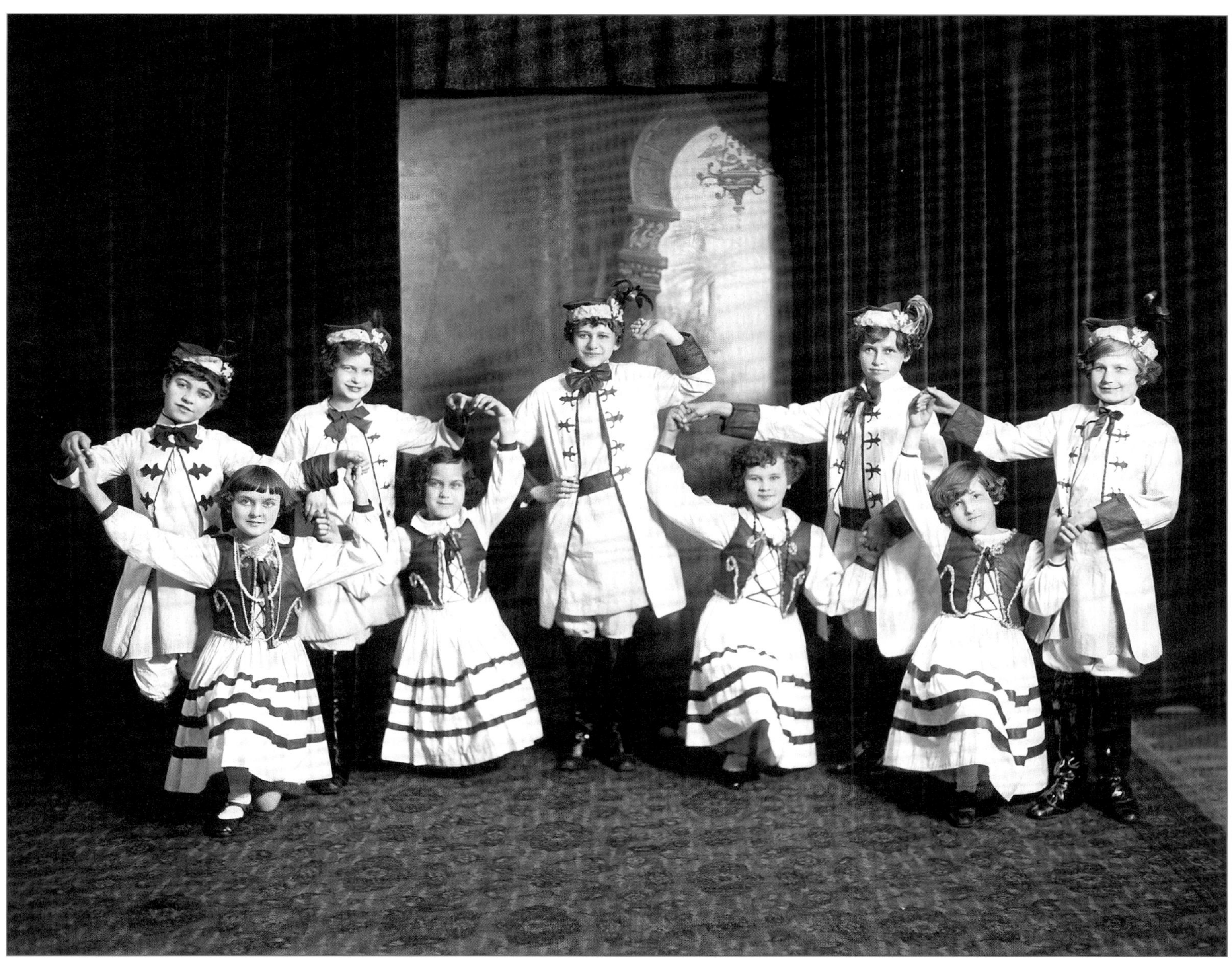

Milwaukee's Poles, like other ethnic groups, passed their customs and traditions on to the younger generation. Dressed in their colorful costumes, this young dance group, active in 1928, learned to perform Polish folk dances. ***Serial # 28082***

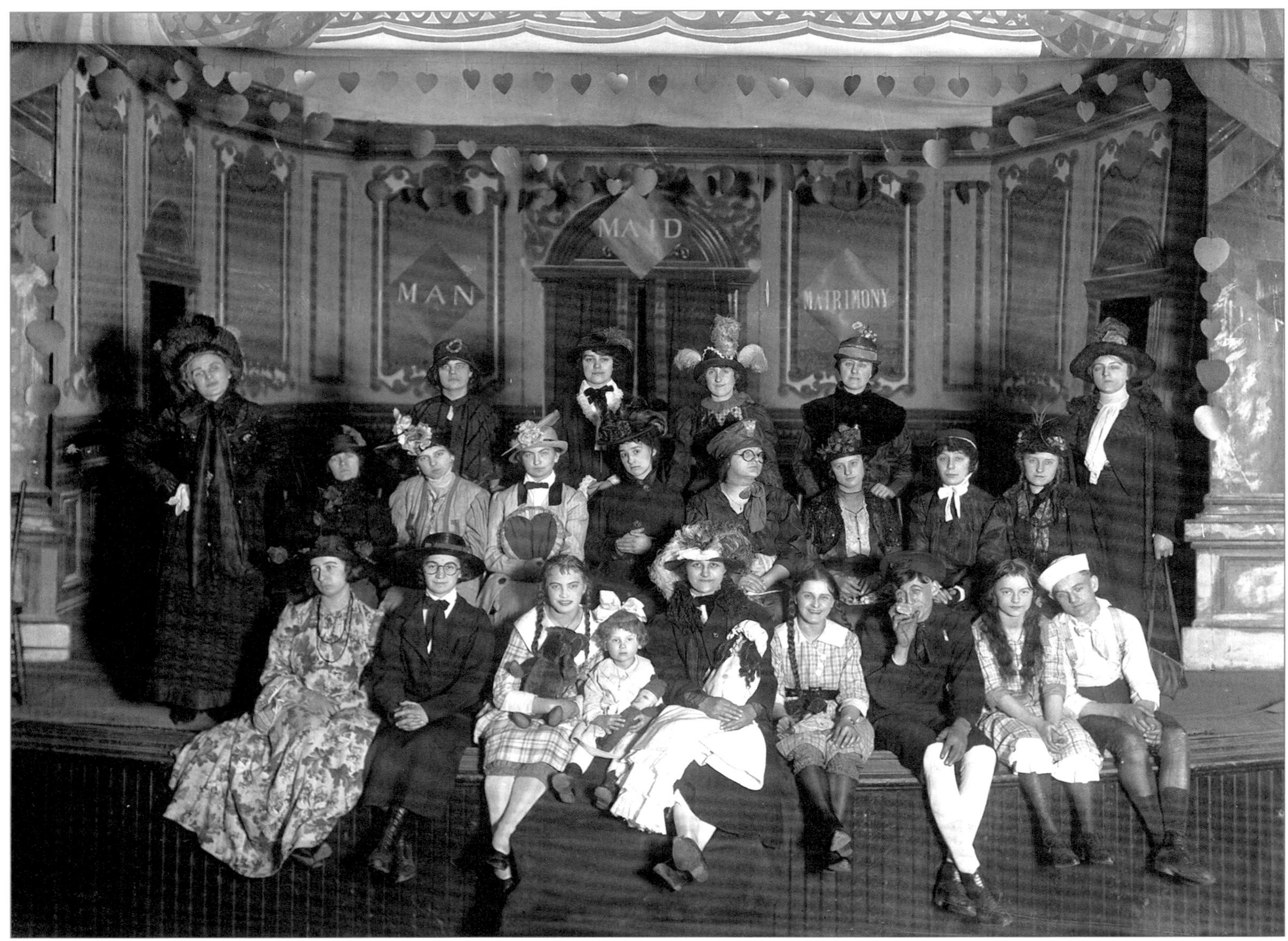

In 1920 the Dramatic Circle of St. Stanislaus staged an "Old Maids Play." Amateur theatrical groups like this one commonly provided local entertainment in an age before television. *Serial # 14532*

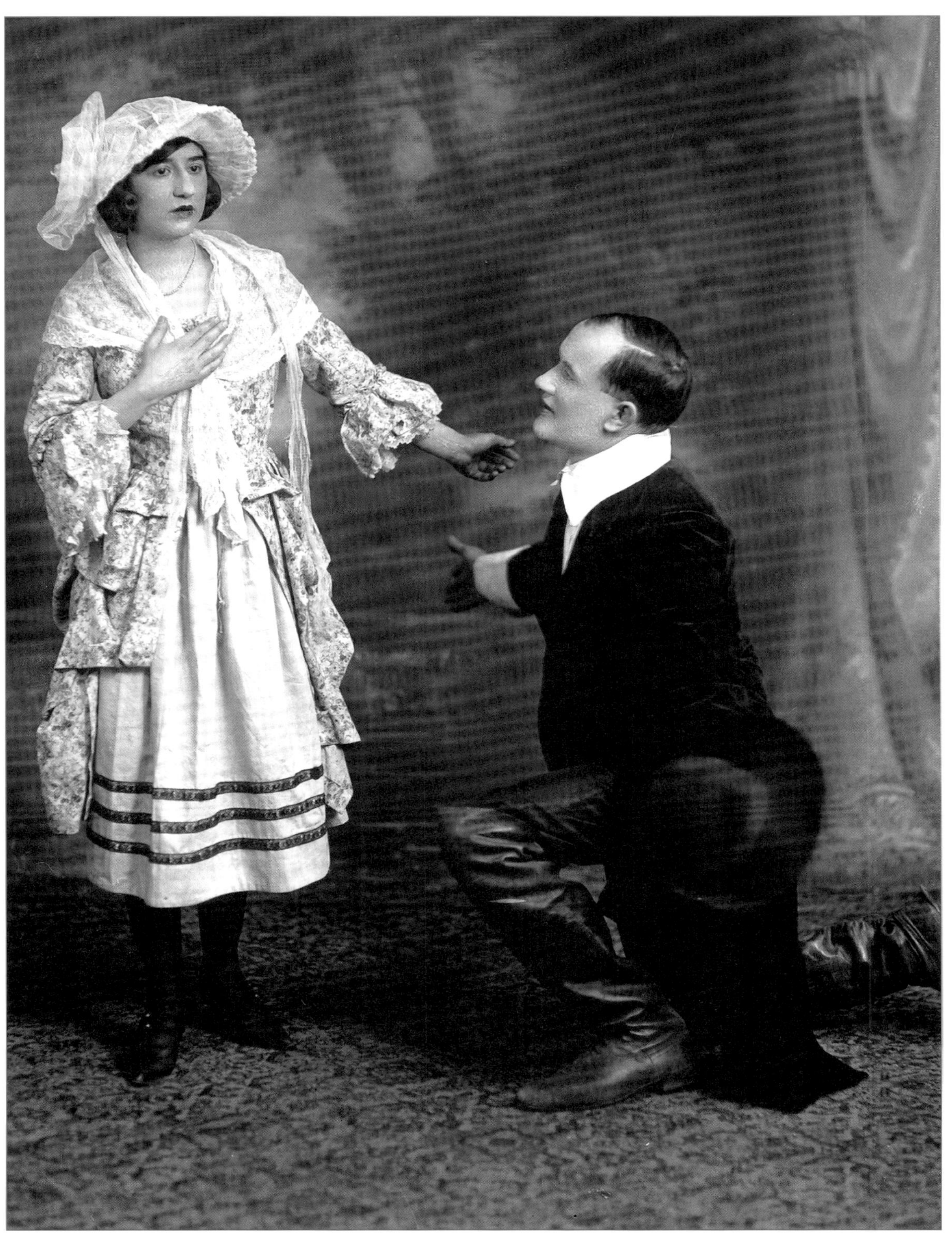

Kwasniewski's clients sometimes had themselves photographed acting out a dramatic moment in the studio. These two performers from the Polish Opera Club, a group of amateur Milwaukee artists, enacted a scene from Friedrich von Flotow's opera *Martha* in 1921. ***Serial # 18036***

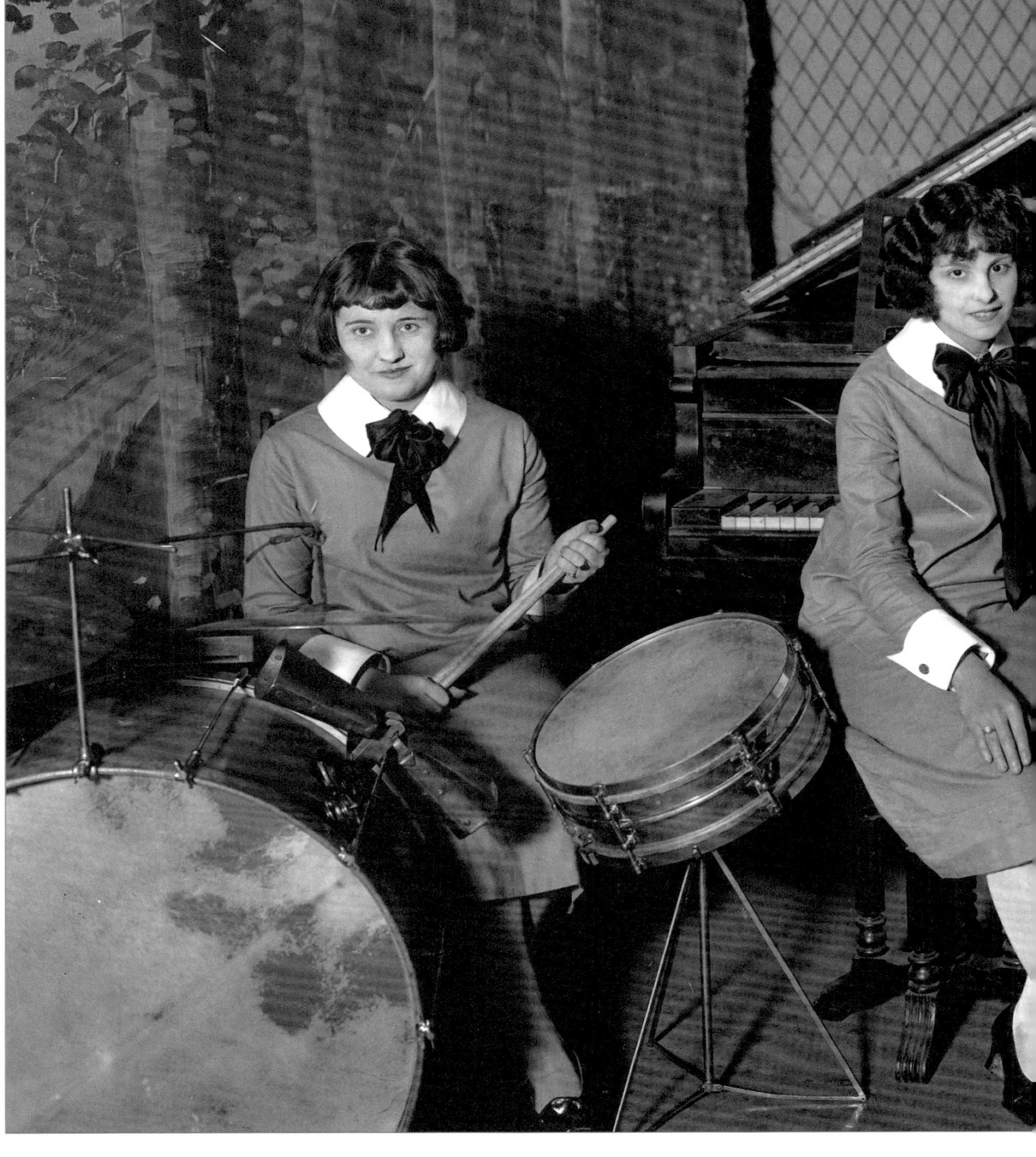

In 1924 bands such as the Sunrise Harmony Queens provided musical entertainment for dancing and singing. The music played would have consisted mainly of traditional folk tunes that were popular in Milwaukee's South Side Polish community.

Serial # 23927

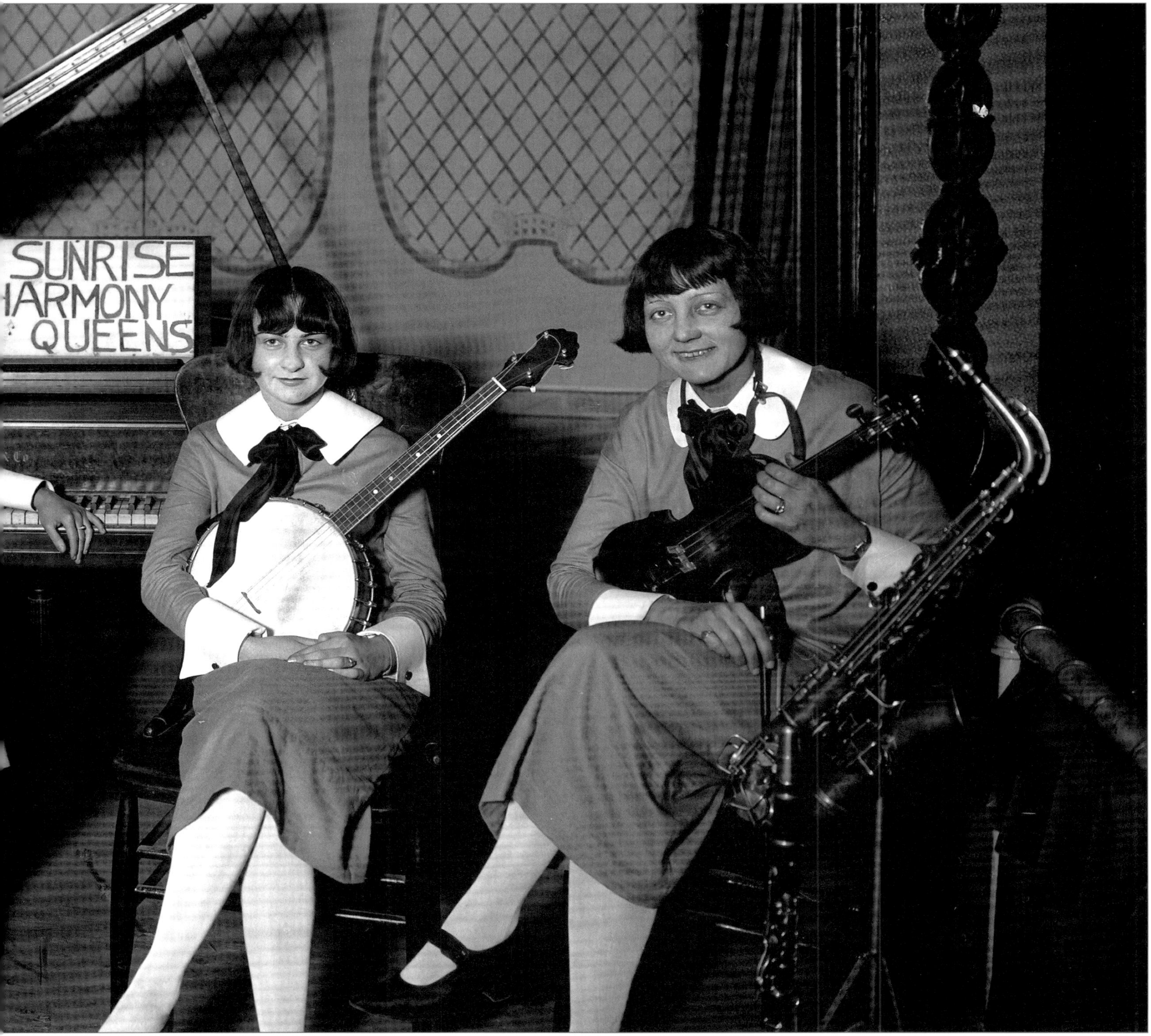

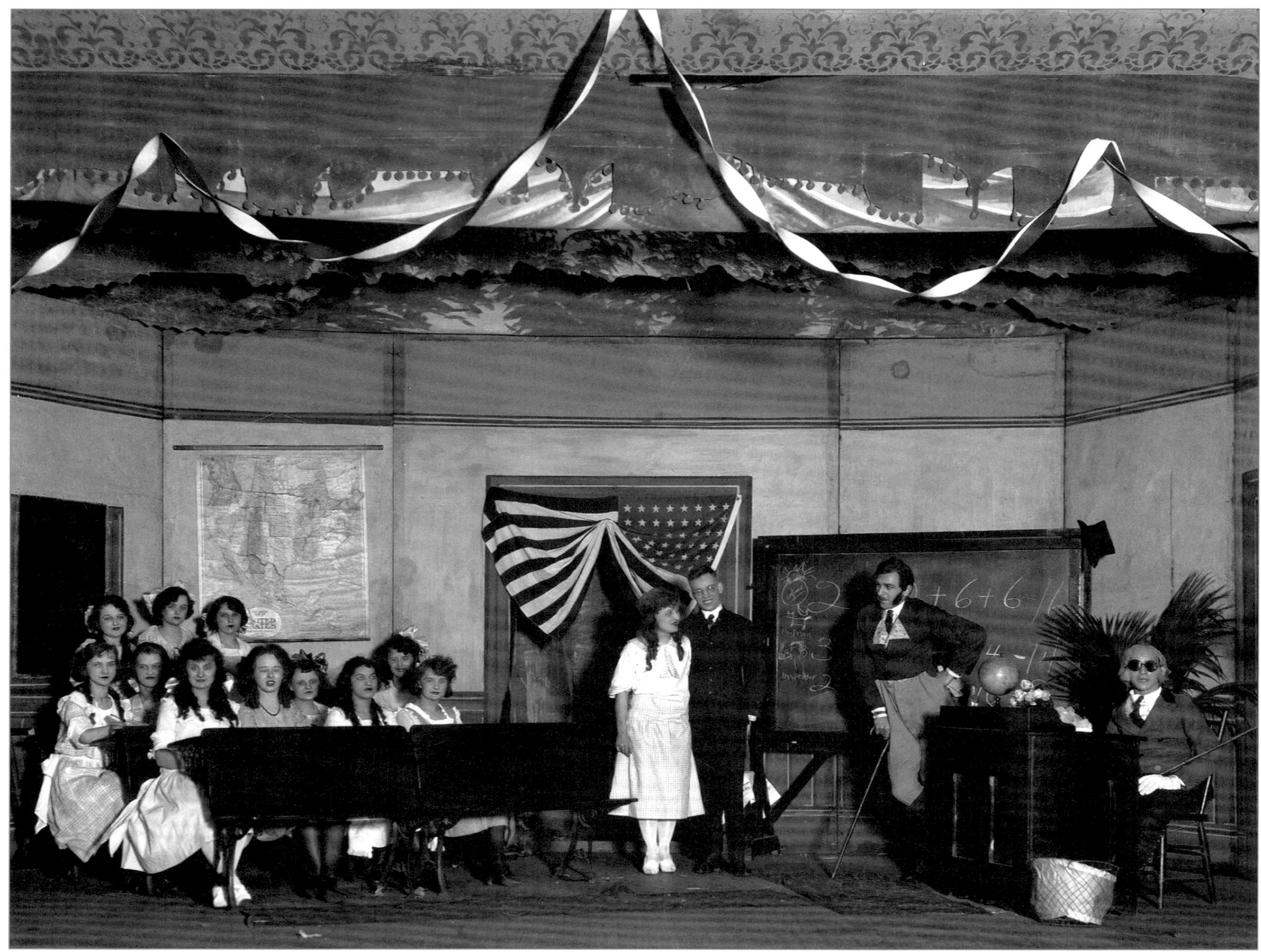

The stage of St. Josaphat's hall was the setting for a 1922 performance of the comical operetta ***Lekcya w Pensyonacie (Lesson in a Boarding House).*** The operetta—subtitled ***No! I Don't Want to Get Married!***—is by Walenty J. Bonk, a little-known writer. ***Serial # 19120***

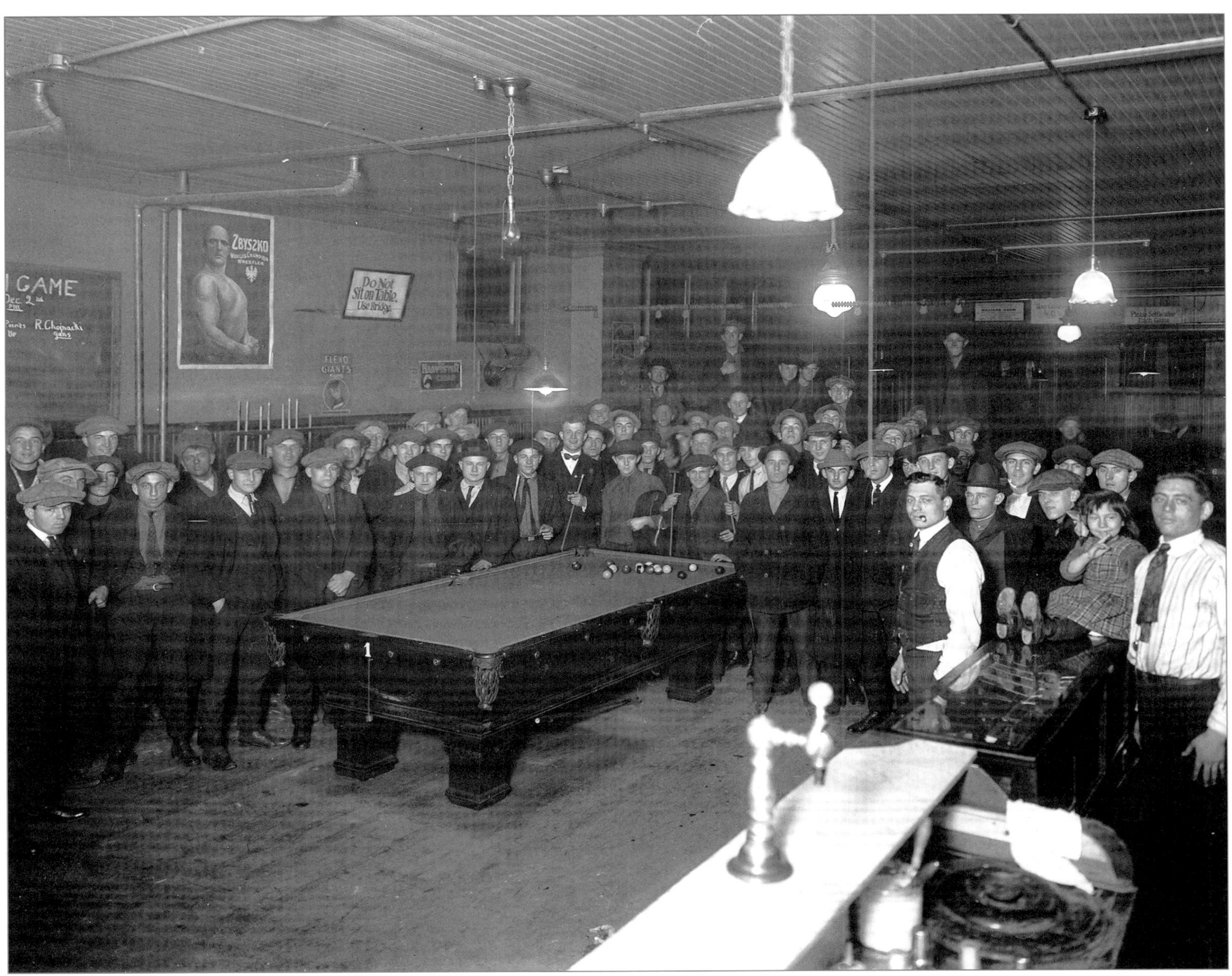

In 1921, when this photograph was taken, the local pool hall was a male-dominated social establishment. From a poster on the wall, Stanislaus Zbyszko, a famous professional wrestler of the time, held a commanding gaze over the room. Although this pool hall on Lincoln Avenue did not allow minors, one young lady made her way into the picture. ***Serial # 18382***

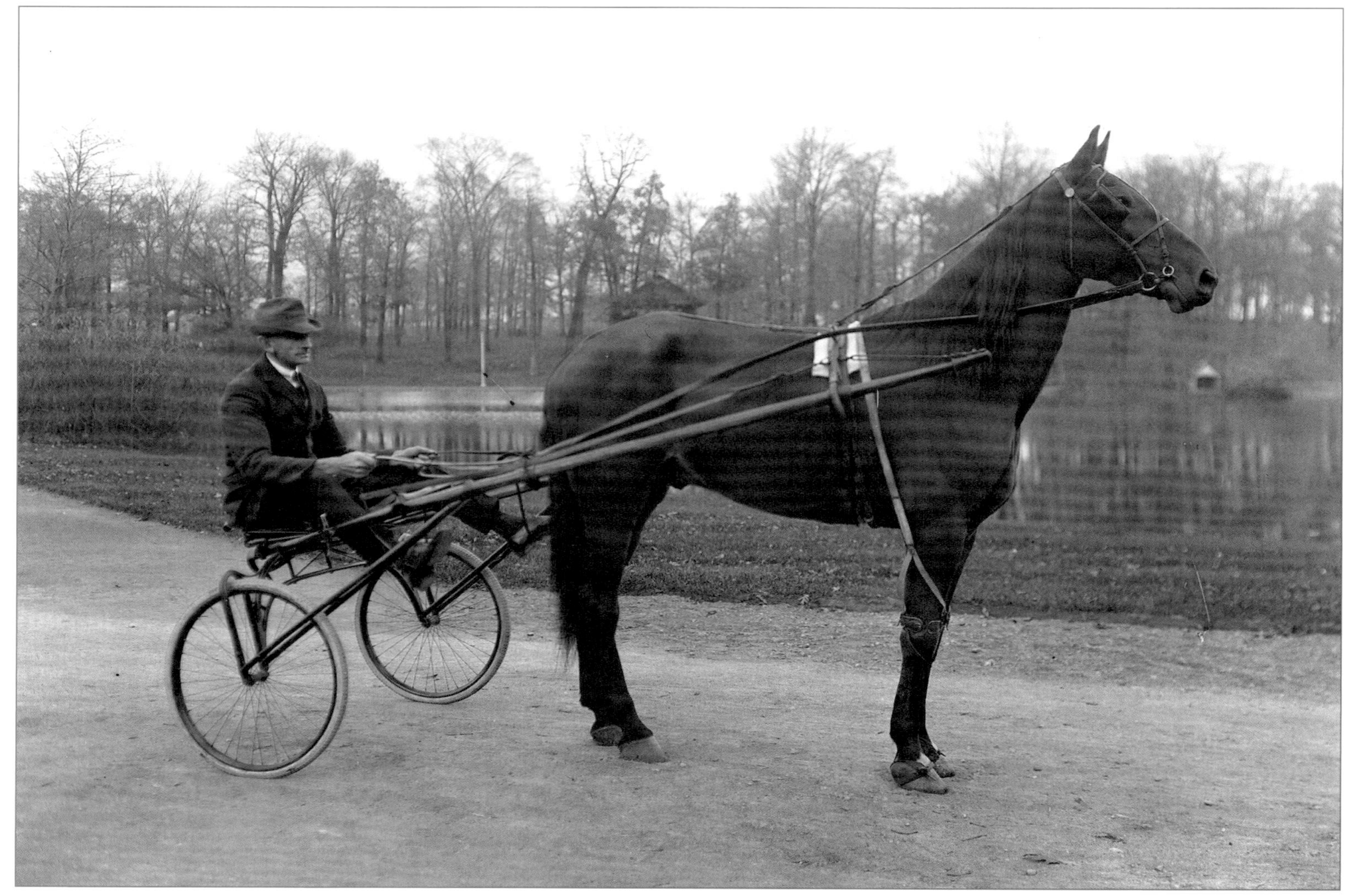

Harness racing was a popular sport in the mid- to late nineteenth century, particularly at county fairs. After reaching its zenith at the turn of the twentieth century, the sport began to decline. The decline was in part attributed to the rise of the automobile and the replacement of the horse as a means of transportation. Kwasniewski took this photograph in one of Milwaukee's parks in 1921. ***Serial # 18316***

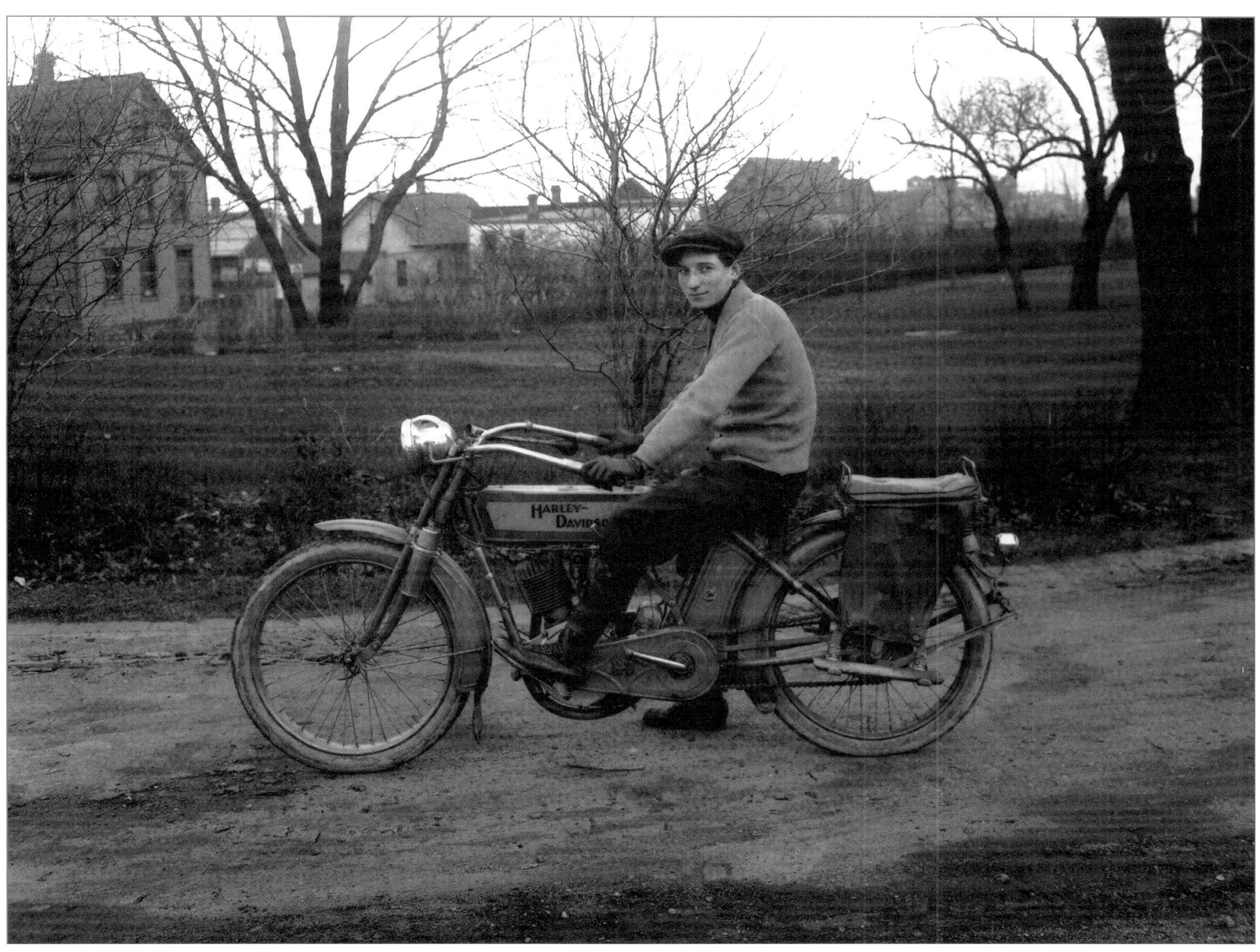

John Urbanski posed on an early model Harley-Davidson motorcycle. The photograph appears to have been taken in Kosciuszko Park, circa 1916. ***Serial # A07102***

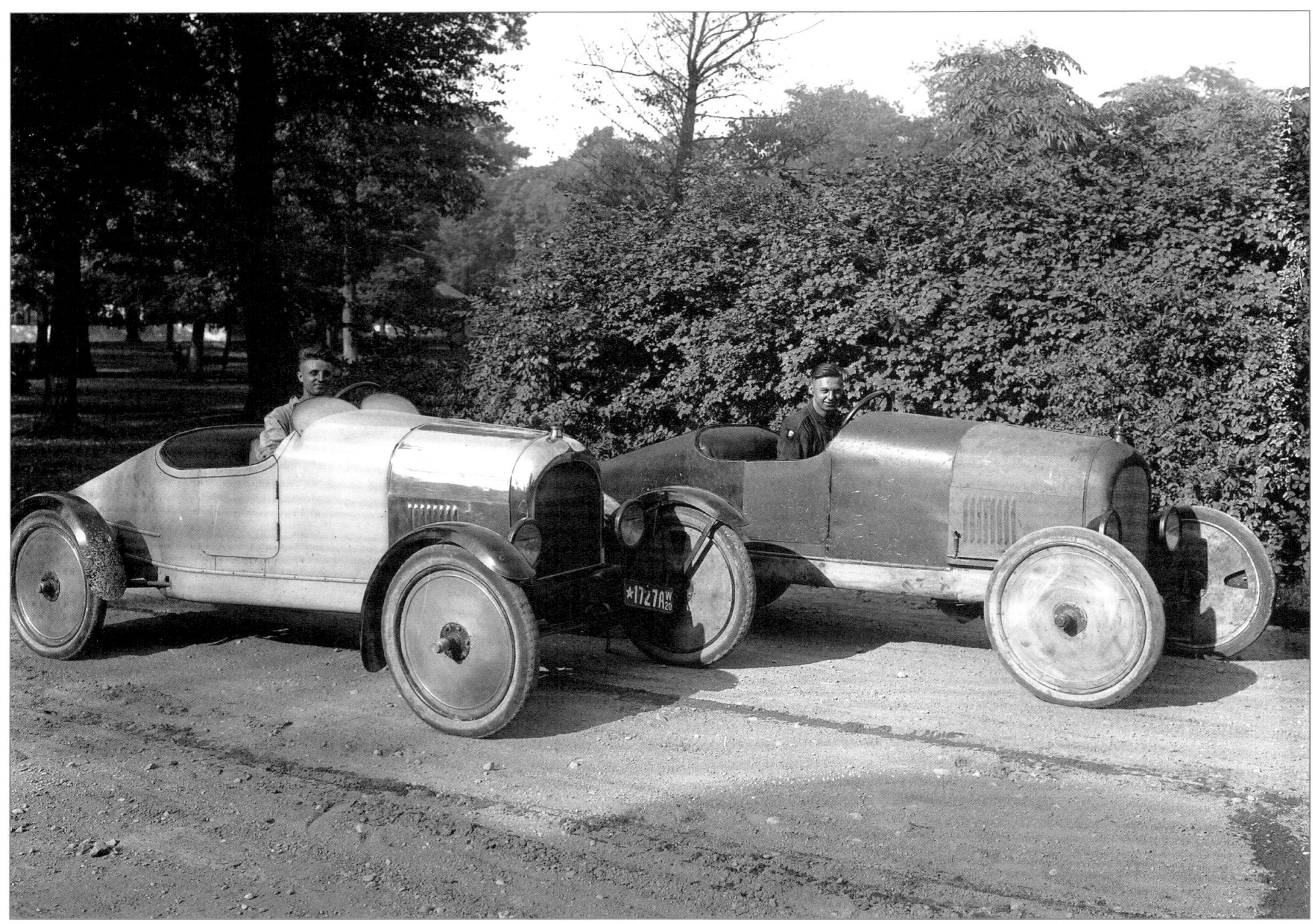

Motor racing grew as a sport soon after the development of the automobile. These two race-car drivers seated in "Ford Speeders" took part in the sport in 1920. One of them may have been Ray Schwacher, a serviceman with the Edwards Motor Car Company, who ordered the photograph. ***Serial # A06753***

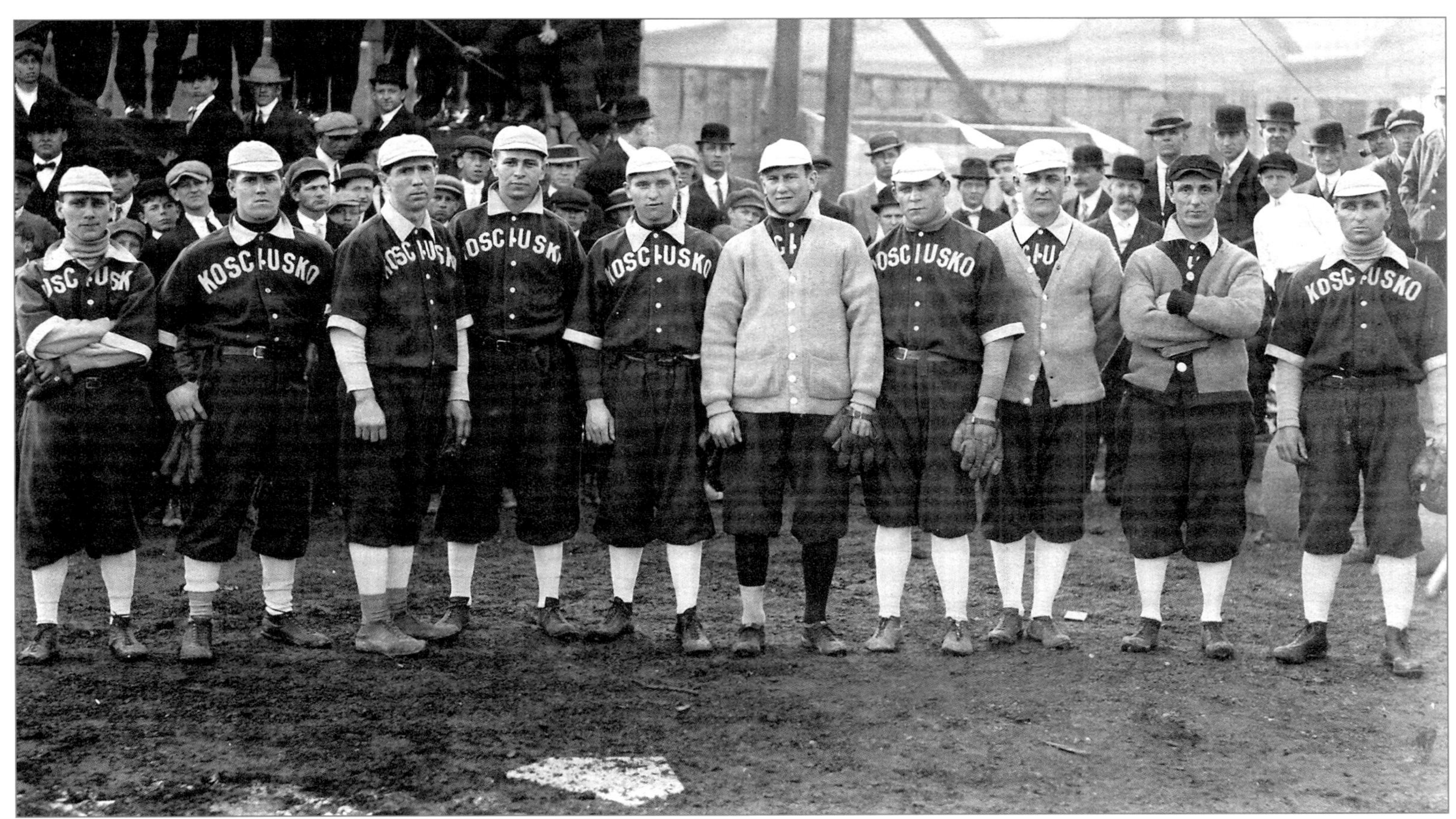

Nearly a century ago the Kosciuszko Reds, a semiprofessional baseball team, played on Milwaukee's South Side. This photograph was taken around 1912, on a day when the Reds took on the Chicago American Giants, a Negro League team.
Serial # A06764-1

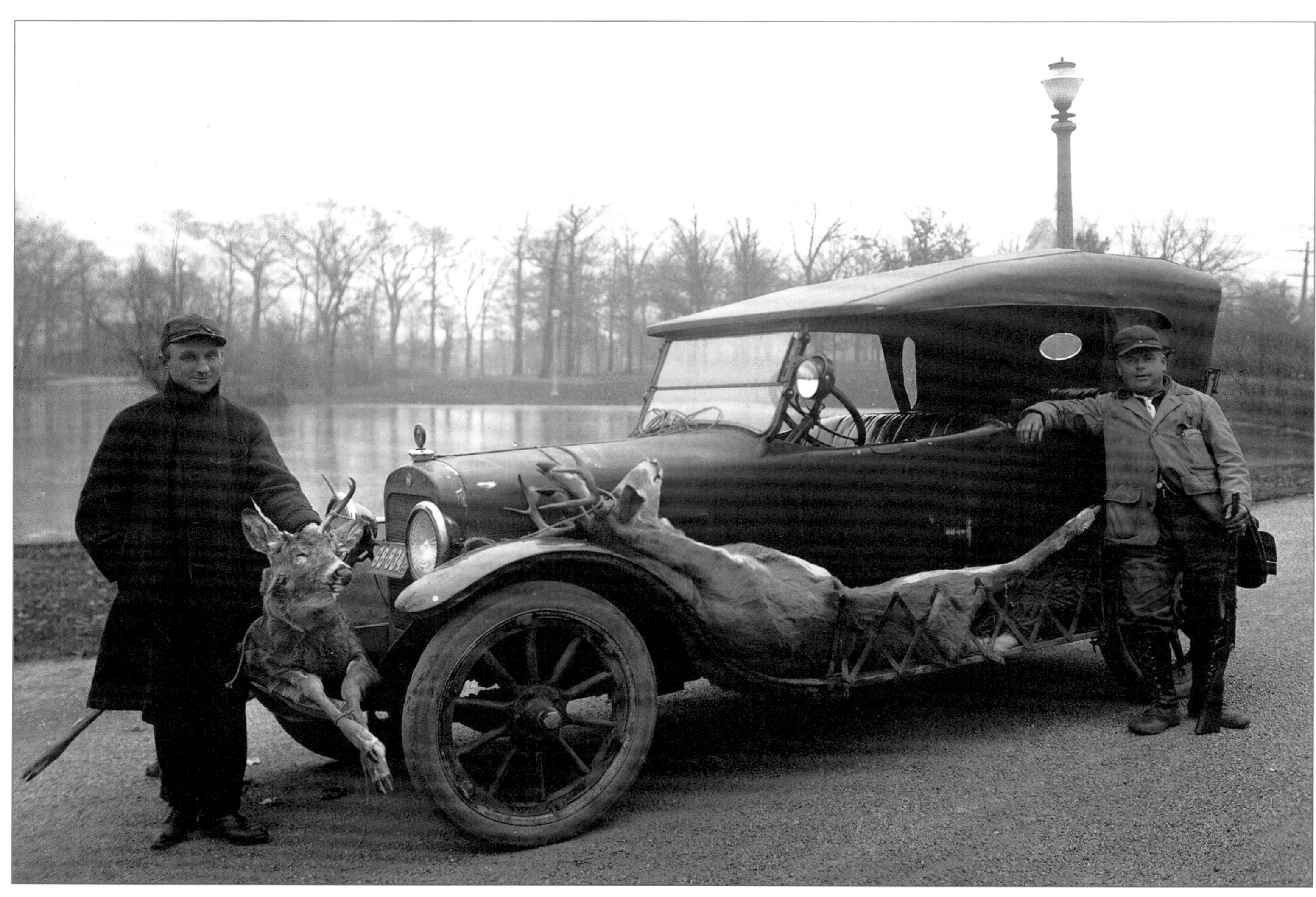

1922 was a successful deer-hunting season for these fellows. *Serial # 20192*

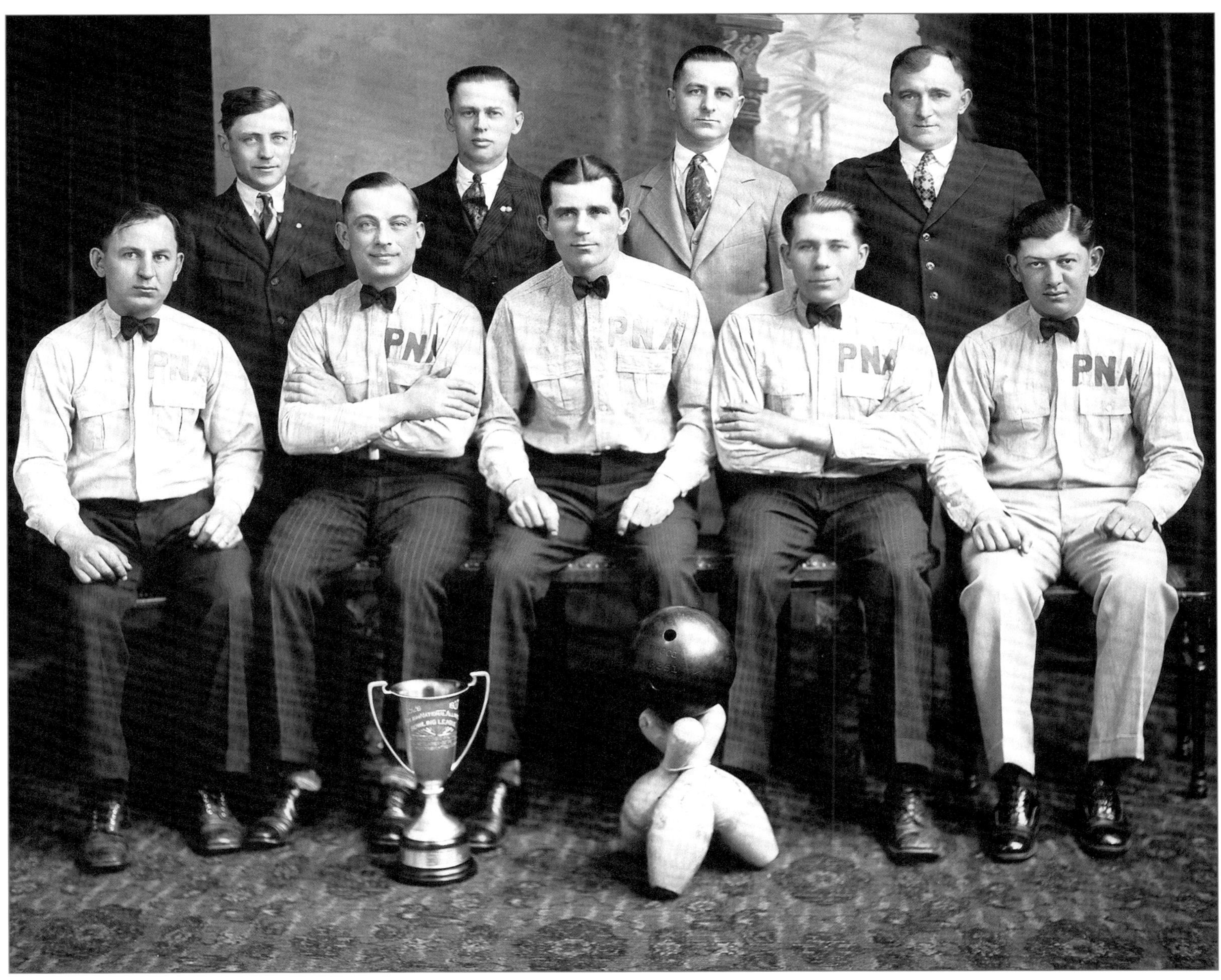

This 1926–1927 Polish National Alliance bowling team posed for a studio portrait after a winning season, as the trophy attests. For Americans of Polish descent, fraternal groups such as the Polish National Alliance not only provided life insurance and death and sick benefits but also sponsored social and cultural activities, including instruction in the Polish language. *Serial # 26196*

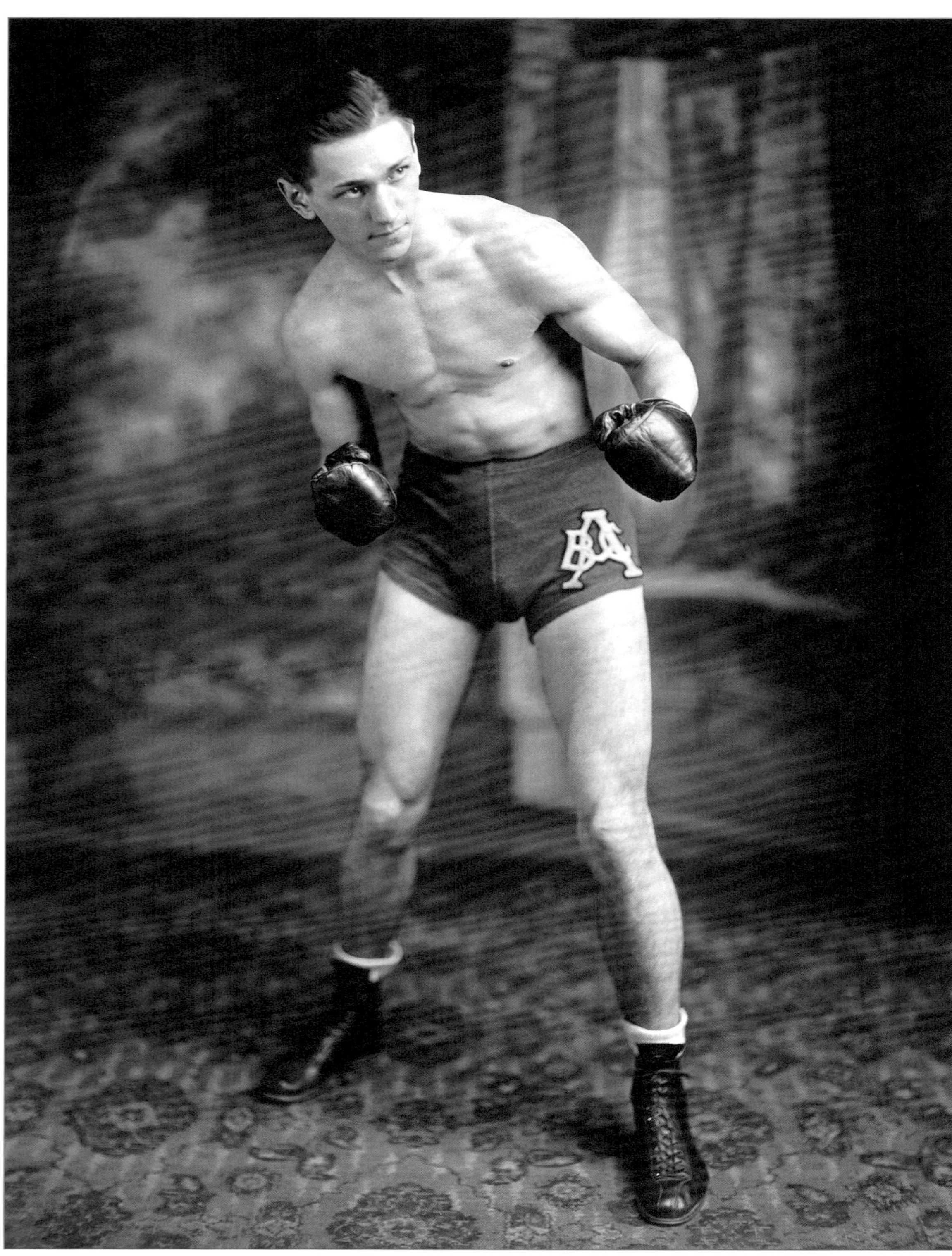

Erwin Frankowiak showed off his boxing form in 1931. That year, when he wasn't boxing, Frankowiak was employed as a millworker.
Serial # 31464

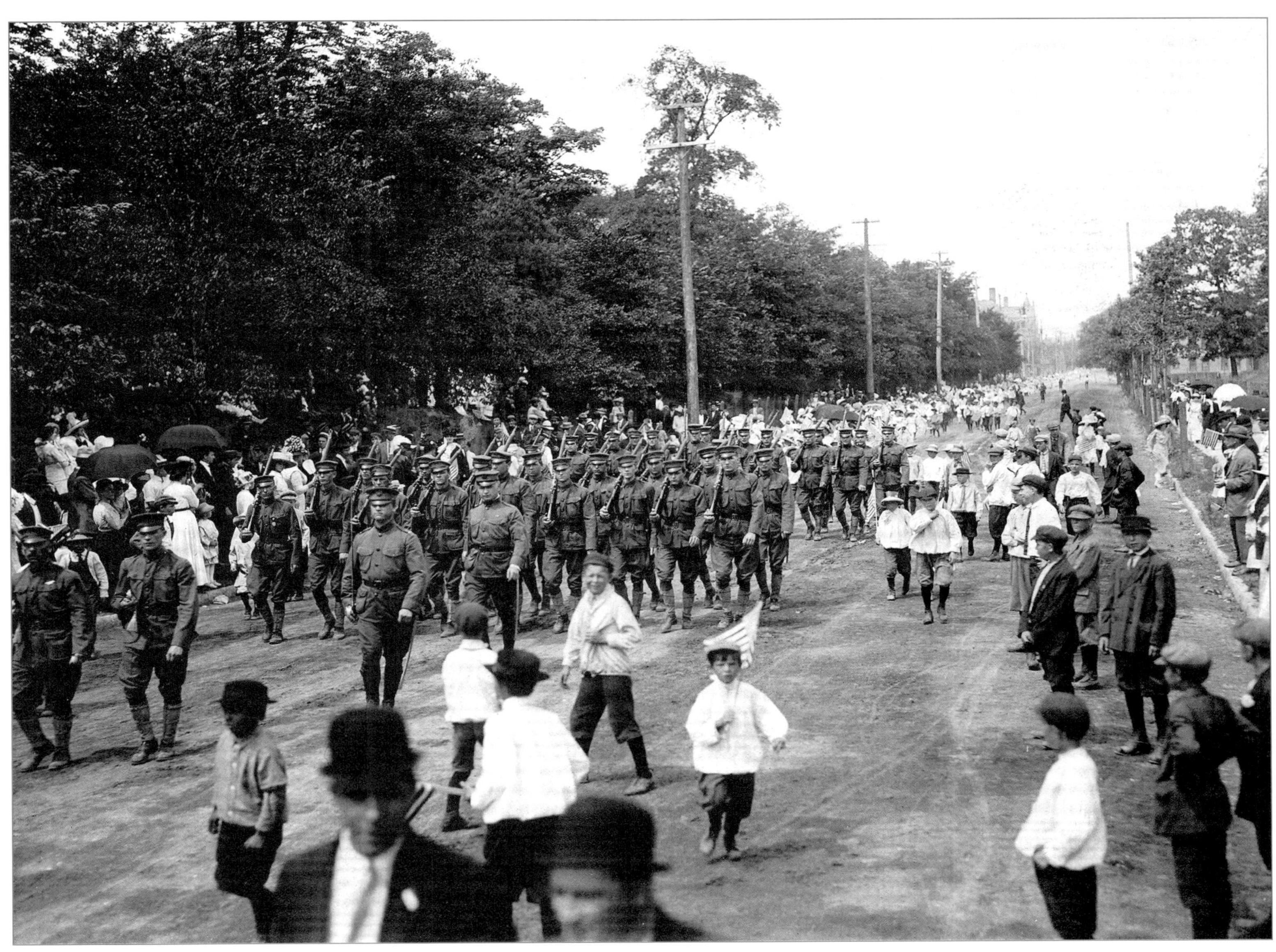

Even before the United States entered World War I, the community showed its support for the men of Company K, who marched by on this day in 1916. *Serial # A10090*

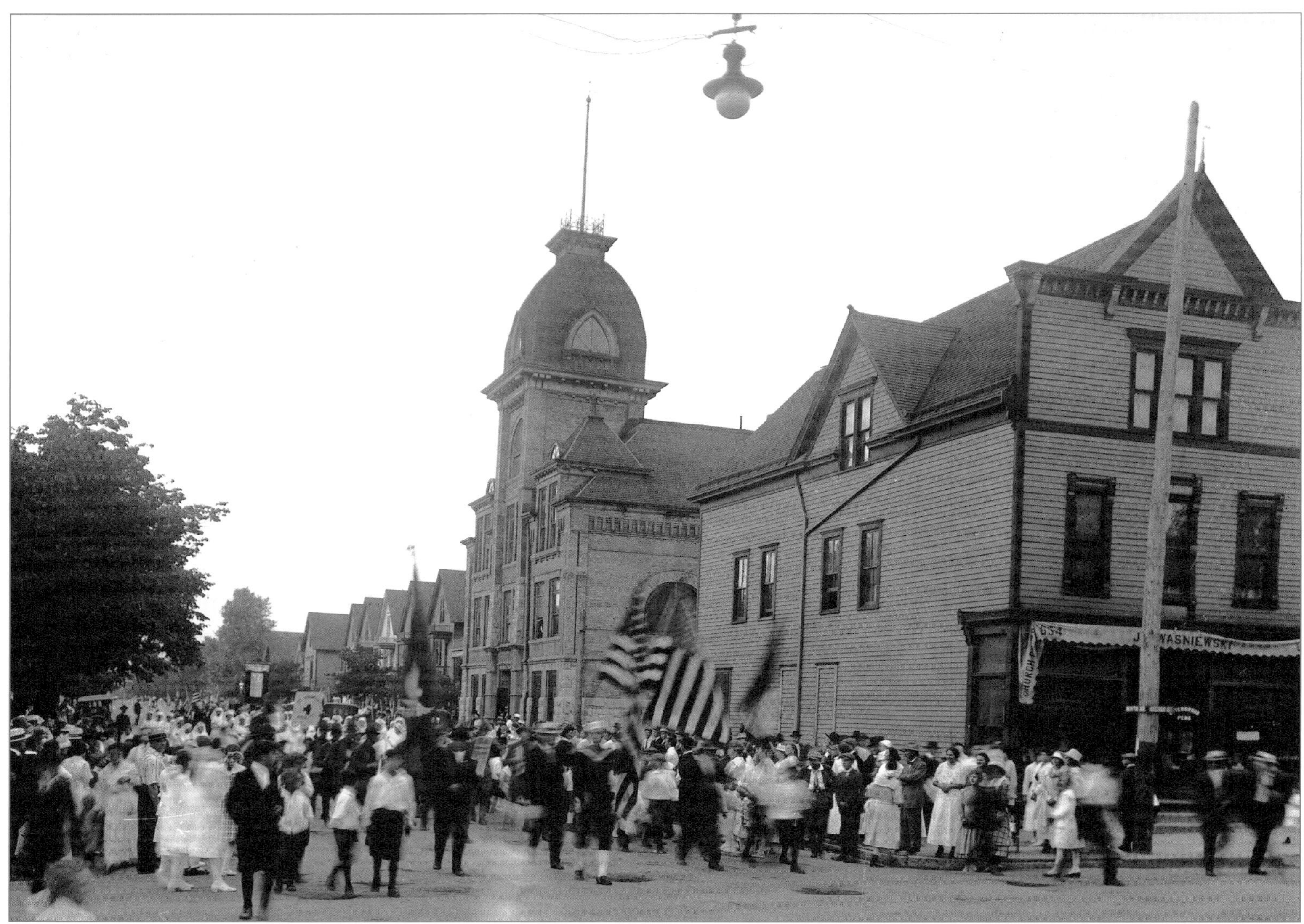

Many Polish Americans viewed World War I as a conflict for Poland's independence. When the United States entered the war, large numbers of Milwaukee Poles enlisted. Those on the home front sponsored various patriotic activities, such fund drives and parades. Here, participants in a parade to rally support during World War I marched up Ninth Avenue (later South Fourteenth Street). Members of St. Hyacinth's Auxiliary were about to pass by when this 1918 photograph was taken. Jozef Kwasniewski, the photographer's father, owned the store on the corner of Becher Avenue. For a seller of church goods, a location near St. Hyacinth's parish must have been good for business. Serial # A00067

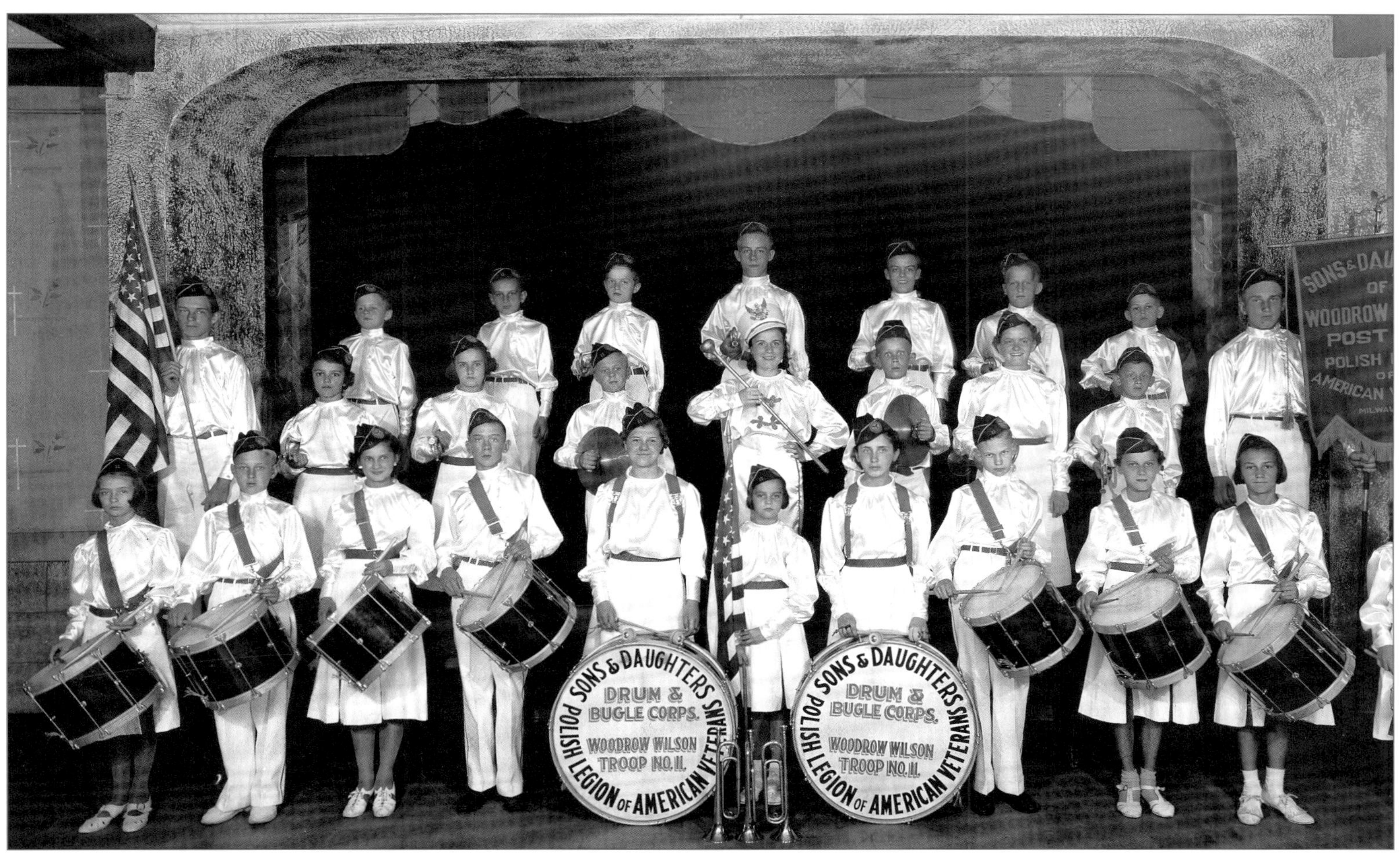

The Woodrow Wilson Post No. 11 of the Polish Legion of American Veterans was established in September 1923. The post was particularly proud of its drum and bugle corps, composed of sons and daughters of its members. This photograph was probably taken sometime shortly after the corps' organization in 1937. *Serial # A05150-1*

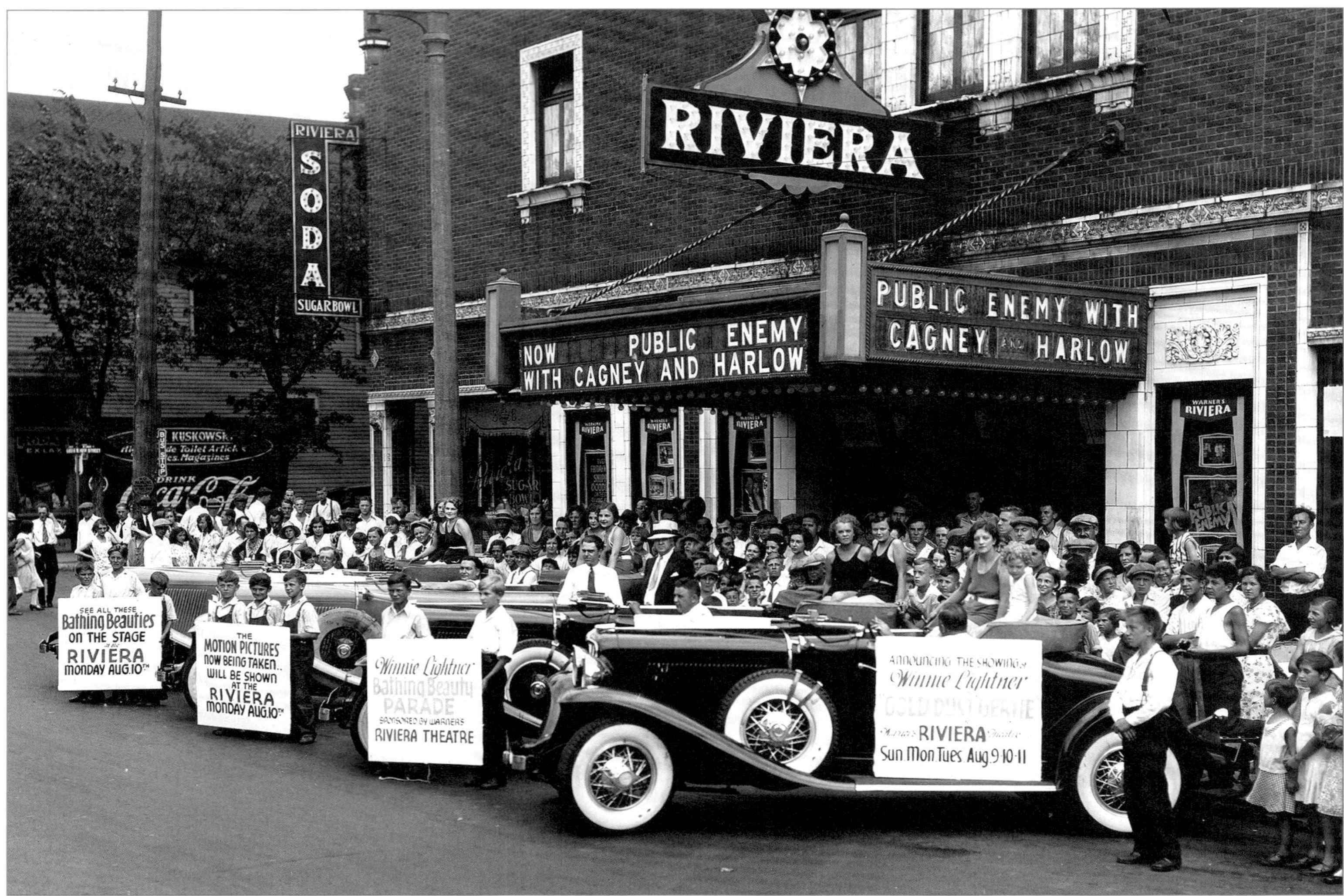

In August 1931 the Riviera Theatre, located at 1005 West Lincoln Avenue, sponsored a "Bathing Beauty Parade." The idea for the parade's theme came from the upcoming movie *Gold Dust Gertie*, which the theater was promoting. Winnie Lightner played Gertie, the ex-wife of two swimsuit salesmen, set on getting as much alimony as she can from the two. Showing in the theater at the time was *The Public Enemy* with James Cagney and Jean Harlow. *Serial # A00127-2*

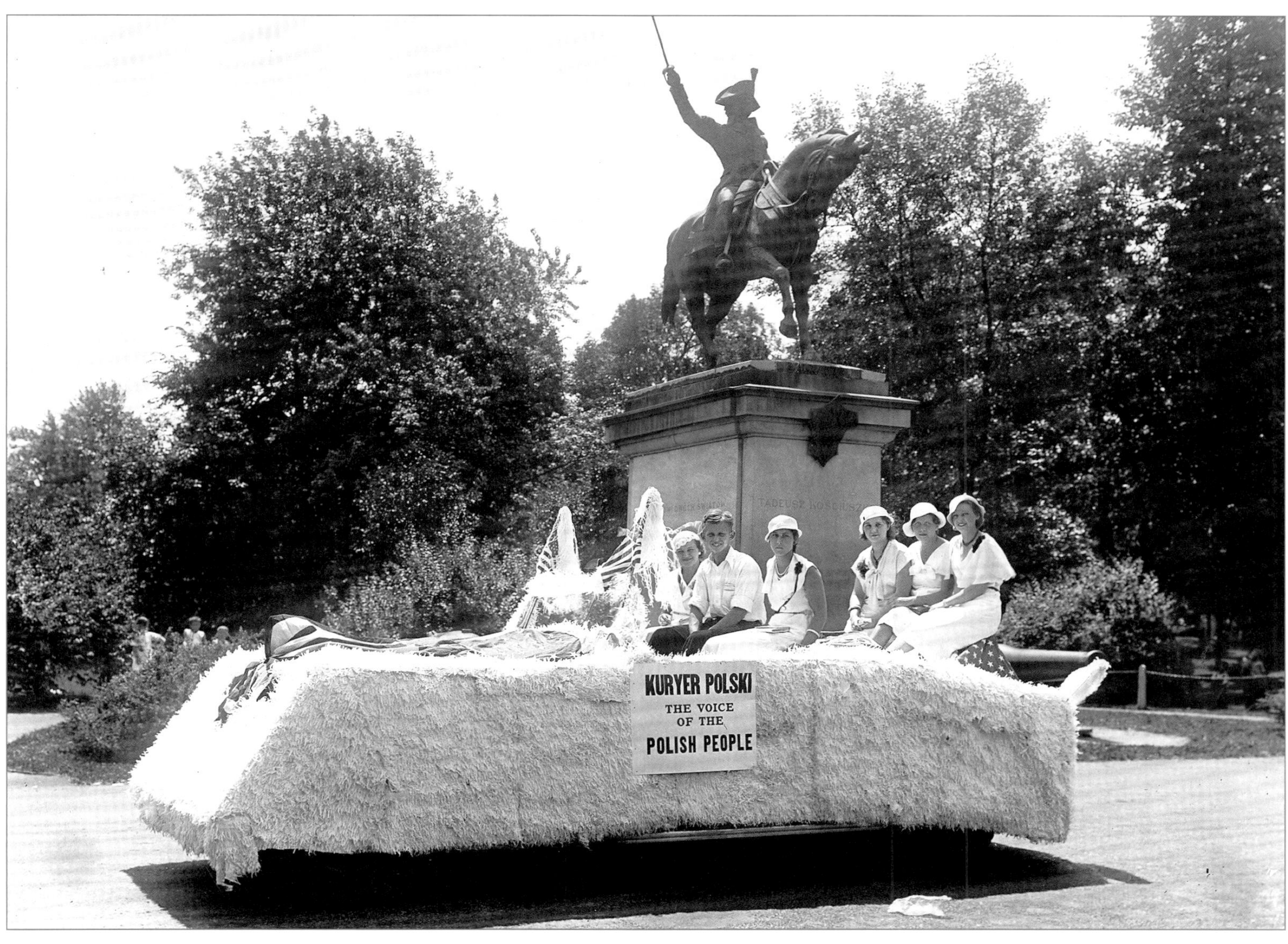

The *Kuryer Polski's* 1933 parade float, carrying some of its employees, made a stop in front of the Kosciuszko Monument in Kosciuszko Park. The *Kuryer Polski* newspaper truly was "the voice of the Polish people," for it was one of the most widely circulated Polish language newspapers in the United States. *Kuryer* newsboys were commonly seen distributing the latest edition to the Poles on Milwaukee's South Side. Michael Kruszka, an immigrant, founded the paper in Milwaukee in 1888. After outgrowing modest quarters on Mitchell Street, the paper moved its production to downtown Milwaukee. The *Kuryer* ceased publication in 1962. *Serial # A15153*

CHAPTER FIVE

COMMERCE

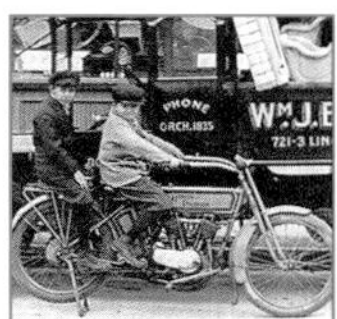

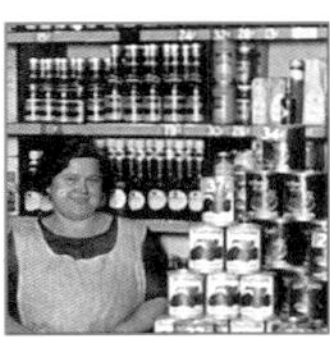

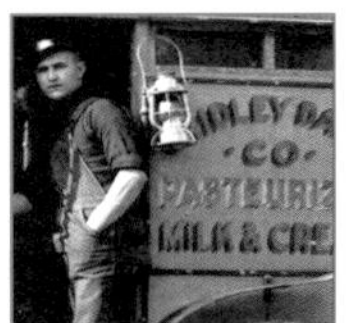

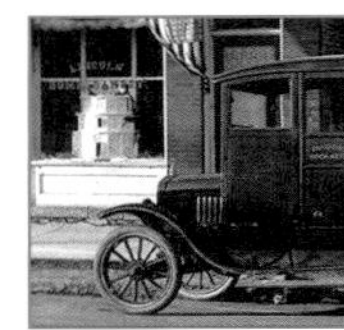

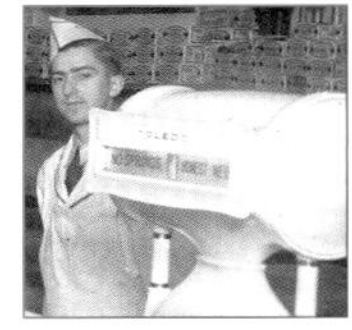

It was industry that brought the Poles to Milwaukee. By the 1860s the city's largest employers were those who turned the bounty of Wisconsin's farms into useful products: wheat into flour, hogs into hams, cowhides into leather, barley into beer. Later in the century the emphasis shifted to metal bending, and Milwaukee became the self-styled "Machine Shop of the World." Polish South Siders spent long days turning out steam engines at the E. P. Allis Company (a forerunner of Allis-Chalmers), overhead cranes at Harnischfeger, electrical controls at Allen-Bradley, precision gears at Falk, automobile frames at A. O. Smith, tractors at International Harvester, and construction machinery at Chain Belt. The newcomers generally started at the entry level, rising only slowly to the foreman class, but a few became industrialists in their own right. The most notable was Sylvester Wabiszewski. Already a successful building contractor, he took over a struggling steel foundry in 1914 and made it a regional powerhouse. Maynard Steel, still a family enterprise, remains a fixture on South Twenty-seventh Street.

Although industry was its economic backbone, the South Side's Polonia developed a sizable society of entrepreneurs. An 1895 survey turned up 73 grocers, 51 butchers, and—a clear sign of the working-class community's thirst—164 saloon keepers. The neighborhood spawned hun-

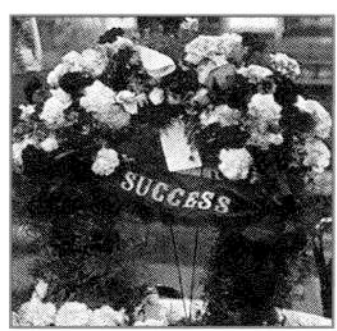

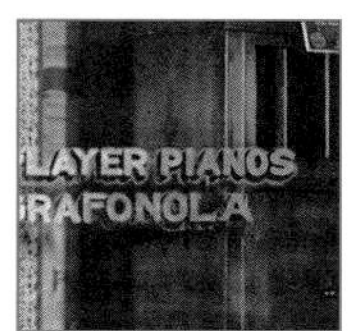

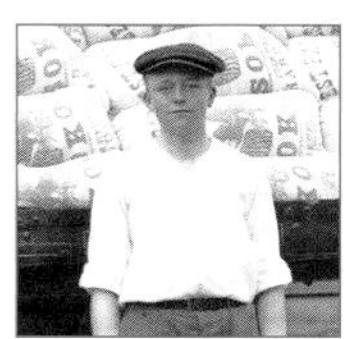

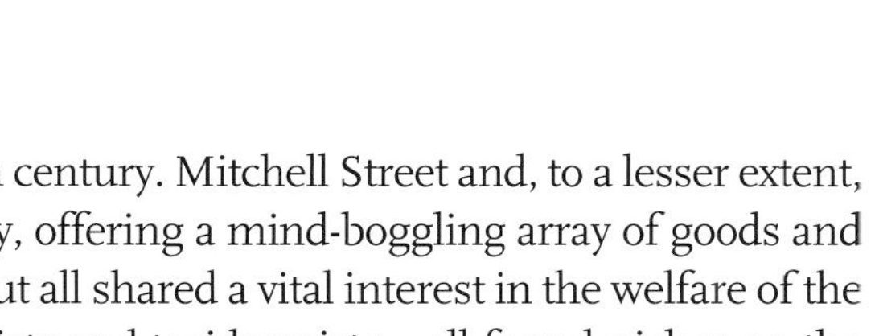

dreds of other small businesses in the early twentieth century. Mitchell Street and, to a lesser extent, Lincoln Avenue were the shopping malls of their day, offering a mind-boggling array of goods and services. Each business was independently owned, but all shared a vital interest in the welfare of the street. Haberdashers and hardware stores, tobacconists and taxidermists—all found niches on the South Side. Small businesses multiplied on the side streets as well, so that no one had to walk far for bread or beefsteak.

Roman Kwasniewski's studio reflected the same entrepreneurial spirit. His fellow business owners were some of his steadiest customers, and the photographer's coverage of Lincoln Avenue's storefronts is practically complete. Kwasniewski also provided ample documentation of a new force in the economy: the automobile. By the 1920s car showrooms, body shops, and filling stations were rapidly replacing the livery stables, carriage works, and hay markets of the horse-drawn era.

For many Polish Milwaukeeans ownership of a small business, despite the high risks and long hours, was considered a ticket to prosperity. Kwasniewski was summoned to any number of grand openings during the economic boom of the 1920s. The going-out-of-business sales he photographed in the next decade demonstrated that not everyone made it, but the entrepreneurial itch remained a constant in the community. When better times returned, South Side businesspeople, and their customers, continued the slow but steady climb into the middle class.

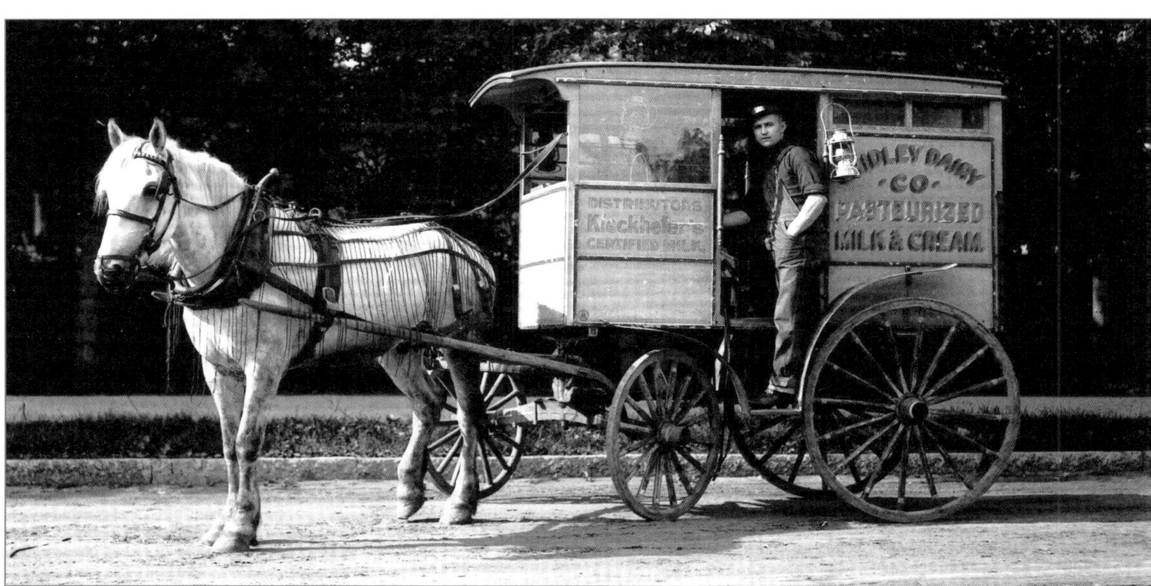

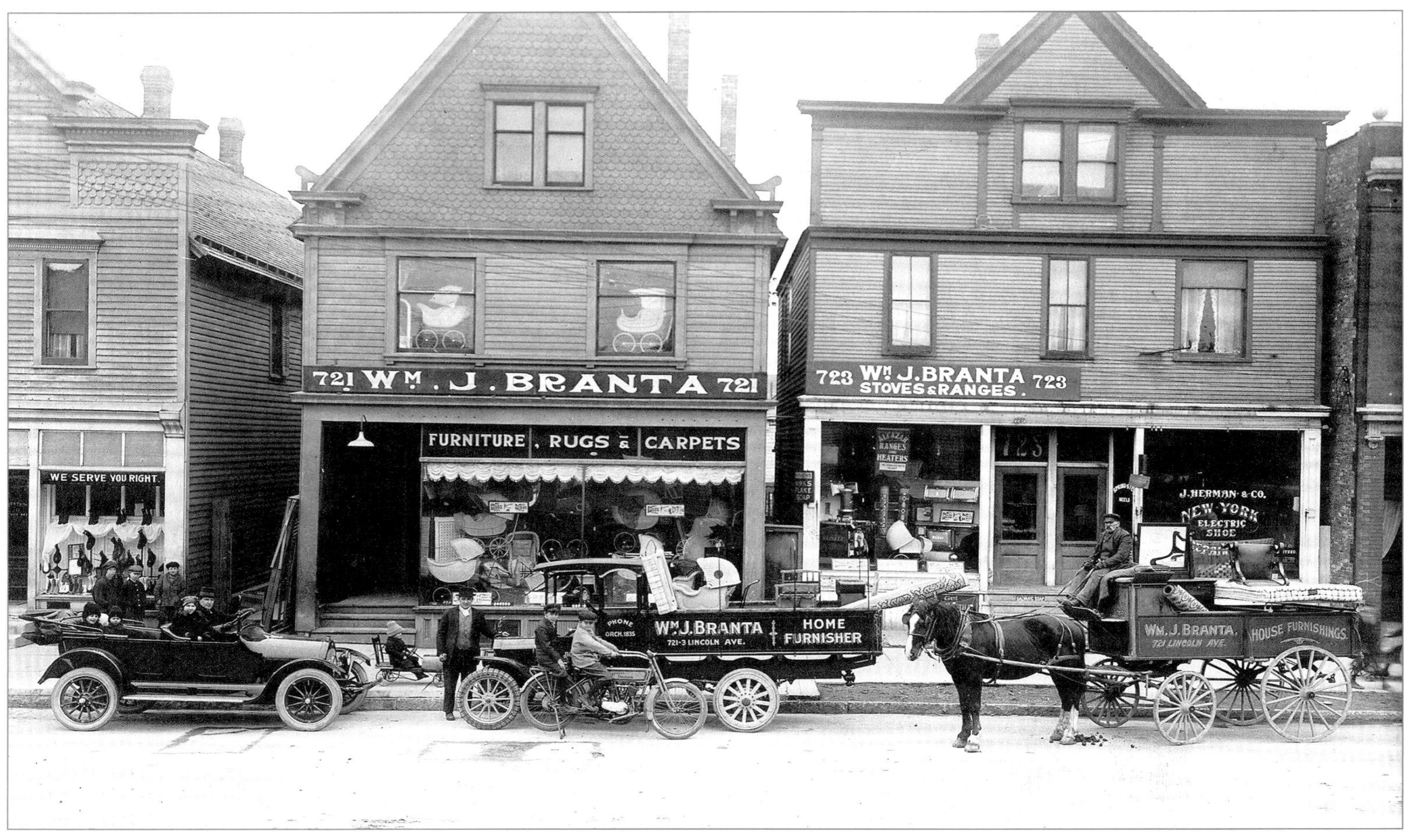

The William J. Branta home-furnishings store was established circa 1915 at 721 Lincoln Avenue (now 1561 West Lincoln). The store's horse-drawn delivery wagon and motorized delivery truck, the family car, and the early Harley-Davidson motorcycle demonstrate the transition in the modes of transportation that was taking place in the 1920s. The business closed shortly after 1930. ***Serial # A07008***

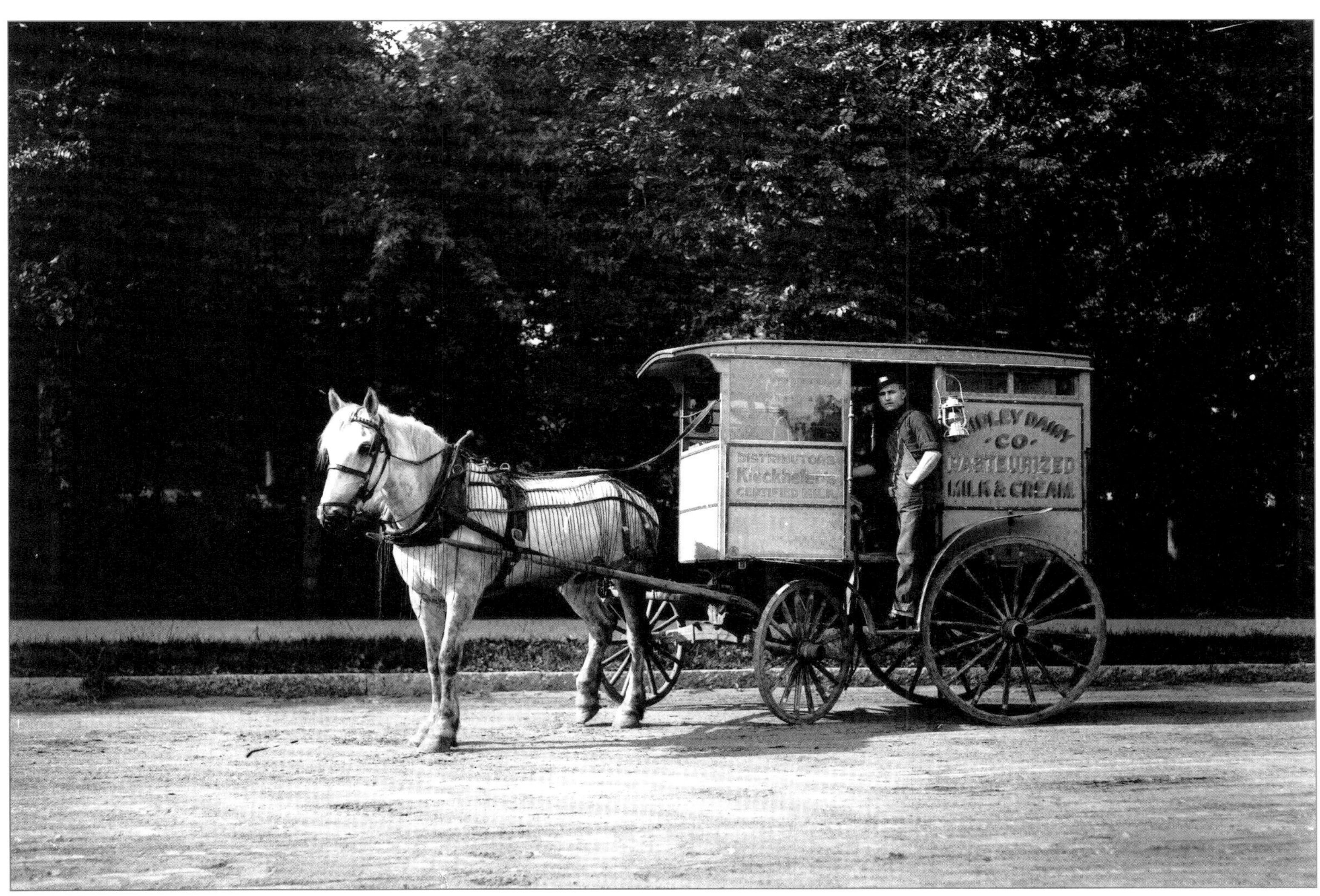

Milkmen delivering dairy products to area homes by horse-drawn wagon were a familiar sight in Milwaukee around the turn of the twentieth century. The Gridley Dairy Company, which was founded in 1886, distributed the first bottled milk and cream sold west of New York City. The lantern located on the side of the delivery wagon in this undated photograph helped light the milkman's way as he traveled his route in the early morning hours. In 1928 Gridley became a part of Borden.

Serial # A07096

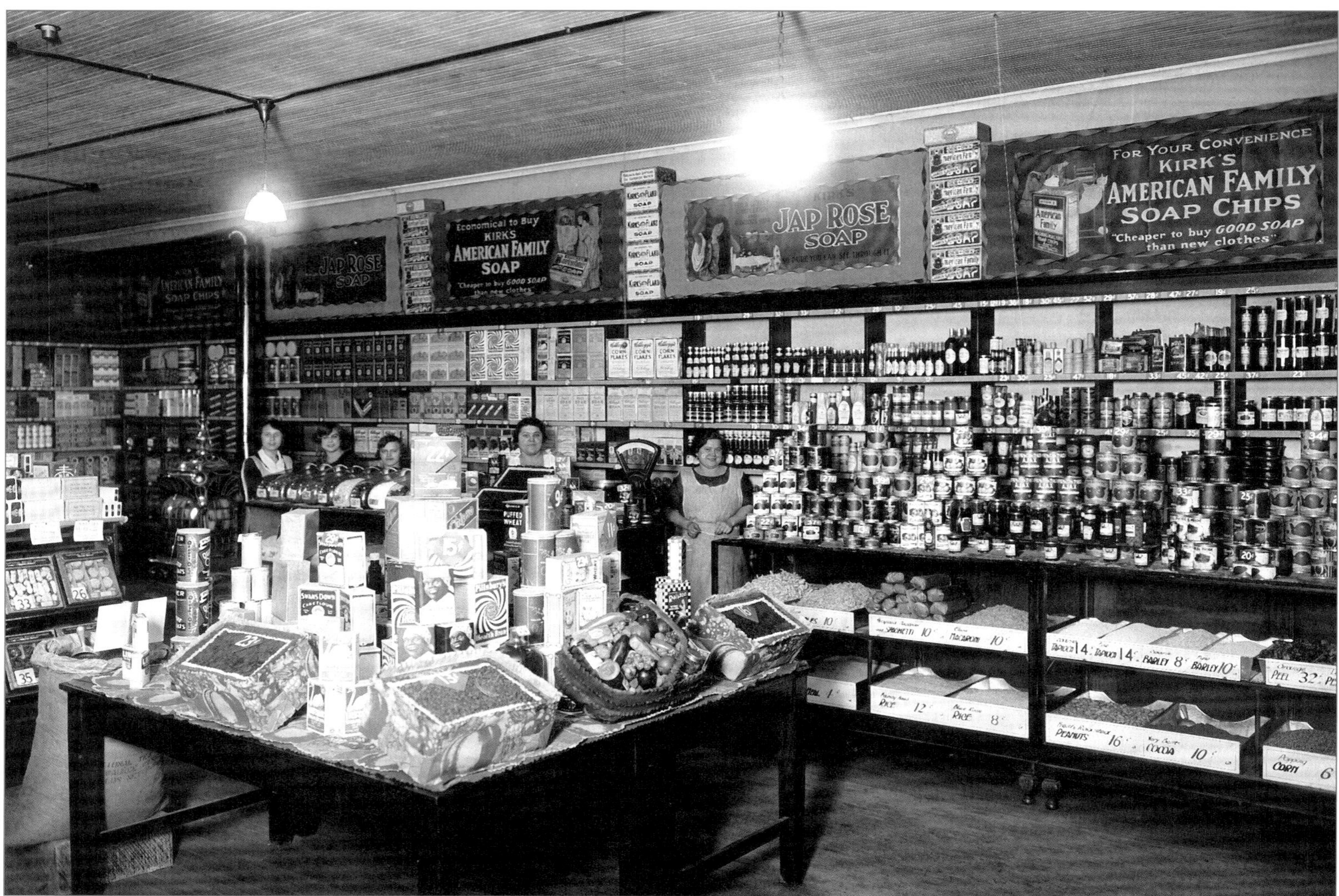

Grocery stores have changed noticeably since the early twentieth century. Merchandise prices once were much lower, and at a time when dry goods didn't always come prepackaged, service was important. Store clerks weighed and measured foods like macaroni, rice, barley, tapioca, cocoa, and popcorn for customers. This unidentified store also sold cleaning supplies, including Kirk's brand soaps, which it advertised. ***Serial # A15380***

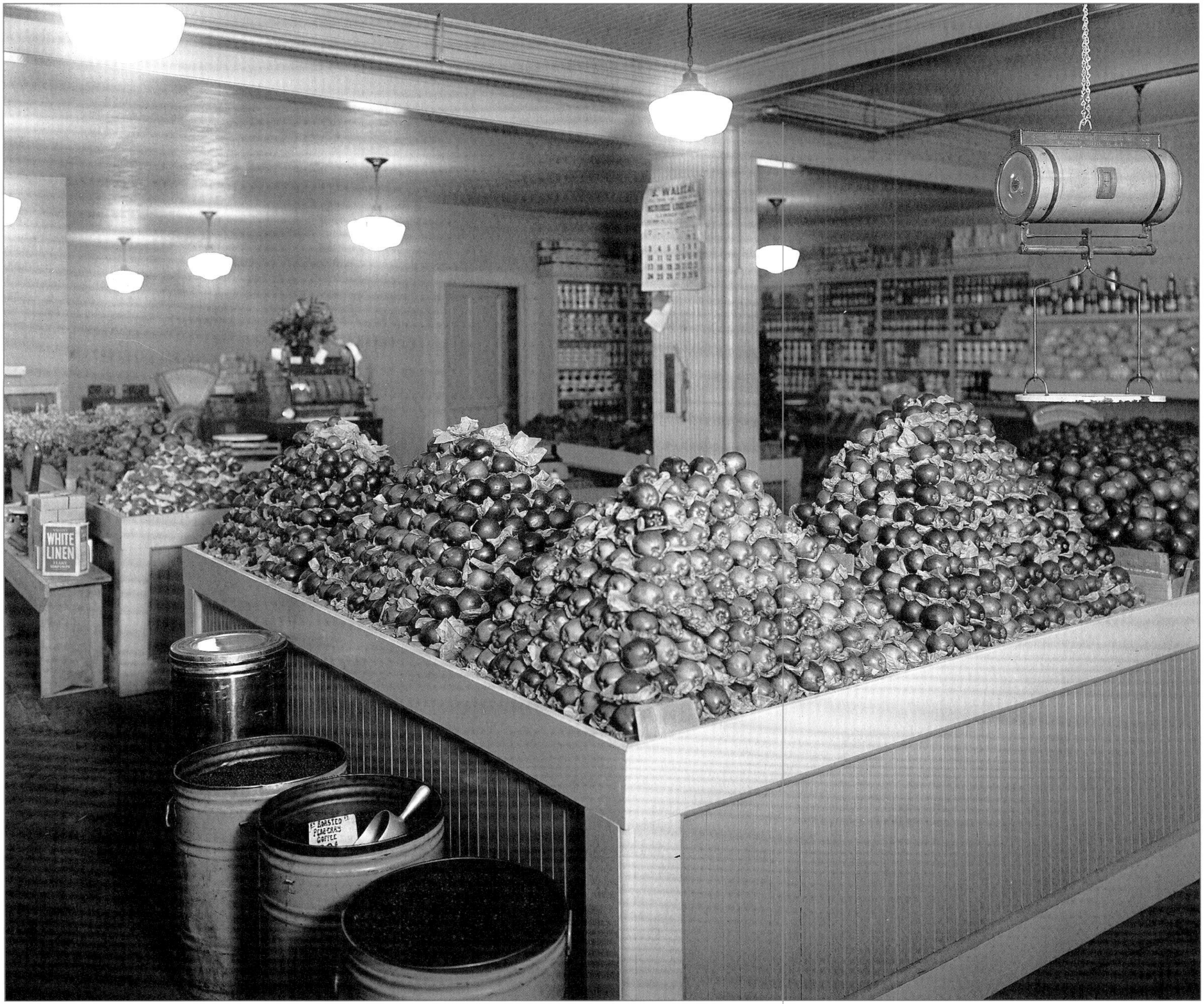

This photograph was probably taken in 1921 or 1922, around the time that the Lincoln Fruit Store was undergoing a change in ownership. The store, located at what was then 652 Lincoln Avenue, stocked a bountiful supply of fresh fruit. Roasted coffee could also be purchased at this market. ***Serial # A07314***

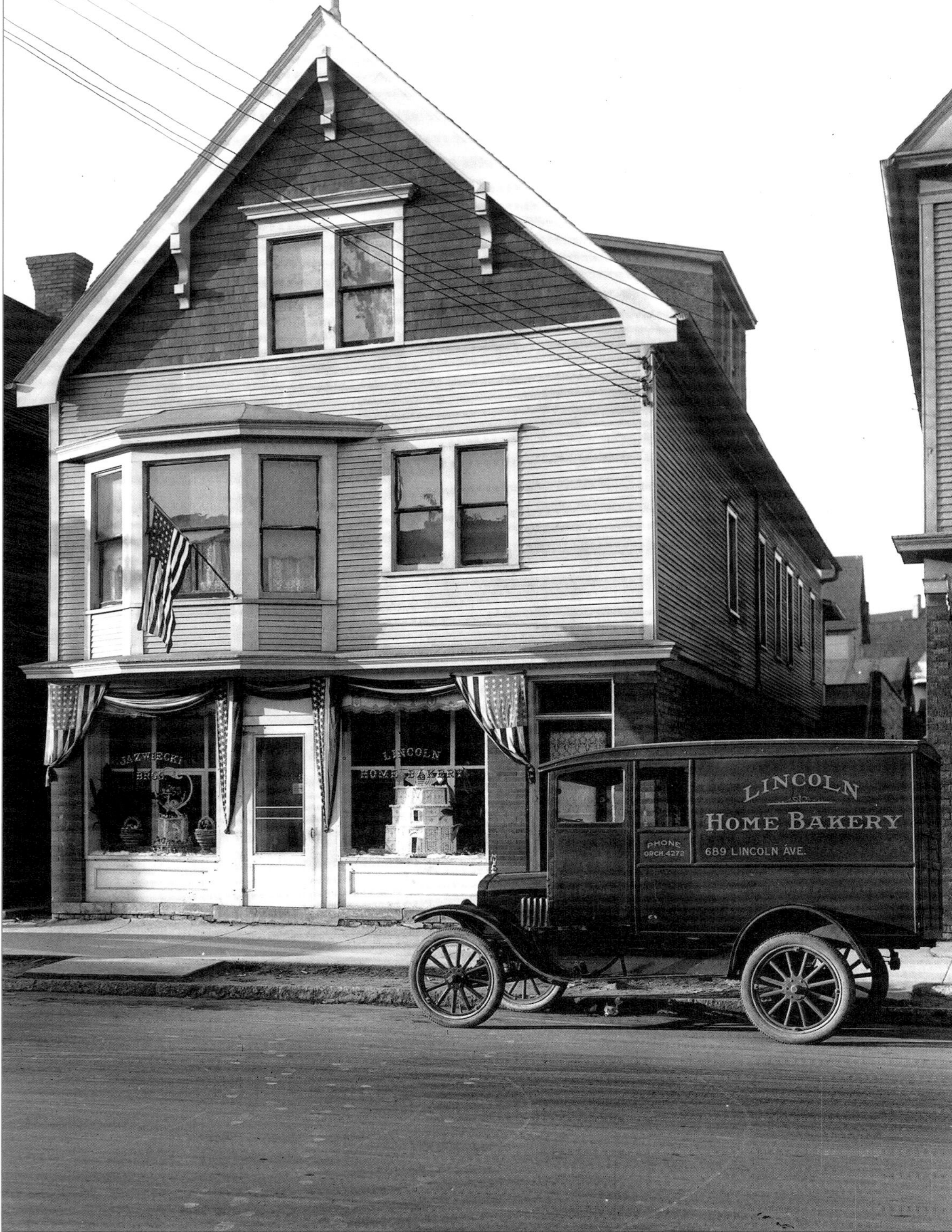

No doubt, the aroma of delicious home-baked goods drew customers into the Lincoln Home Bakery. Delivery service was also available, and when this 1922 photograph was taken during the nuptial month of June, the bakery may frequently have used its truck to transport wedding cakes. The store was decorated for the upcoming Fourth of July holiday.

Serial # 19347

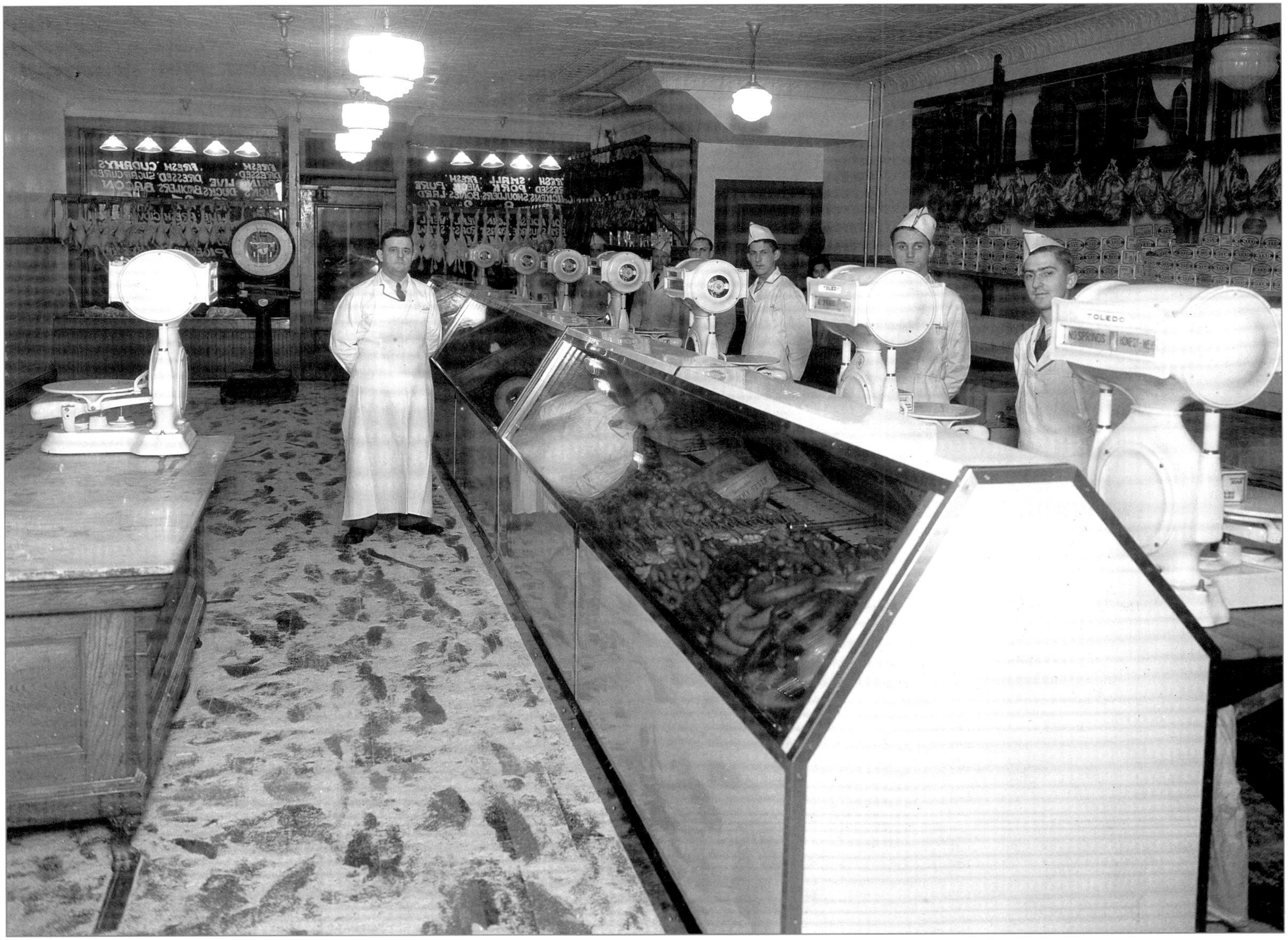

Frank Bzdawka (on the left) and his employees posed for the camera in 1931 at the Bzdawka meat market, located on Lincoln Avenue near Eleventh Street. Butcher shops like this one once covered their floors with sawdust to soak up spatters. Fowl hanging in this store's windows must have attracted the attention of pedestrians passing on the street. *Serial # 31325-1*

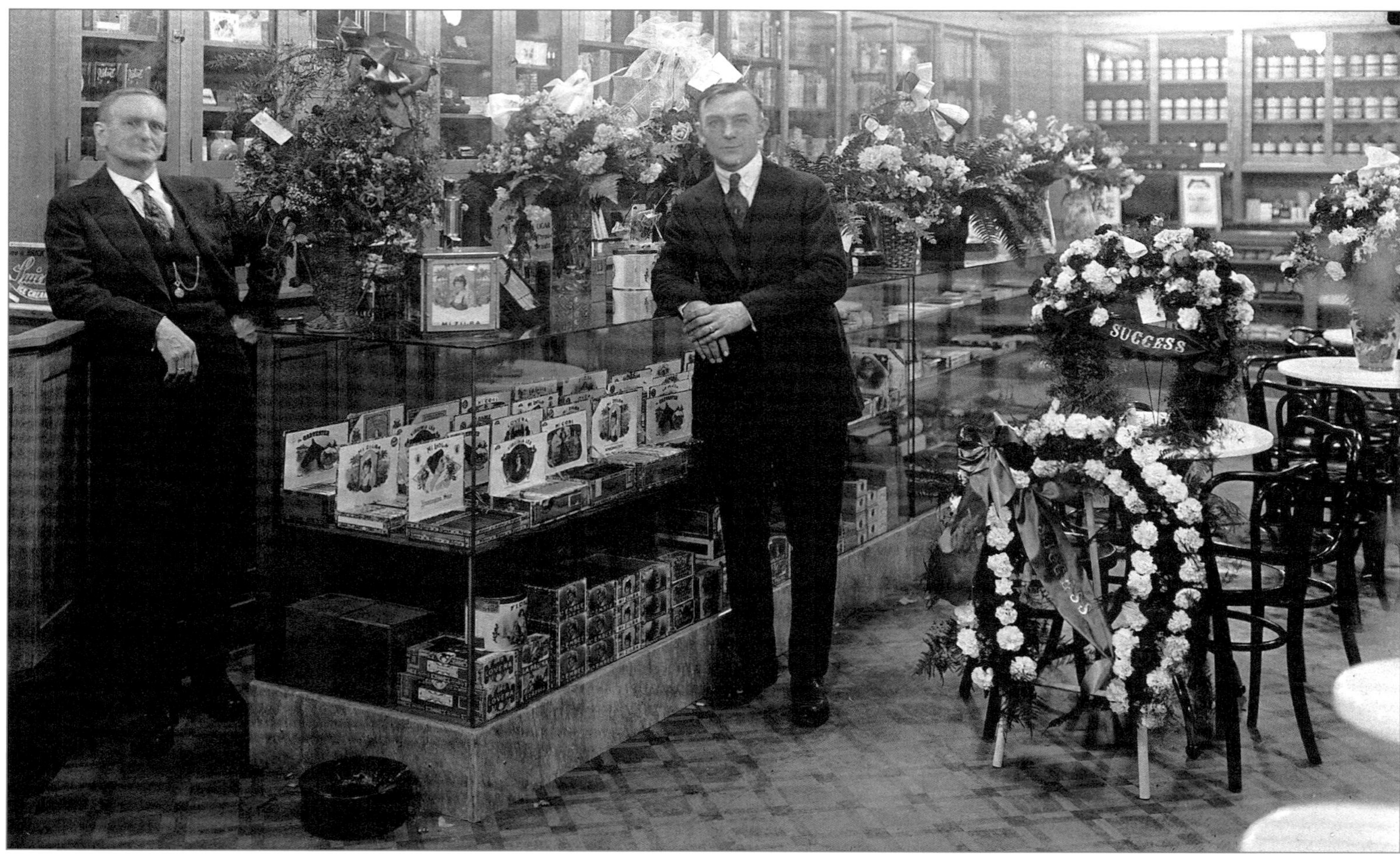

Well-wishers sent bouquets of flowers and "success" banners to Henry F. Czerwinski to commemorate the opening of his drugstore on Lincoln Avenue in 1920. Before establishing his own business Czerwinski worked for his uncle Frank Piszczek, a well-known druggist on Milwaukee's South Side. Czerwinski remained in business until his death in the mid-1950s. The individuals in this photograph are not identified, although the man on the right most likely is Henry Czerwinski.
Serial # 16117

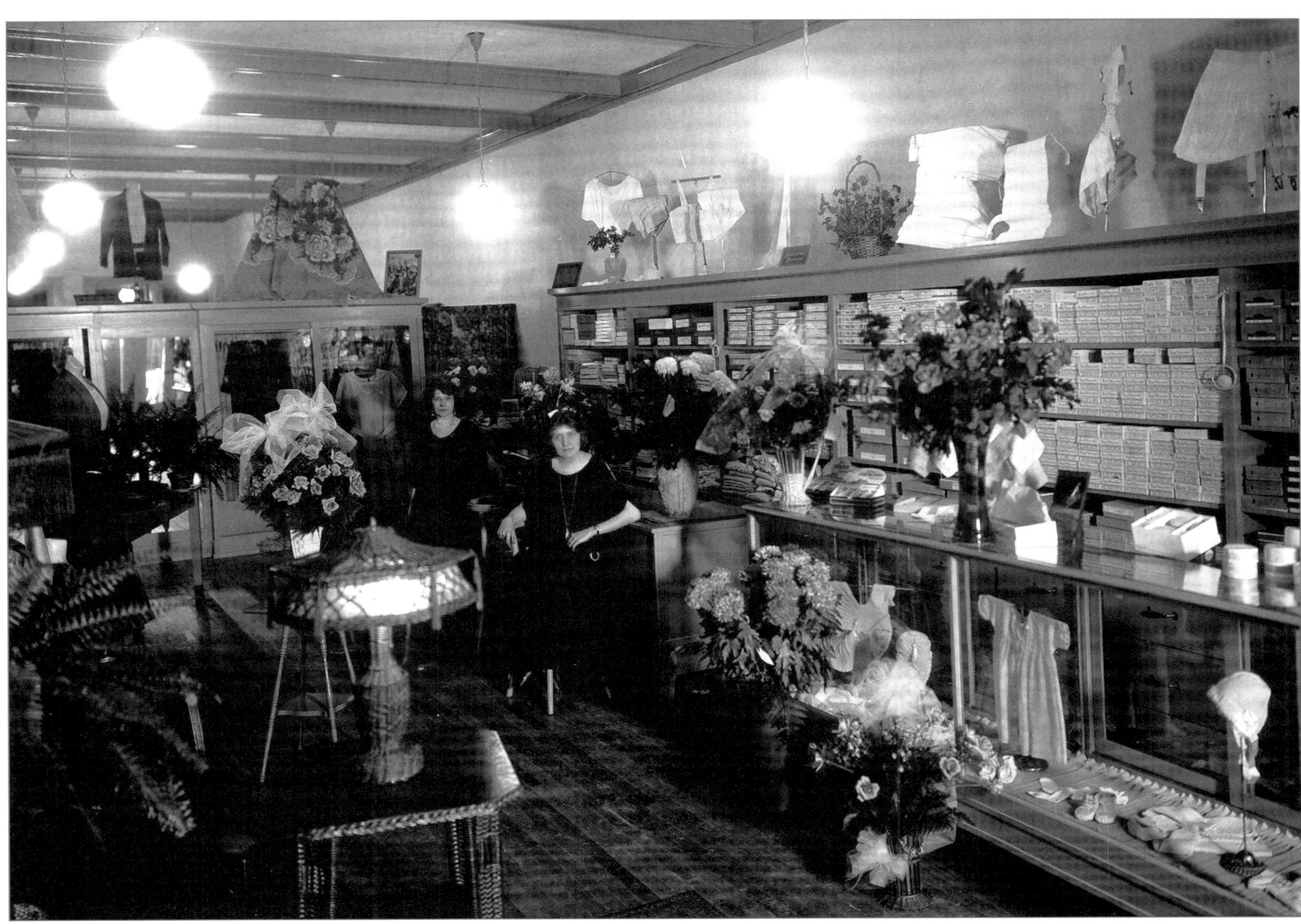

The Swientek Lingerie and Children's Wear Store on Lincoln Avenue formally opened for business in September 1922. Theodora Swientek established another dry-goods store on Greenfield Avenue a number of years later. Shortly after that she closed the Lincoln Avenue shop. *Serial # 20061*

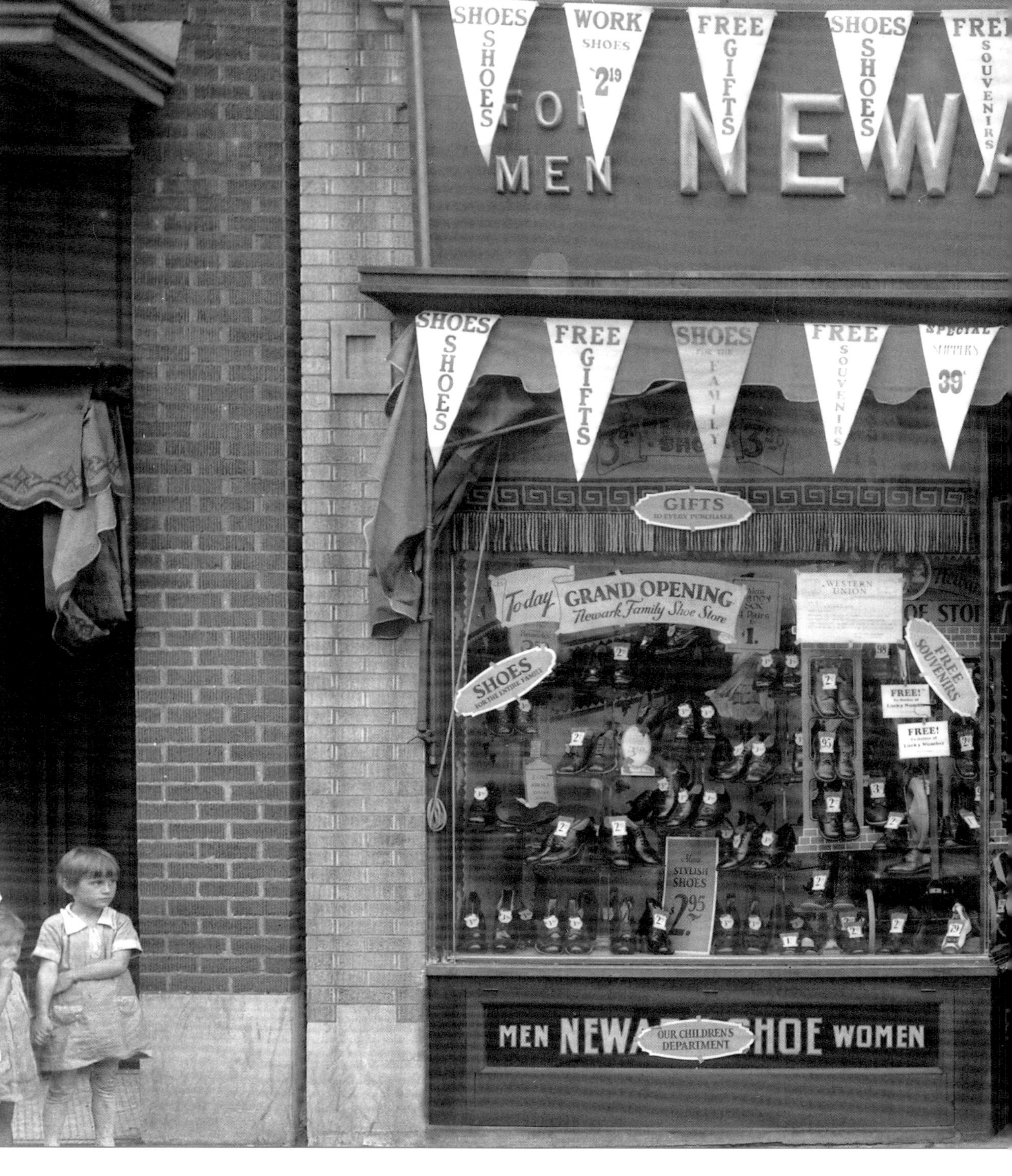

With several locations already throughout Milwaukee, in October 1929 the Newark Family Shoe Store marked the grand opening of another store on Milwaukee's South Side. The store featured shoes for the whole family: men's work shoes, women's stylish shoes and slippers, and children's play shoes. Hungry shoppers could stop for lunch next door, where liver sausage sandwiches cost only ten cents. ***Serial # 29656***

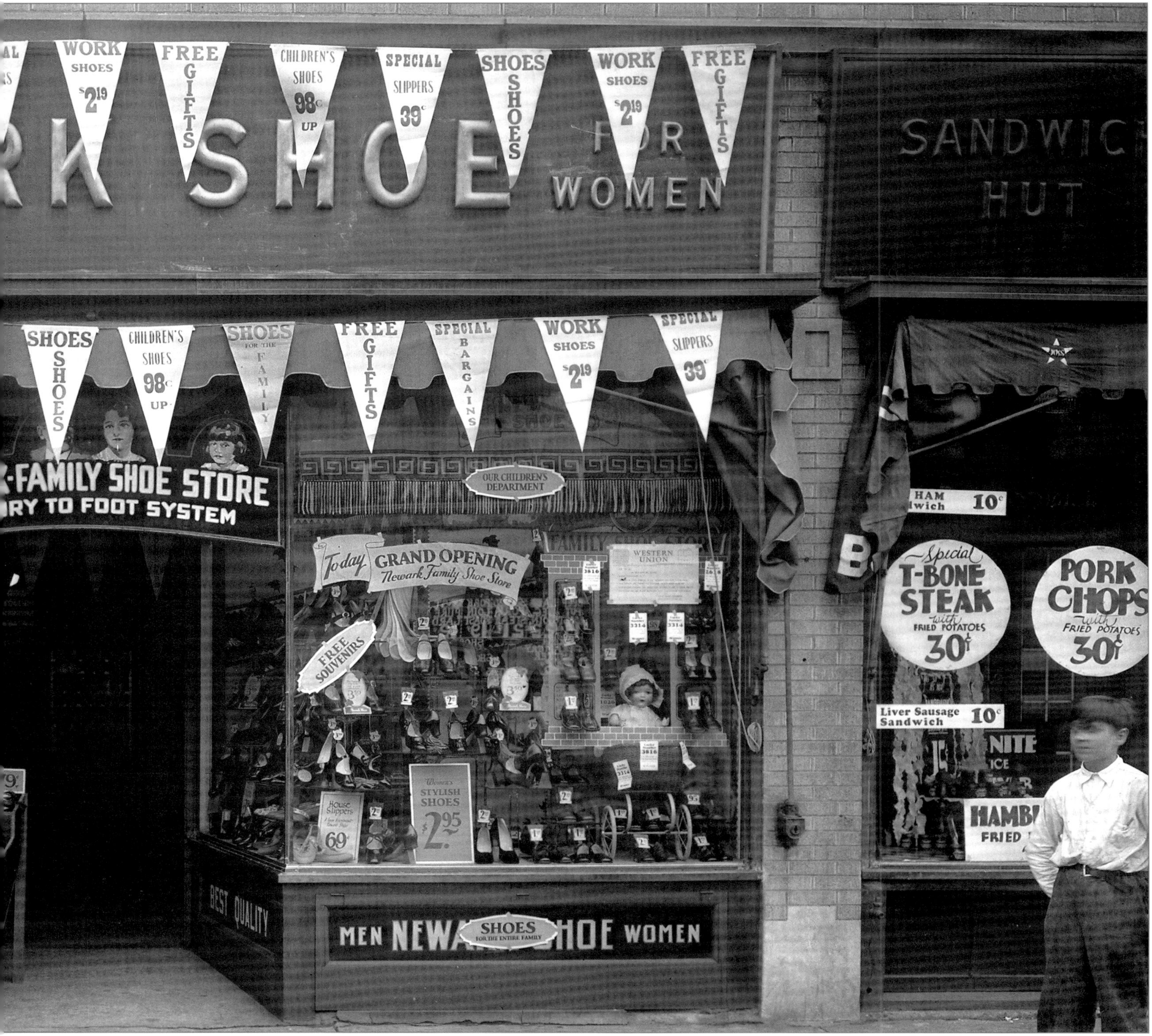

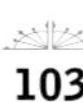

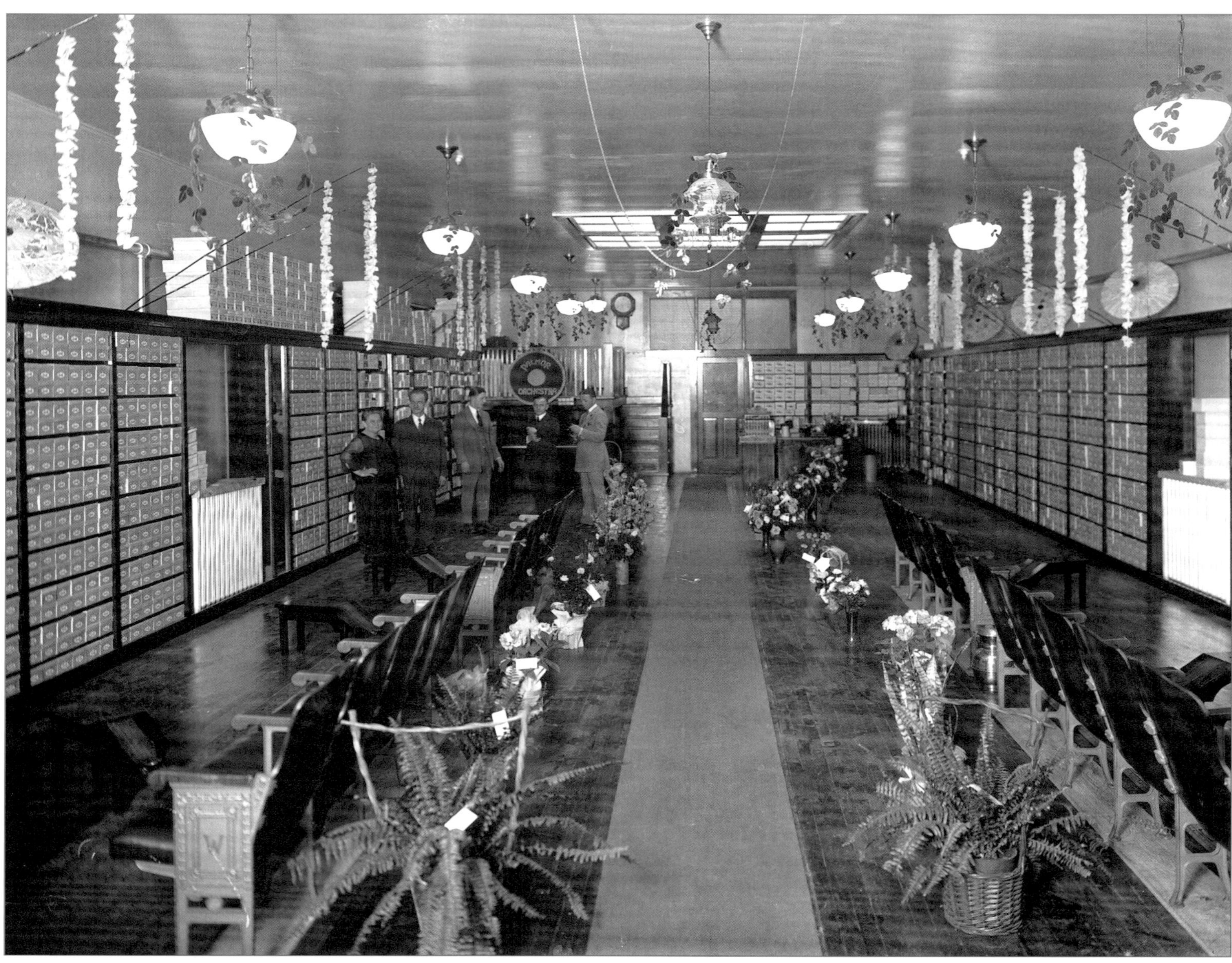

The Lincoln Bootery's sales staff waited for their first customers following the store's grand opening in the mid-1920s. Shoppers browsed through an extensive shoe display in the windows before entering the store. Once customers selected a shoe style they liked, a salesperson assisted and ensured that footwear fit properly. *Serial # A07066*

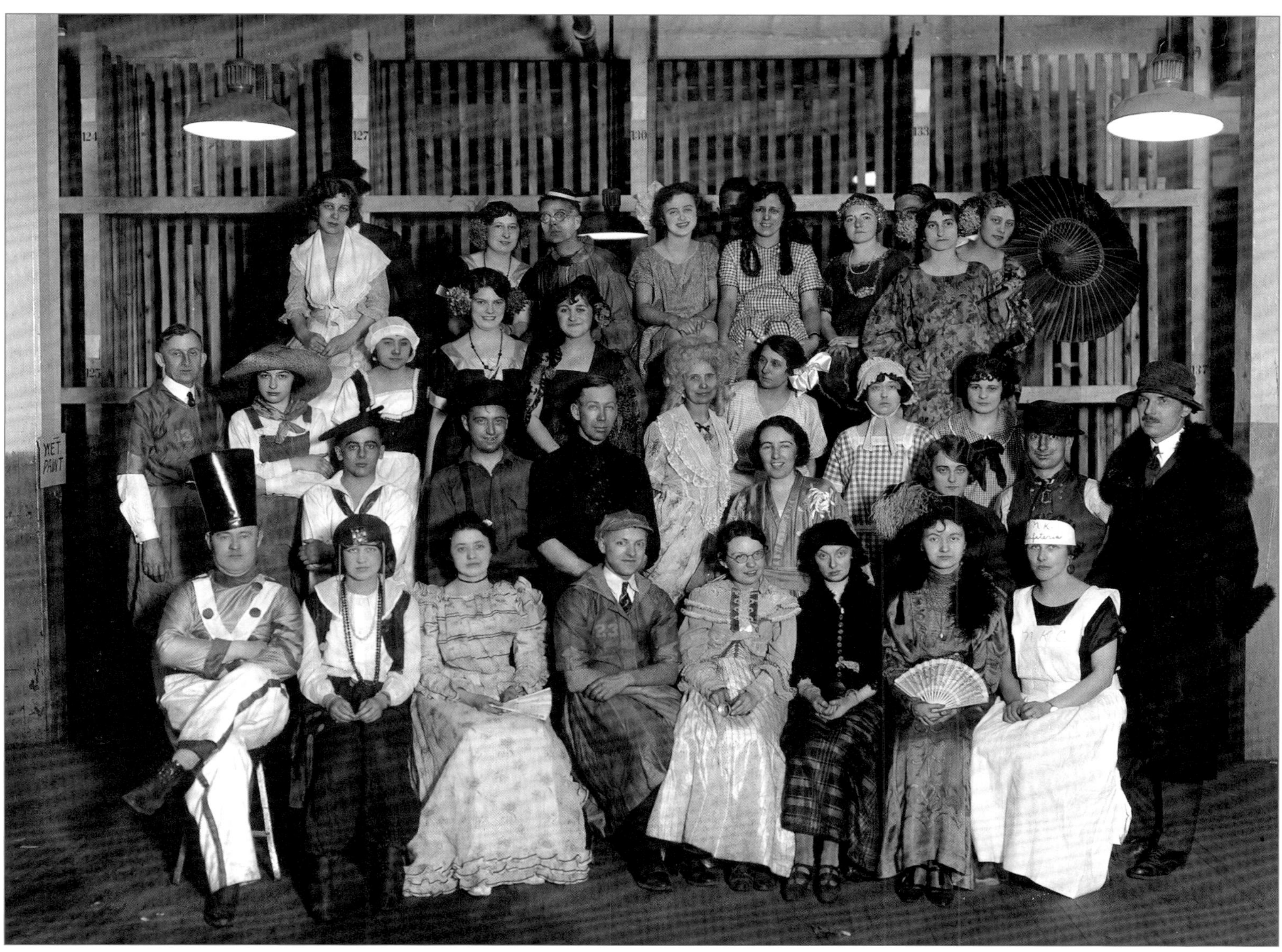

Costumed employees of the National Knitting Company assembled for a photograph in February 1924. The company was established as the National Knitting Works in 1880 and was renamed and incorporated as the National Knitting Company a few years later. Located on Clinton Street (later South First Street) by the Kinnickinnic River, the company manufactured gloves, mittens, and heavy socks. In its heyday the National Knitting Company enjoyed a worldwide reputation for its woolen goods. ***Serial # 23060***

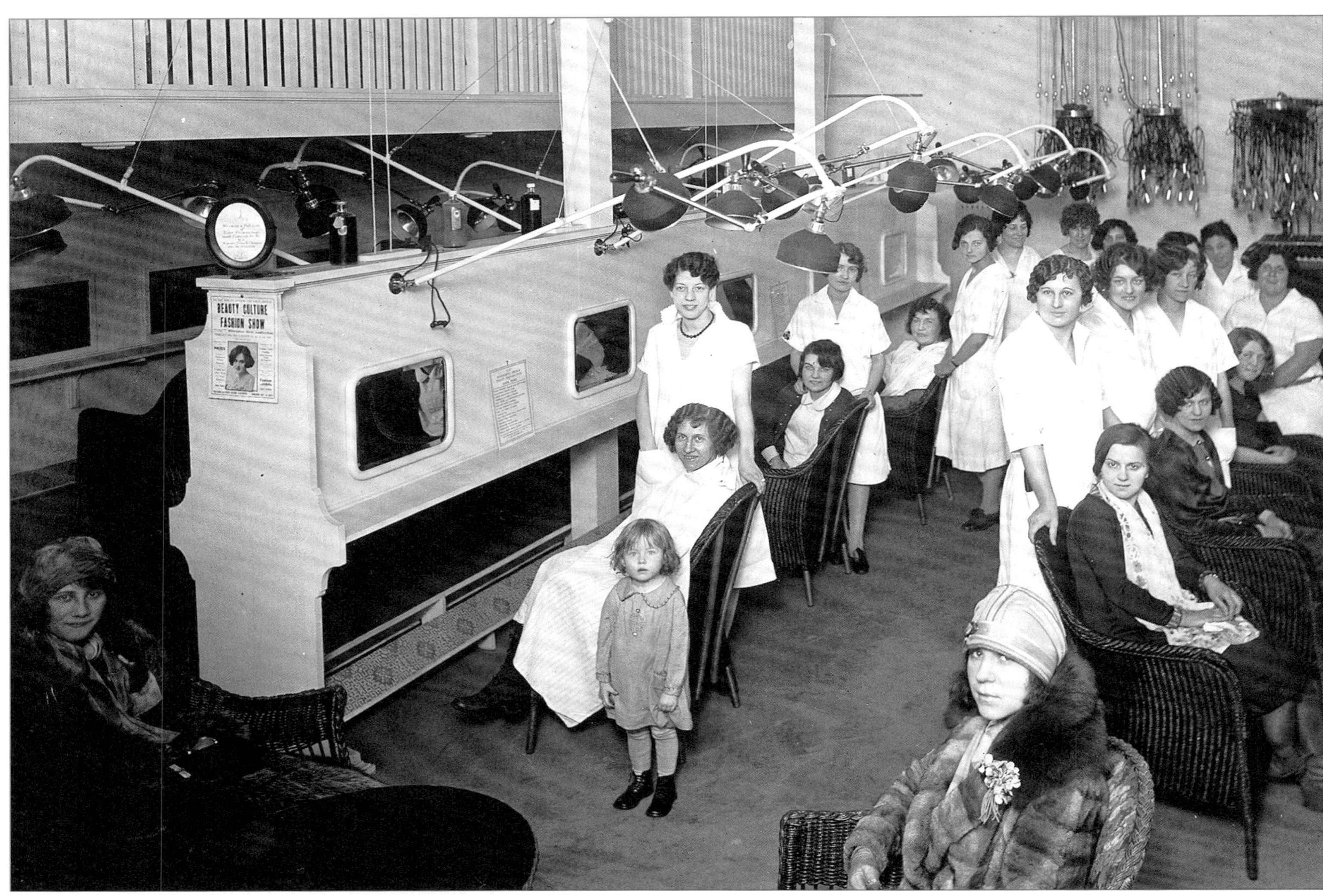

The Klotz Beauty Shoppe touted itself as the "South Side's largest" and "most modern equipped." Perhaps these women were visiting the beauty shop to get a "permanent wave" and prepare for the Beauty Culture Fashion Show advertised on the sign in the left of the photograph. Circa 1927. ***Serial # A07007***

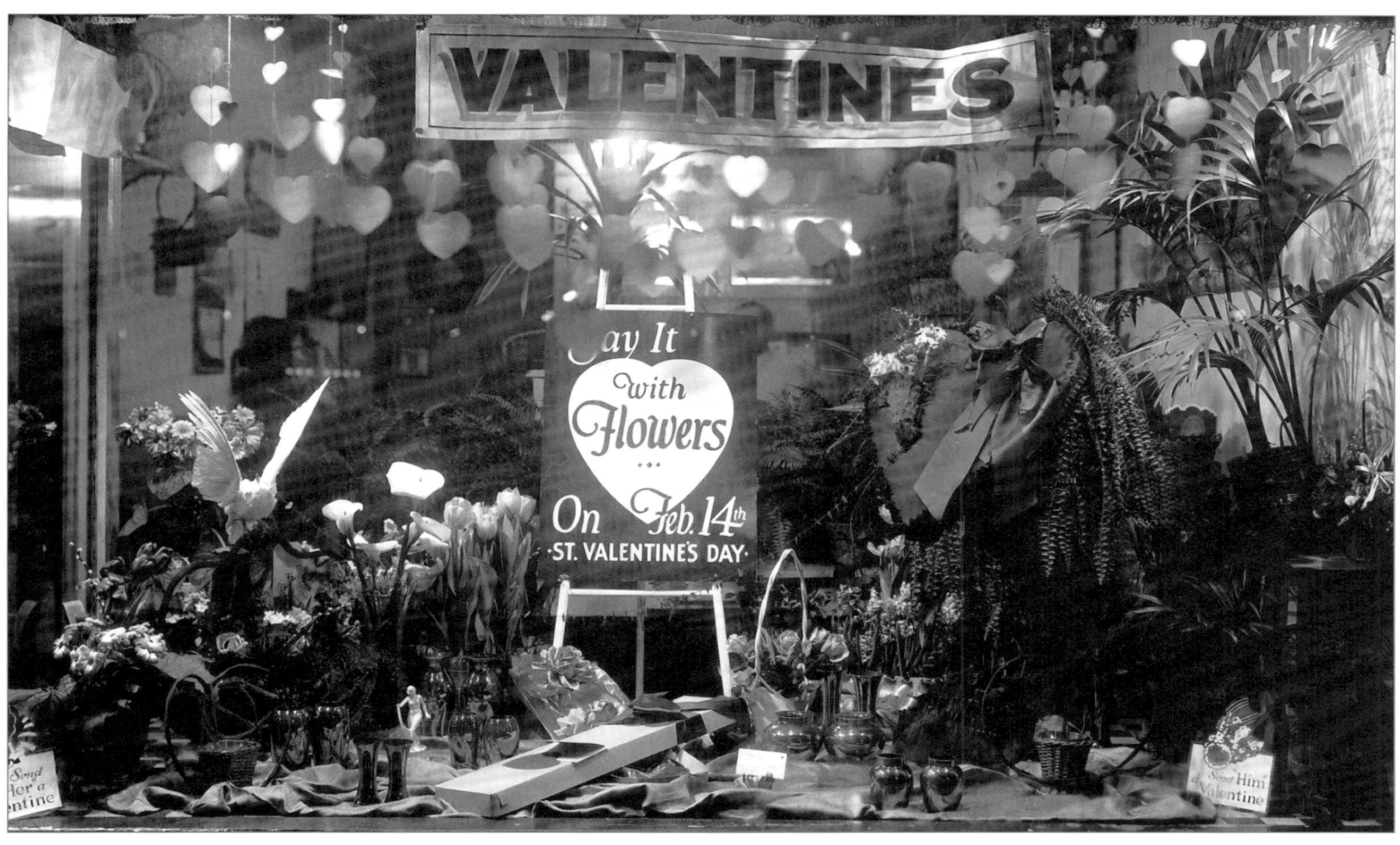

The South Side Art and Floral Company's window display encouraged sweethearts to "Say it with Flowers" on Valentine's Day in 1927. The flower store was located on Lincoln Avenue. ***Serial # 26055***

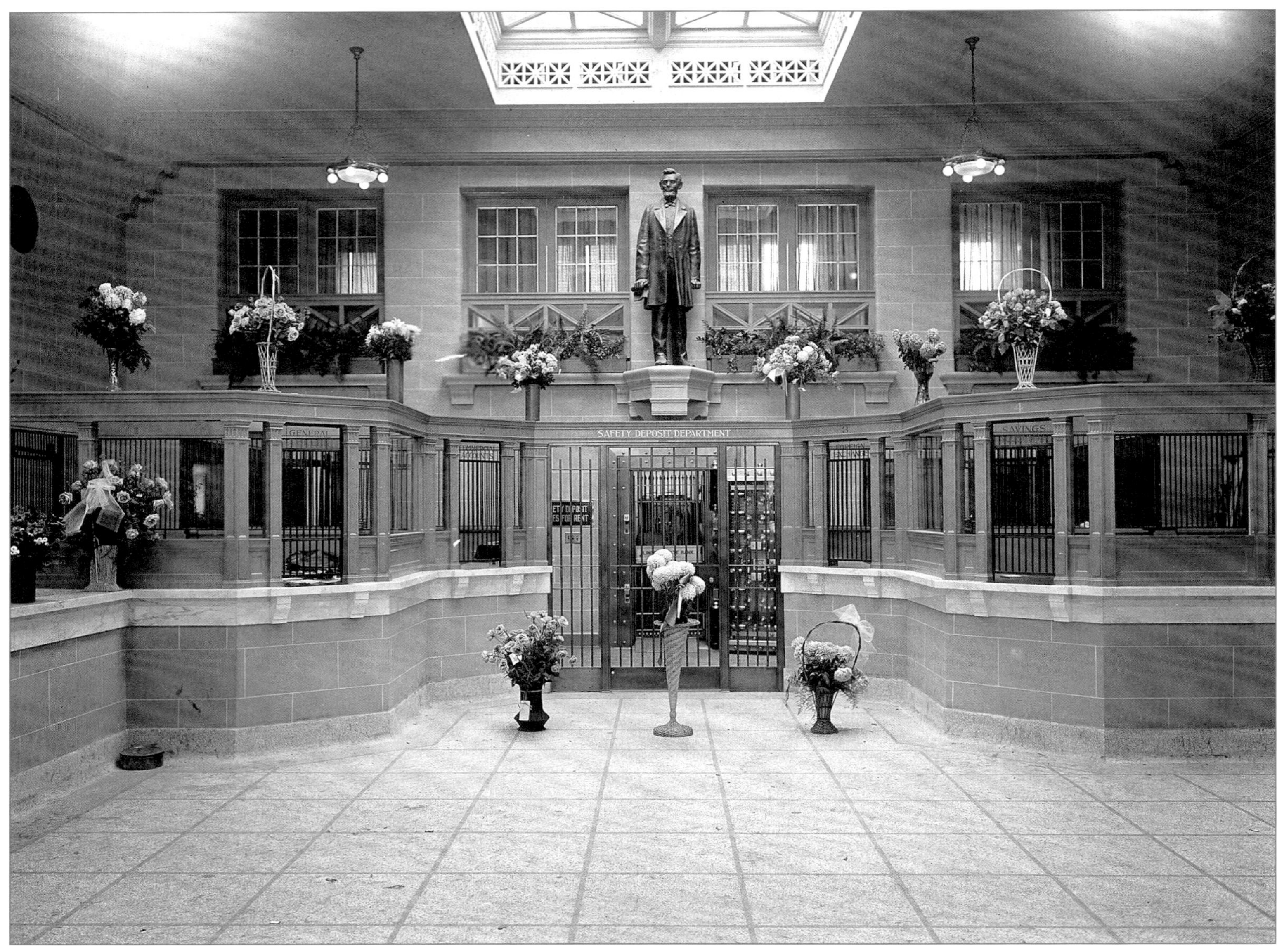

The Lincoln State Bank formally opened for business on December 1, 1920, after completion of a new building at 612 Lincoln Avenue (now 1216 West Lincoln Avenue). The bank was once known as the "first Polish bank in Wisconsin."

Serial # A07005

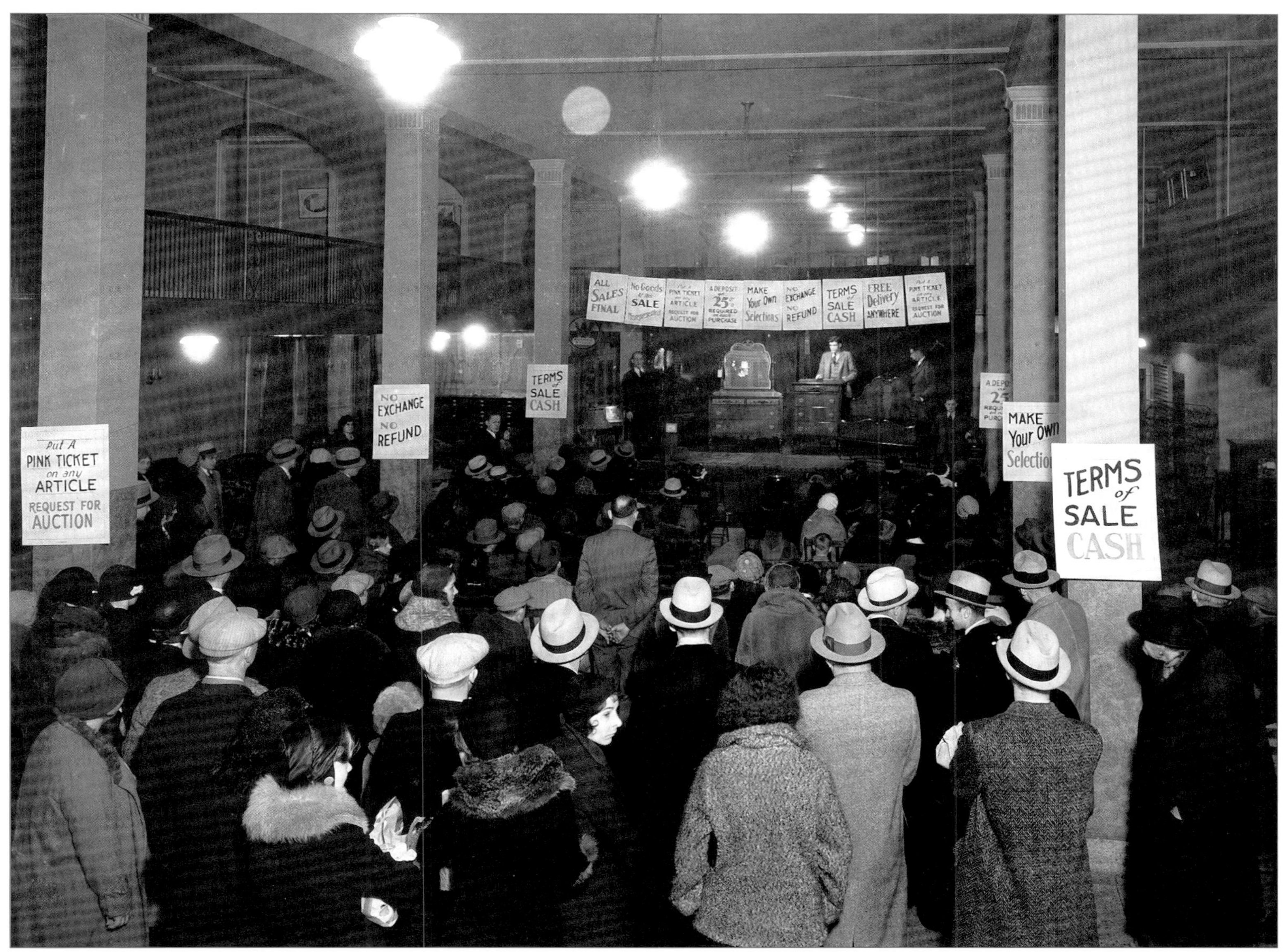

Many businesses were liquidated during the Great Depression, including the Branta-Rechlicz Furniture Company, which was located on Lincoln Avenue. Quite a crowd gathered during the auctioning off of the company's merchandise in the early 1930s.
Serial # A07060-2

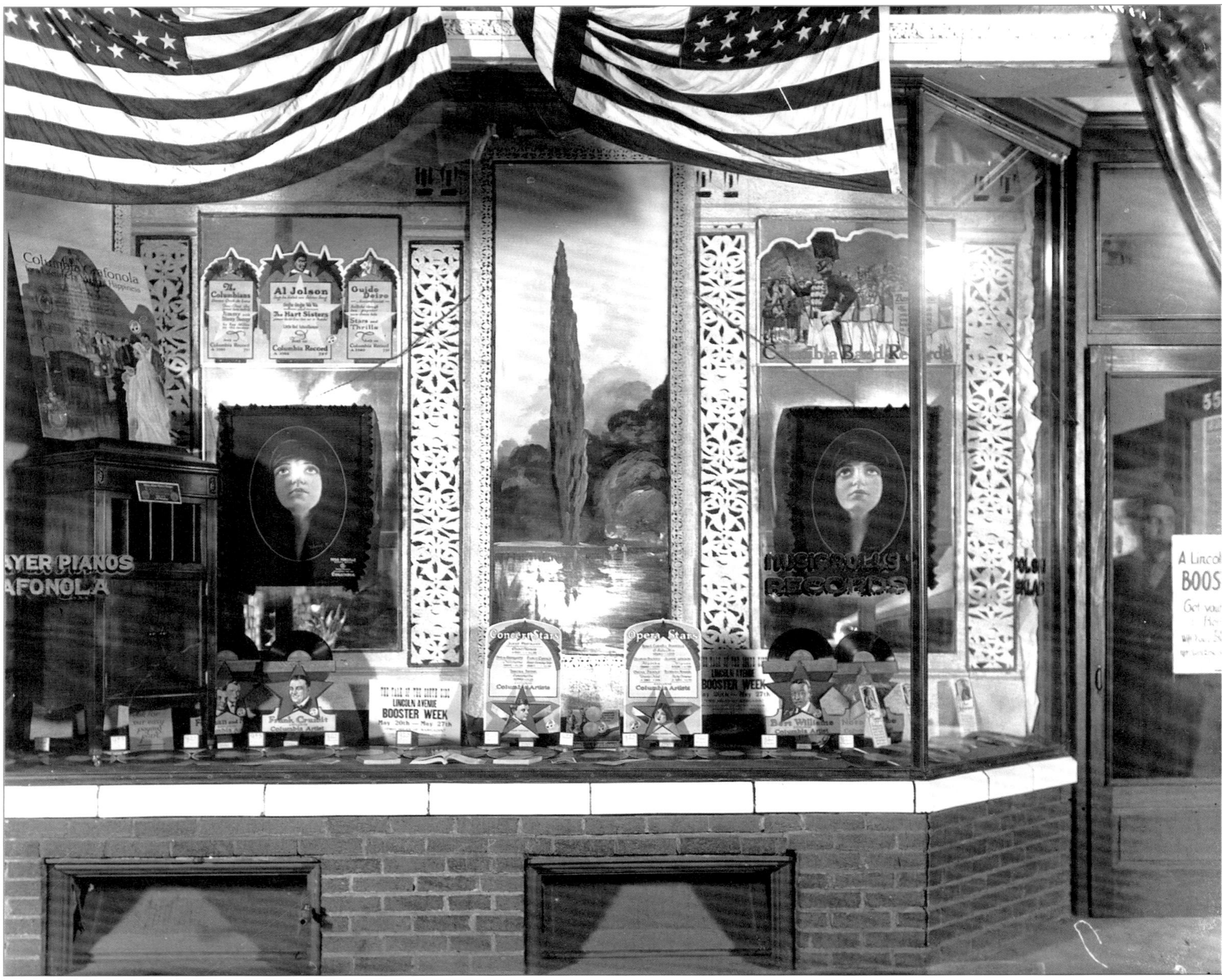

During Booster Week in May 1922 Walter Przybylski's Modern Music Shop, located at what was then 557 Lincoln Avenue, advertised and displayed the latest music equipment and recordings in its store window. Columbia's Grafonola, a record player, shown on the left, was one of the many items for sale during the short time that the store existed. ***Serial # 19326***

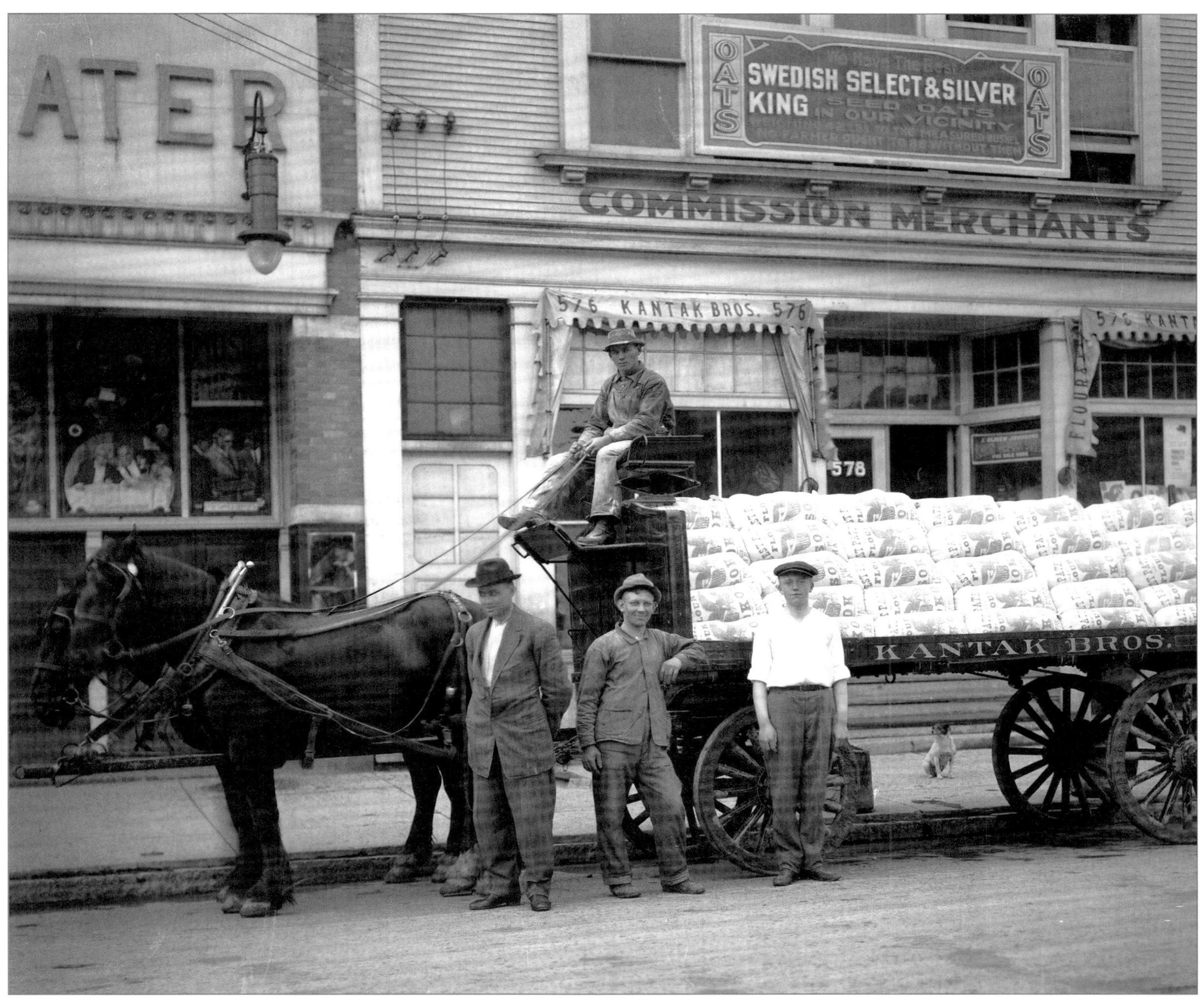

Seed oats and flour were just two of the products for sale at the Kantak Brothers store located next to the Lincoln Theater on Lincoln Avenue. The photograph of these men with a horse-drawn wagon load of flour was taken around 1912.

Serial # A07330

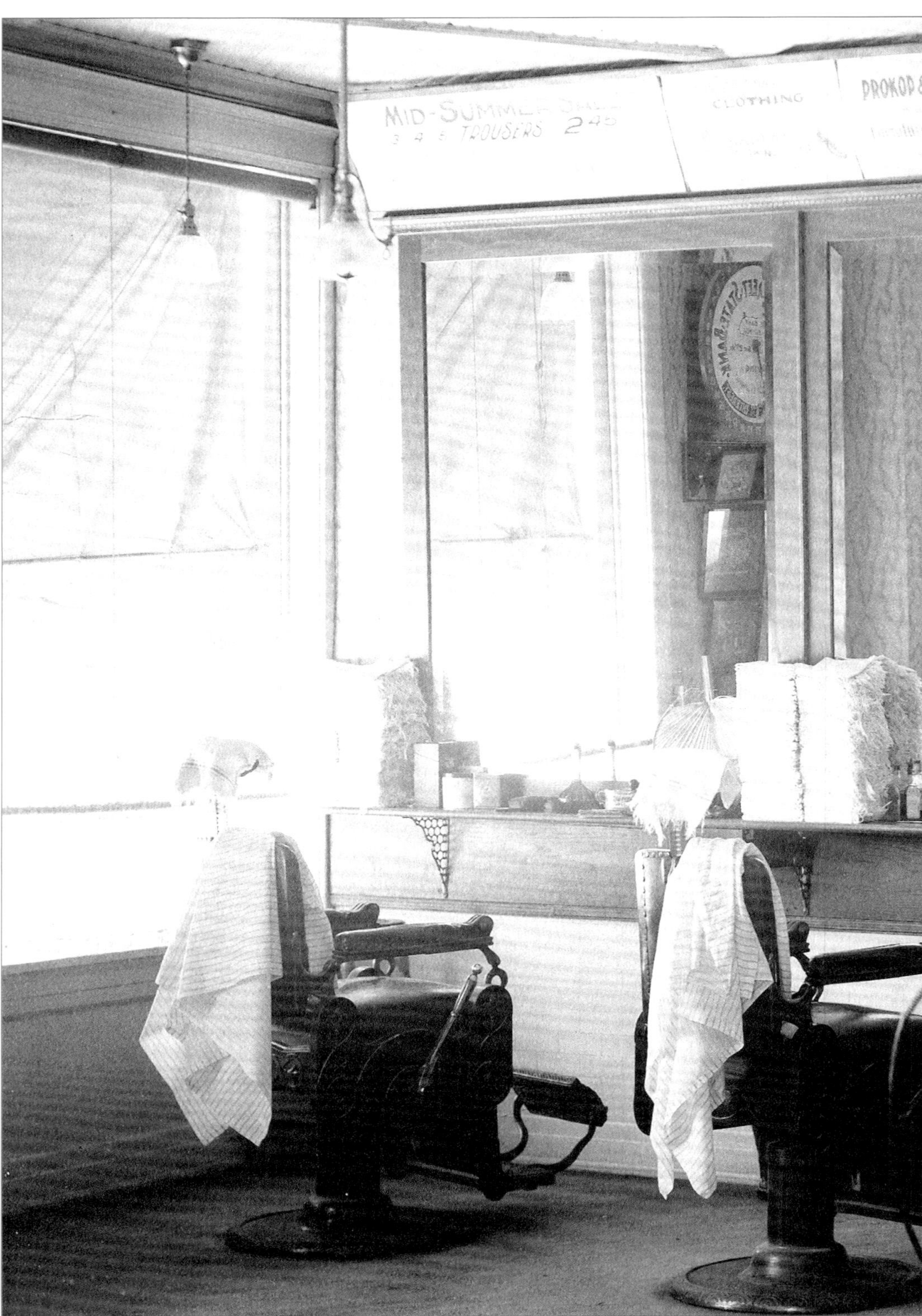

Joseph Michalski opened his barbershop on Windlake Avenue around 1903. At the time when Kwasniewski took this photograph, circa 1915, spittoons were placed throughout the shop for customer convenience.
Serial # A15189

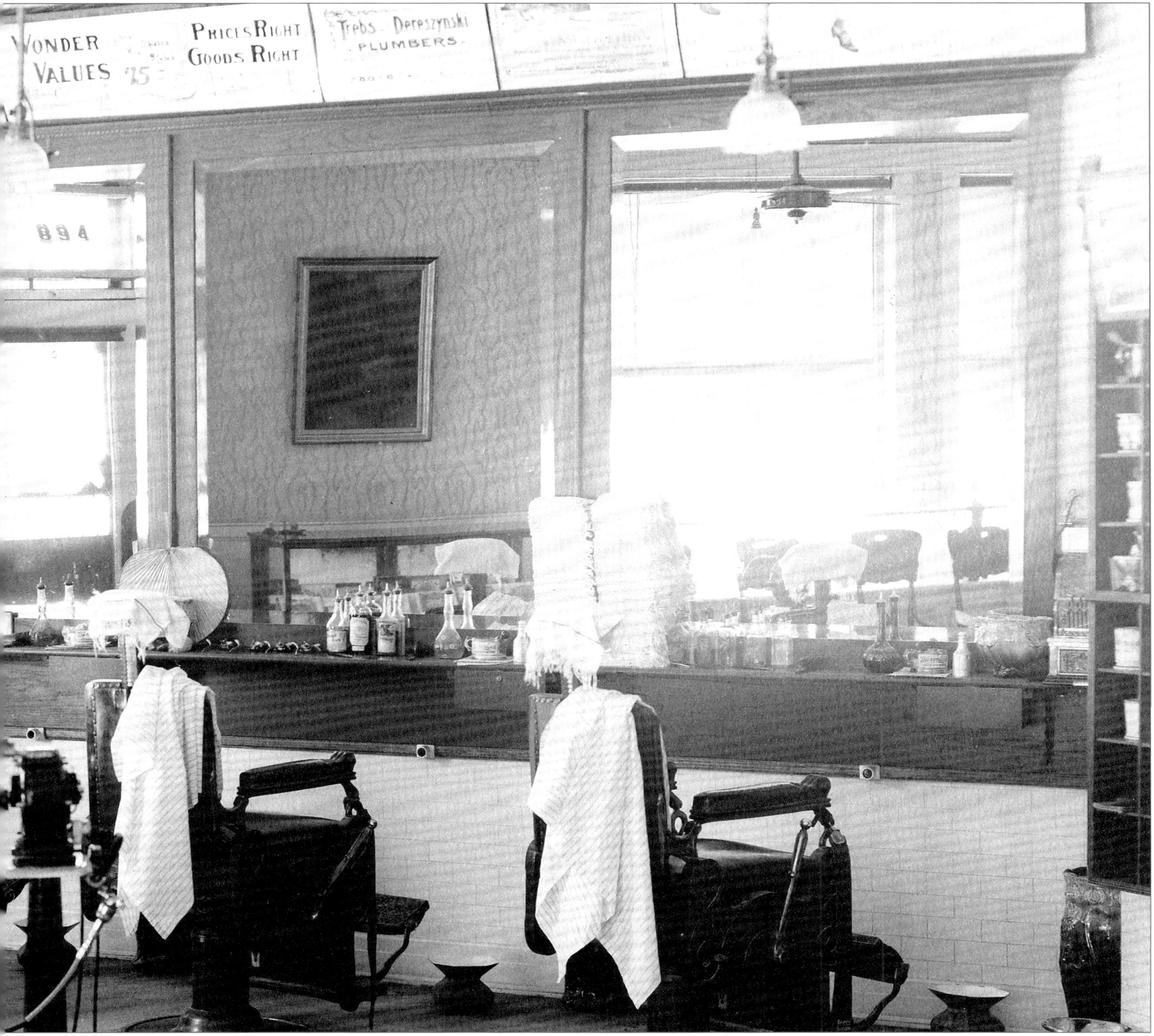

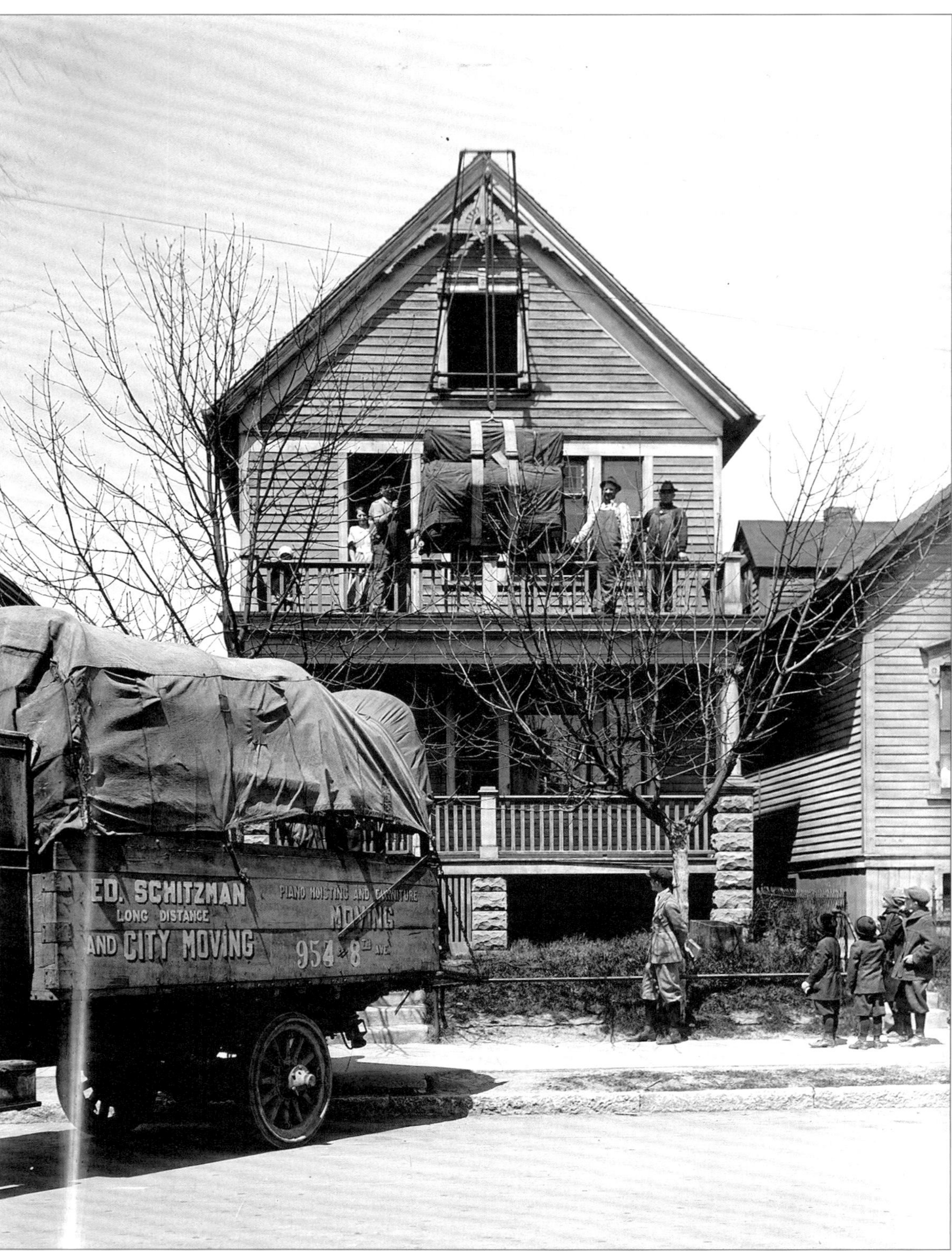

Neighborhood kids looked on as the Ed Schitzman moving company of Milwaukee hoisted a piano into the upper story of this house in 1921.

Serial # 18060

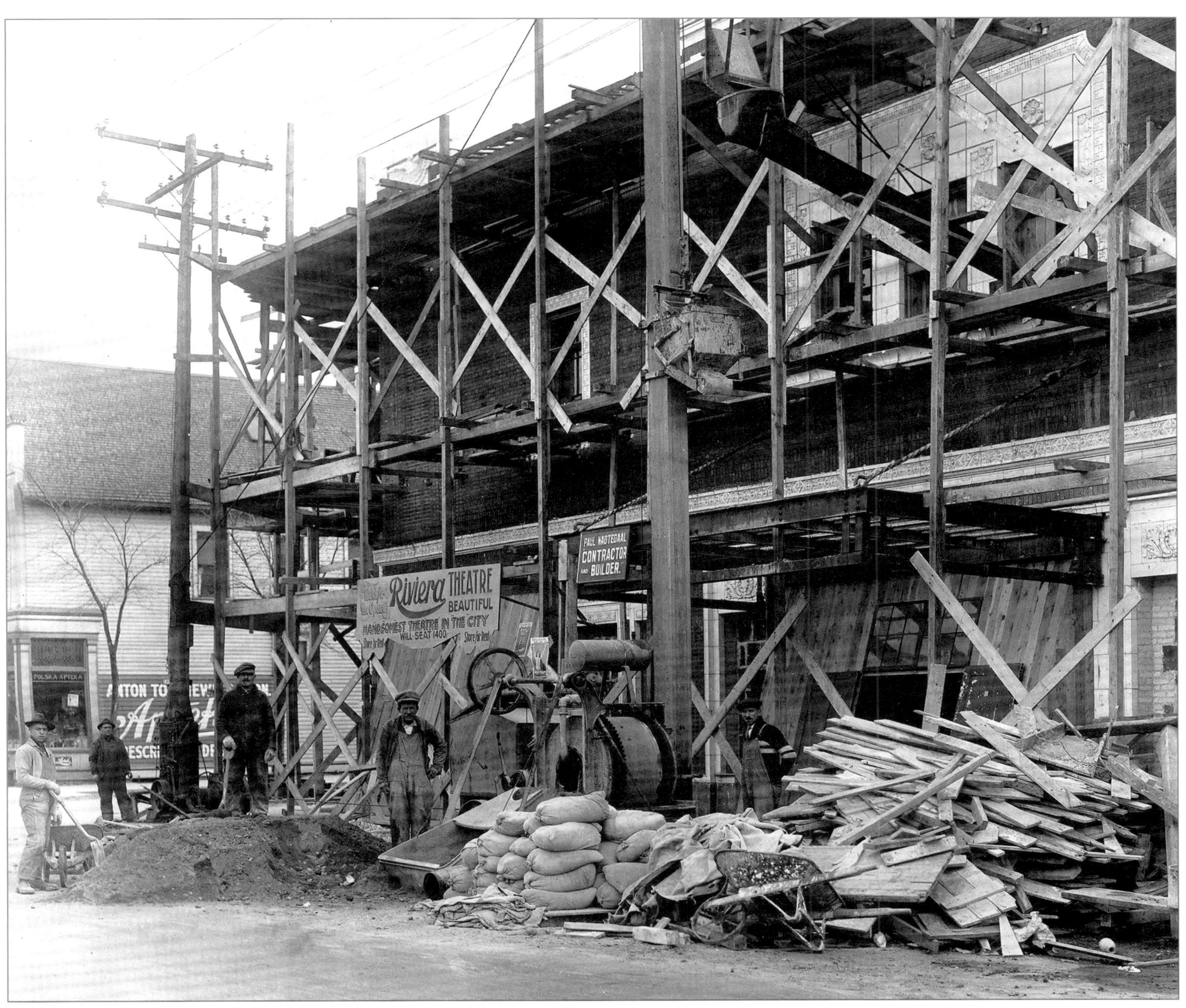

These men working on the construction of the Riviera Theatre paused for a photograph in November 1919. The Riviera, located at what was then Fifth and Lincoln Avenues (today 1005 West Lincoln), was billed as the "handsomest theatre in the city" before it was even completed in 1921. The theater closed in 1954. ***Serial # A07334***

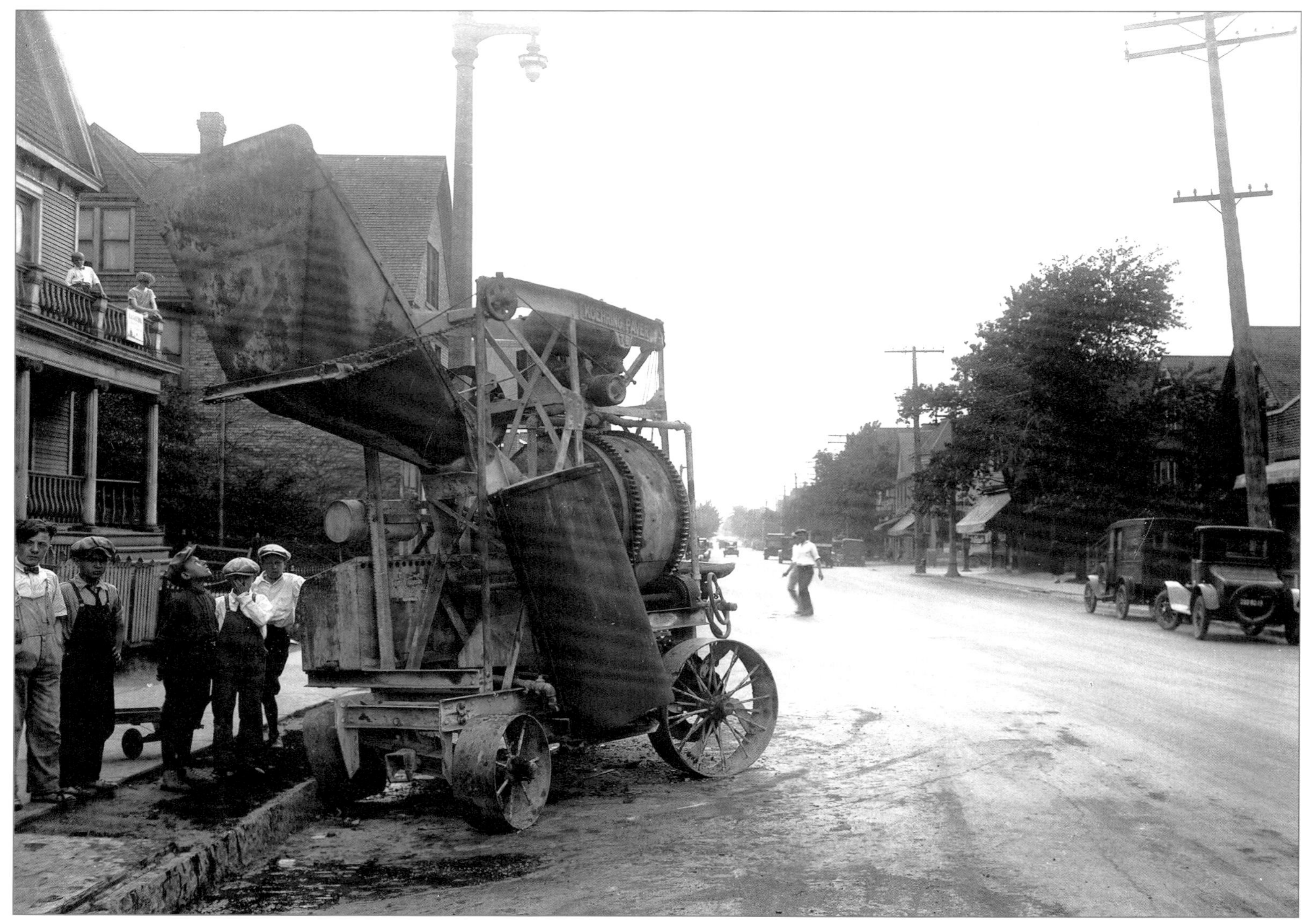

In June 1927 boys from the neighborhood examined a damaged concrete paver made by Milwaukee's Koehring Company, a manufacturer of heavy-duty construction equipment. ***Serial # 26626***

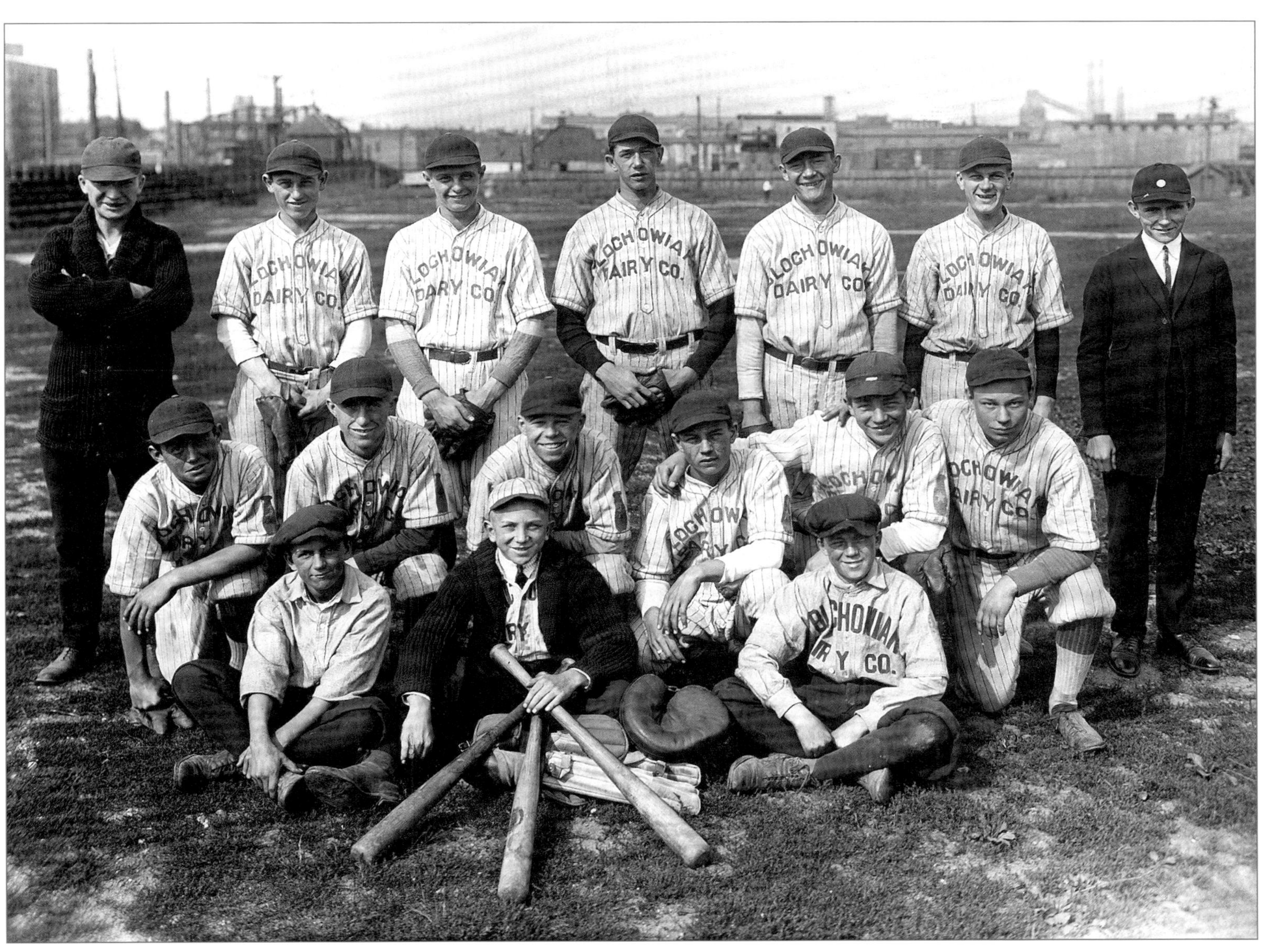

Sponsored by the Blochowiak Dairy, these young baseball players took up one of America's favorite pastimes in 1923. Milwaukee's industrial growth is clearly visible beyond the playing field. ***Serial # 22034***

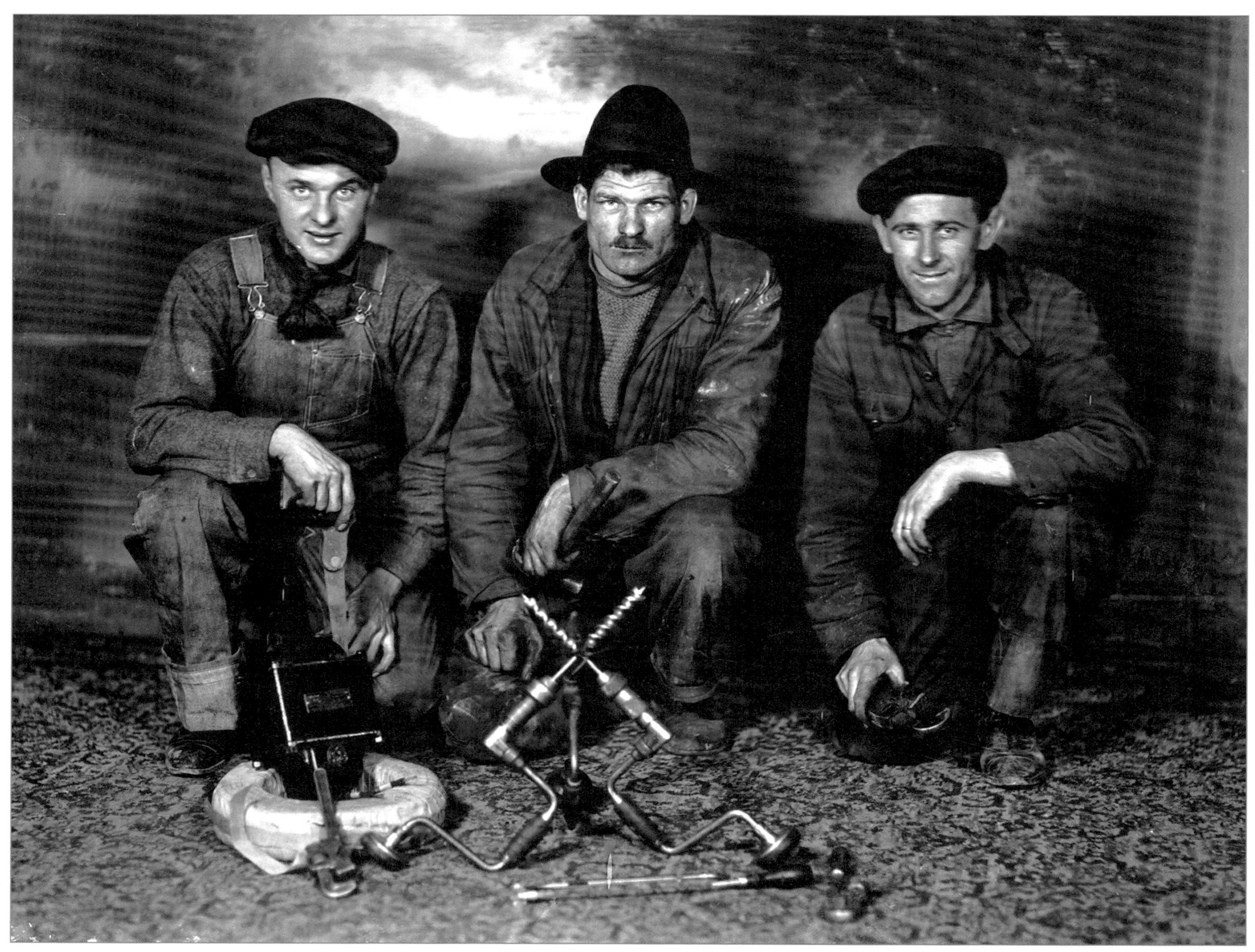

Identified as "the three electricians," these men posed in the photographer's studio with the tools of their trade in January 1921. *Serial # A05612*

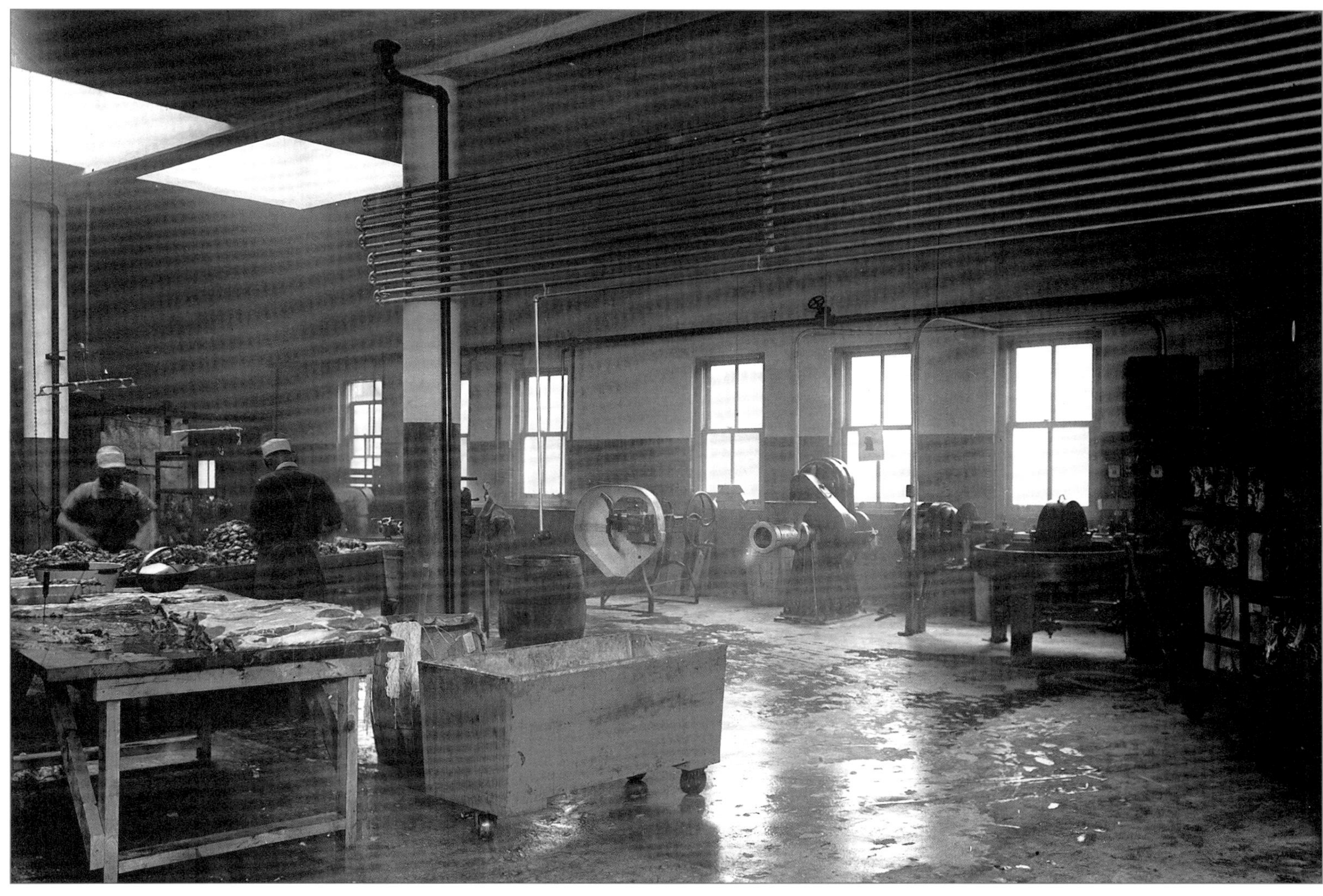

Sausage-making operations were under way at the Badger Sausage Company in February 1928. Stanley Imanski, a Polish immigrant, was one of five entrepreneurs who had organized the company the previous year. Arriving in the United States with some sales experience, Imanski got his start in the sausage business working as a sausage salesman for Frank and Company and for Quality Products Company, two other Milwaukee sausage manufacturers. As company president, Imanski no doubt ensured that the Badger Sausage Company's products had that real Polish flavor. ***Serial # 28070***

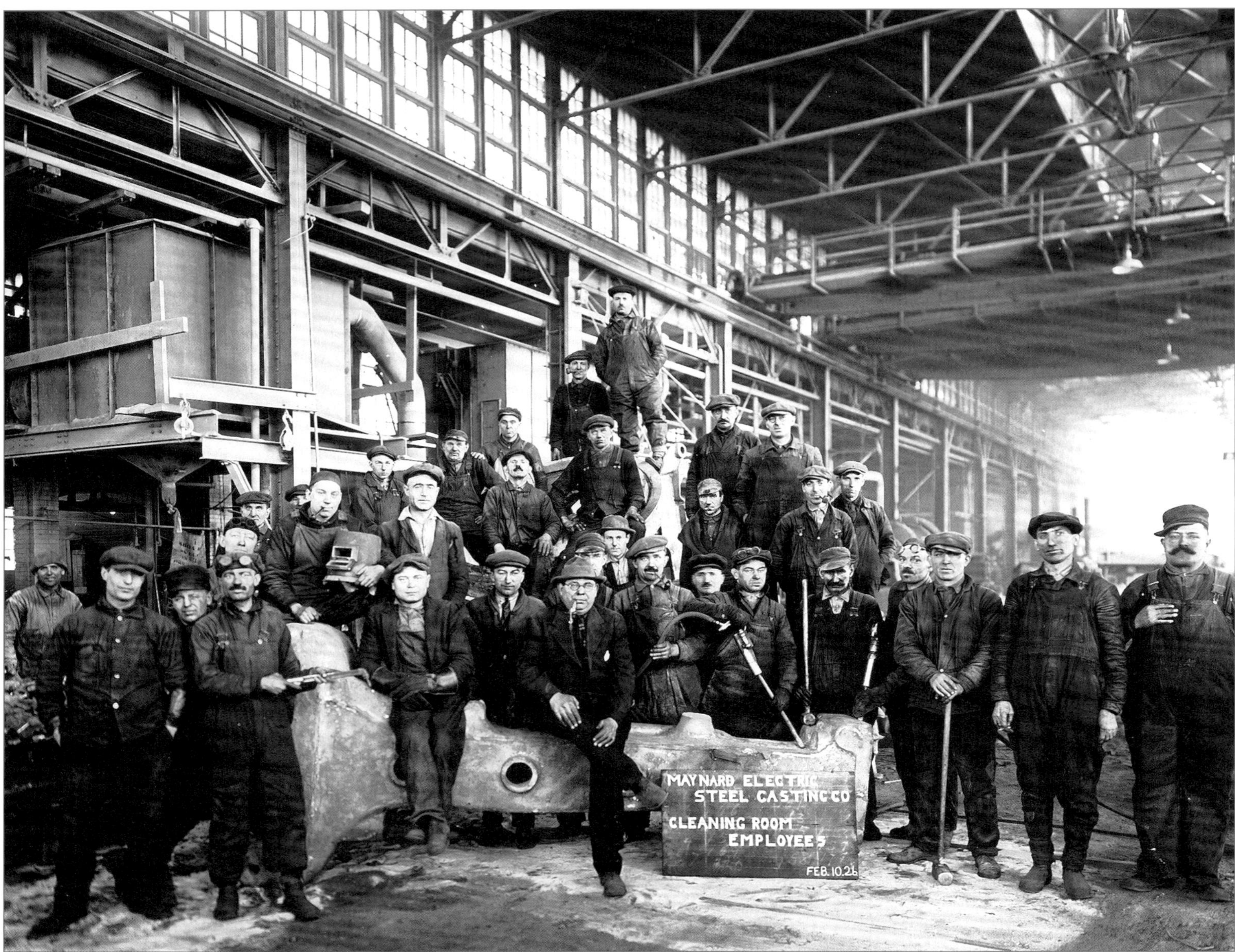

Many South Side Milwaukeeans found jobs in factories. One area employer was the Maynard Electric Steel Castings Company, established in 1907 by Charles Maynard. Sylvester Wabiszewski, a Polish immigrant, acquired the foundering company in 1914. Maynard eventually became one of the largest electric steel casting plants in the Midwest. These Maynard employees gathered for a photograph in 1926, in a cleaning room that had been constructed the previous year.

Serial # 25049

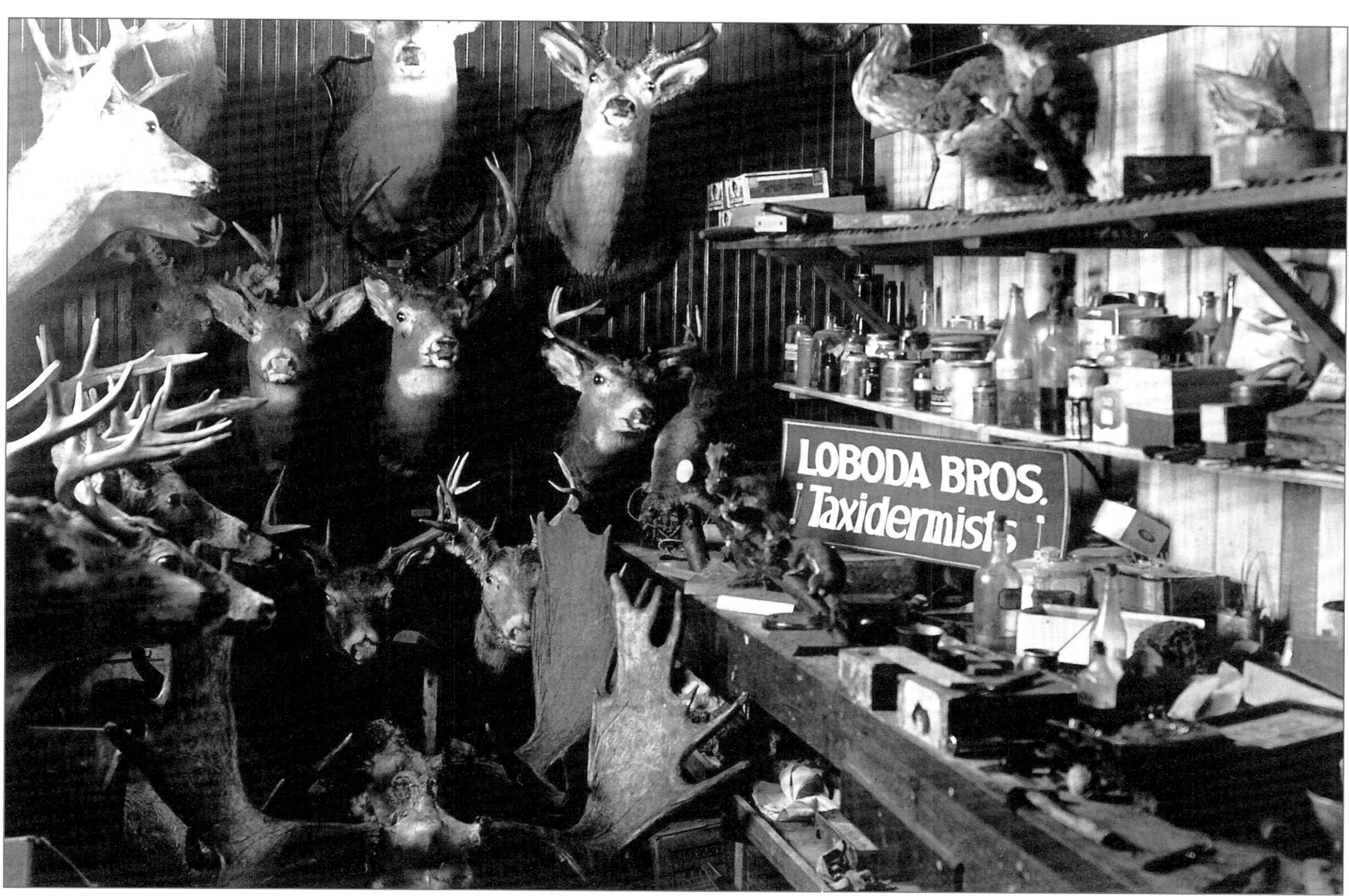

In the mid-1920s Milwaukee-area hunters could take their trophies to the Loboda Brothers Taxidermists. This photograph shows the interior of the taxidermy shop as it looked after what appears to have been a particularly successful deer-hunting season. ***Serial # 23780***

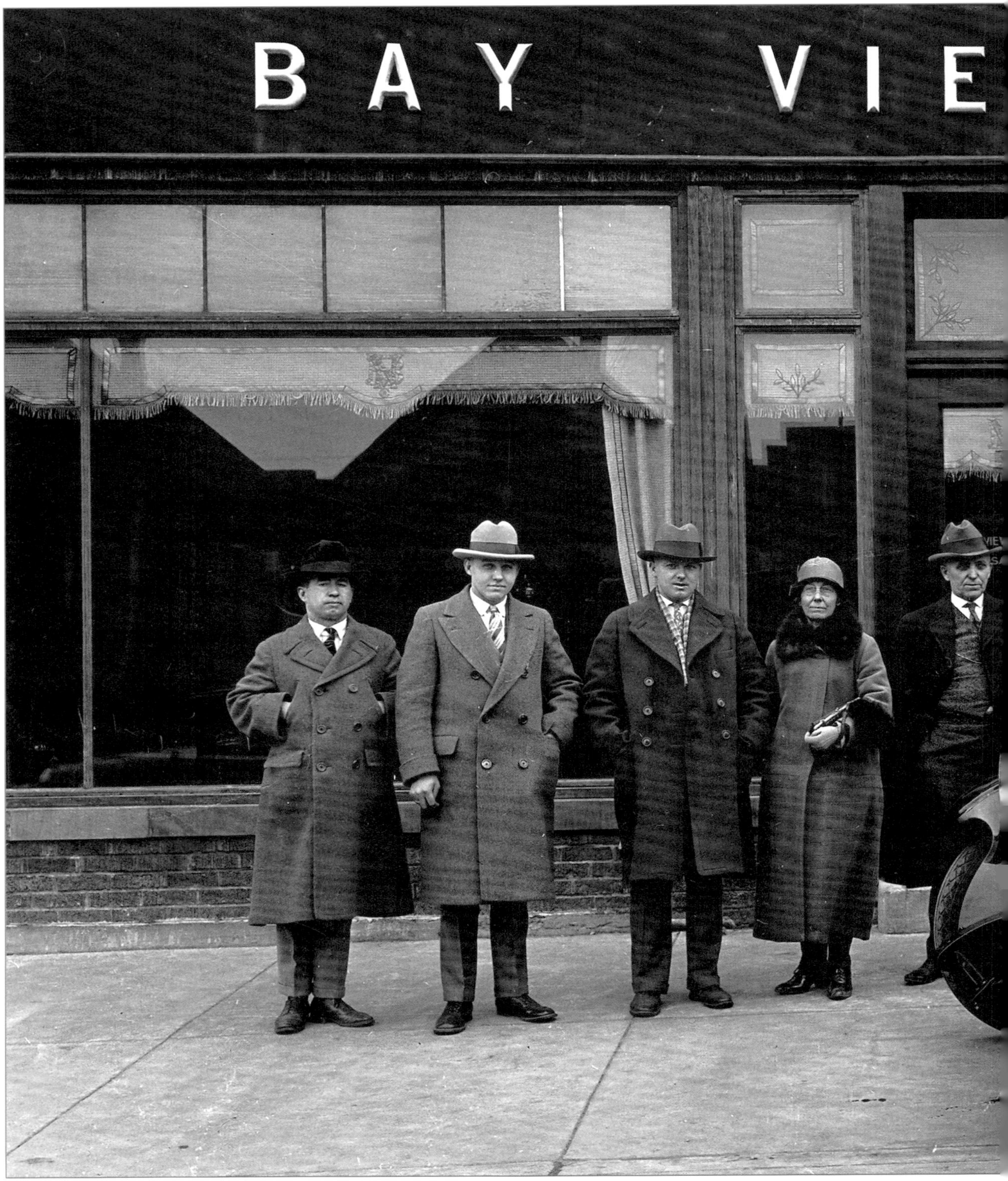

The Bay View Nash Company automobile dealership operated on Lincoln Avenue in the mid- to late 1920s, during what were the Nash Motors Company's most prosperous years. Kwasniewski took this photograph of what he indicated was a "prize car" in 1925. *Serial # 24899*

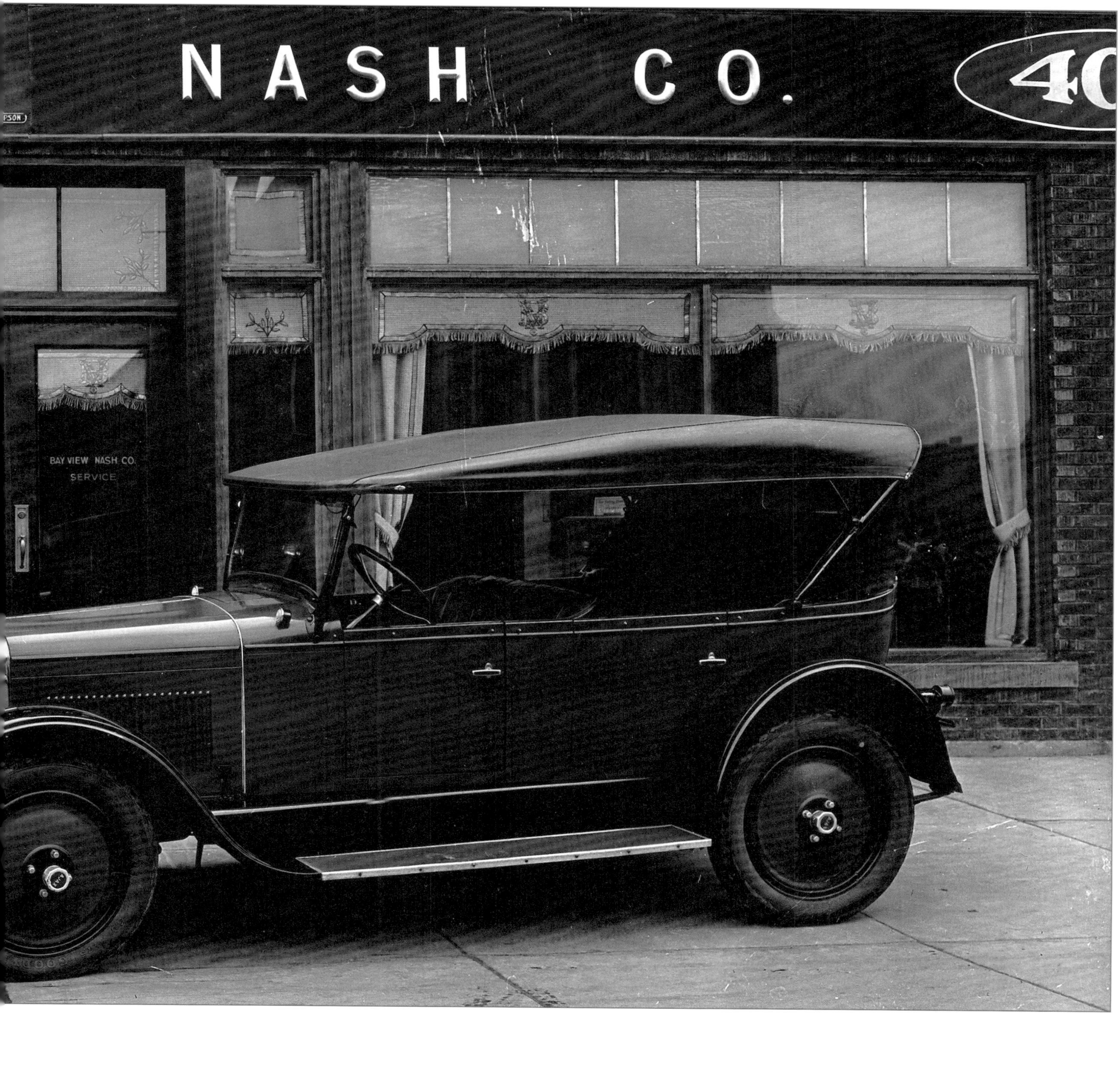

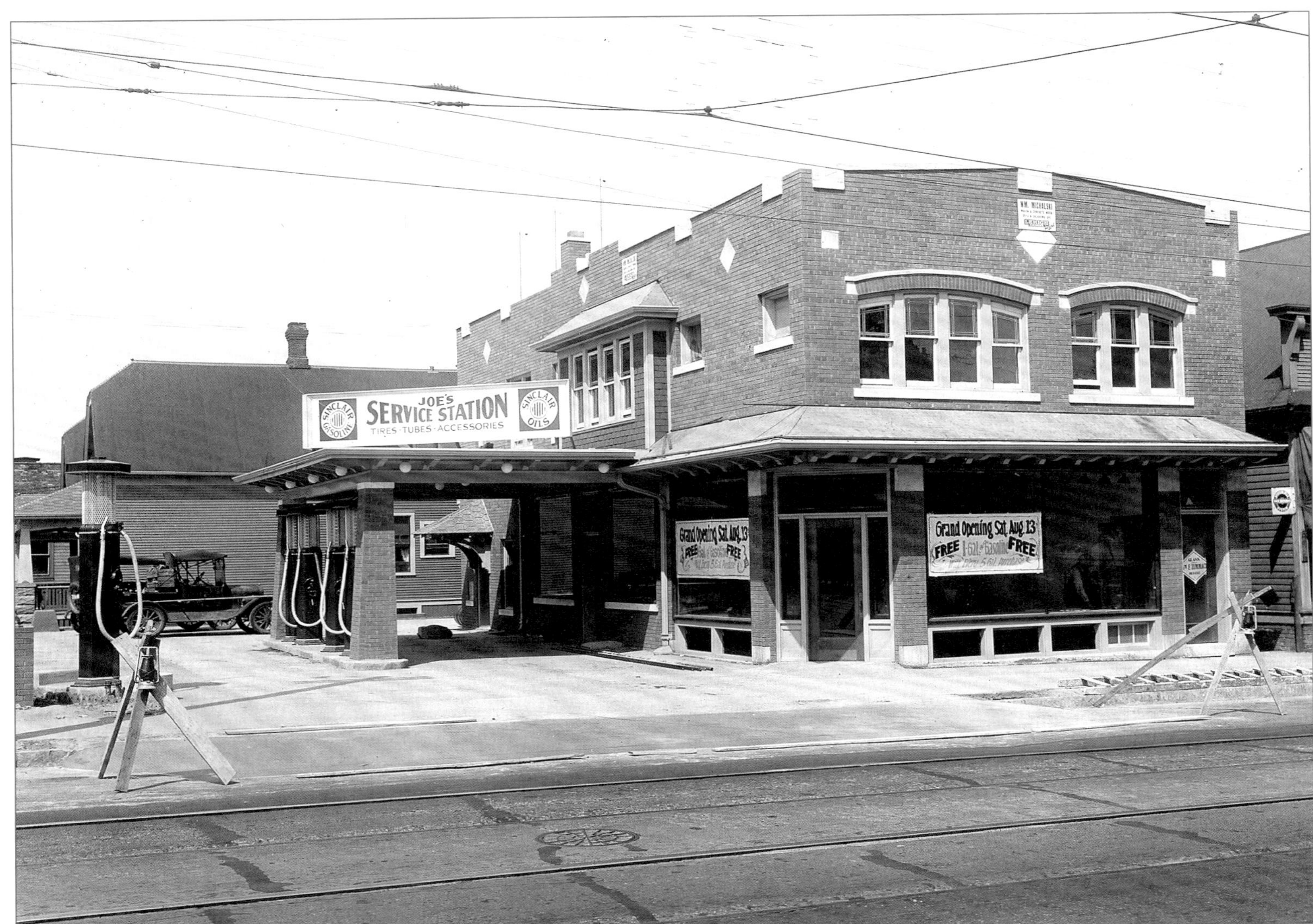

In the late 1920s Joe Zielinski opened Joe's Service Station located at what was then 1205 Eighth Avenue (later 2689 South Thirteenth Street). The signs in the windows announced that on the day of its grand opening the station was giving away a free gallon of gasoline with every five gallons purchased. Zielinski's service enterprise changed somewhat in later years, and by the 1940s he was running a "tavern and filling station." ***Serial # A07056***

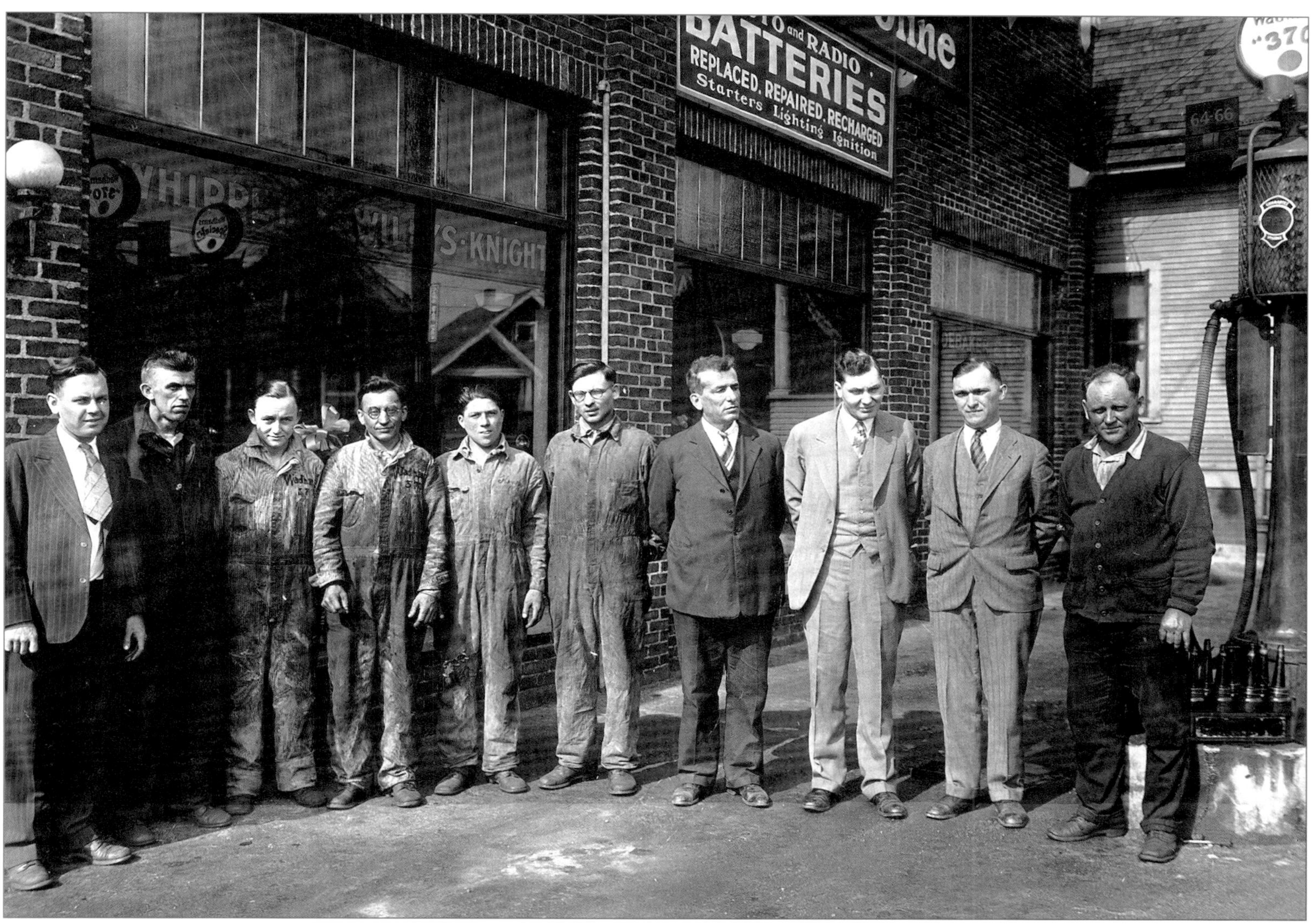

The men in this 1929 photograph specialized in customer sales and service at Bay View Auto Sales and Repair, located at what was then 1415 Kinnickinnic Avenue (today 2797 South Kinnickinnic Avenue). American automobile makes in the sales department included Whippet, Willys-Knight, Studebaker, and Erskine. The station also sold Wadhams gasoline.

Serial # 29124

EPILOGUE

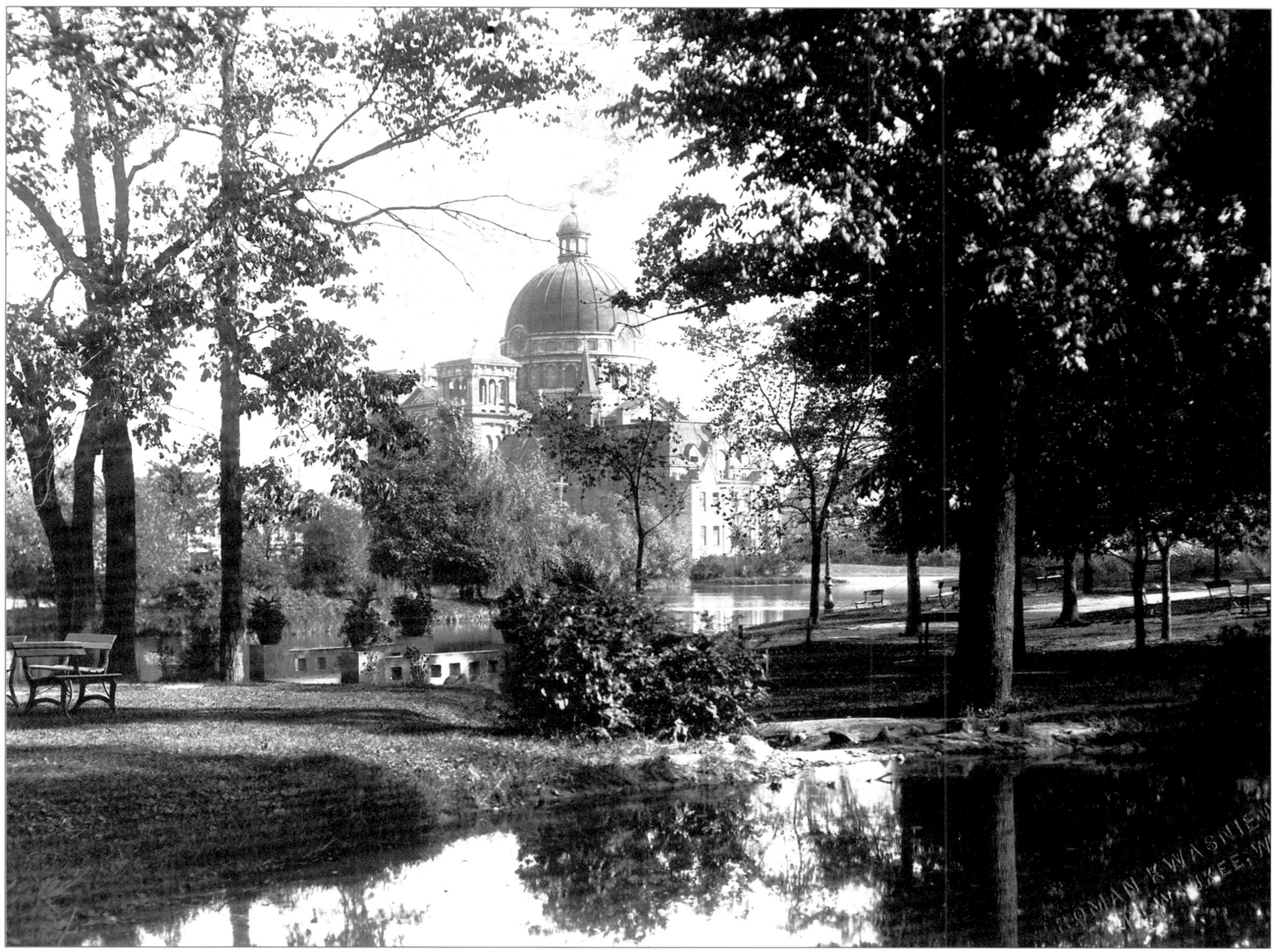

Although the neighborhood has changed from photographer Roman Kwasniewski's day, the Basilica of St. Josaphat, as seen from Kosciuszko Park in this undated image, today stands as a strong reminder of Milwaukee's South Side Polish community.
Serial # A11395

A NOTE ON THE COLLECTION

During the past decade, staff members at the University of Wisconsin–Milwaukee Archives have done an excellent job of preserving, cataloguing, and making the Kwasniewski collection available to interested scholars and the general public. This book represents a culmination of their efforts.

It was my privilege to play a part, along with a number of others, in bringing the Kwasniewski collection to the University of Wisconsin–Milwaukee Library more than two decades ago. In 1974 I was selected to present the Fifth Annual Fromkin Memorial Lecture at the UWM Library. In my talk, "Progressives, Socialists, and the Milwaukee Poles," I discussed the political dynamics of the city's already-substantial Polish immigrant and ethnic community in the years before World War II. In the course of adapting my presentation for publication in the *Wisconsin Magazine of History*, I learned that the Wisconsin Historical Society did not have suitable photographs to illustrate the piece. The editors and I, however, were able to locate a number of appropriate photographs through individuals in Milwaukee who possessed private photograph collections.

The search for photographs inspired me to learn about other collections of photographs of Milwaukee's South Side that might have been preserved. I began to make my own inquiries about whether any of the several area photo studios had saved photographs. But for various reasons none of the shops had saved their old inventories.

It was then that Janet Dziadulewicz Branden, a knowledgeable member of the Milwaukee Polish American community, urged me to contact an old-timer named Roman Kwasniewski who had owned the Park Studio. I tried telephoning Kwasniewski's home several times, with no luck. Then almost as an afterthought I wrote him a brief note. There was no reply, and I forgot about the matter following my article's publication.

One morning in December 1978 I received a note from someone named John Kaczmarowski. It was brief and to the point: "The building is being sold next week. If you want to look at the photographs, let me know as soon as possible."

I immediately telephoned Mr. Kaczmarowski, the ninety-two-year-old Roman Kwasniewski's son-in-law, and we arranged to meet at the former Park Studio. I then contacted William Roselle, then director of the UWM Library. Bill reacted enthusiastically and suggested that several of the library's staff accompany me. A few days later Fromkin bibliographer Stanley Mallach, UWM's resident photographer, John Alley, and I drove to the old studio. There, we were delighted to find a trove of thousands of glass-plate negatives and hundreds of positive prints in amazingly good condition. They were available, Kaczmarowski told us, but only for purchase. Having no authorization to pay for the collection, I telephoned Janet Branden, president of Polanki, the Polish Women's Cultural Club of Milwaukee, who immediately assured me that the club would cover the cost of the collection's purchase. Just days later, Bill Roselle arranged for the collection's transfer to UWM.

In 1982 I worked with Stanley Mallach and Wilbur Stolt at the UWM Library to develop the first exhibit of more than 140 photos from the Kwasniewski collection. Its inaugural display was, most appropriately, at the very first Polish Fest on Milwaukee's lakefront Summerfest grounds on Labor Day weekend that summer.

More than twenty years after that event, I still recall the genuine excitement as crowds four and five people deep pressed forward to gaze at the enlarged photos that depicted community life, work, sports, and ceremony. For the first time, Milwaukee Poles saw their own history. Since then, Kwasniewski's work has been shown on many occasions and has never failed to generate an enthusiastic response.

I know that readers of *Illuminating the Particular* will enjoy this book on several levels. First, of course, the photos depict an important district of the city as it was three generations ago. This sampling is also an entrée by which viewers, whether they are scholars of urban or ethnic history or community researchers, may develop a better appreciation of the collection's contours and dimensions.

Although many individuals have contributed in various important ways to the preservation of the photographic work of Roman Kwasniewski, the greatest credit belongs to Mr. Kwasniewski himself. It was this energetic, enterprising, and talented man who did the photographic work, both in his studio and in his Milwaukee South Side community. But his contribution extends further. Because he kept his work well organized and preserved for the four decades that followed his retirement, we have images today that open a door to a previously almost forgotten world, one filled with the faces and activities of people we can meet again and again. Thank you, Christel Maass, for your work in opening this door even wider!

—Donald Pienkos

SELECTED BIBLIOGRAPHY

Anderson, Byron. "A History of Milwaukee's South Side, 1834–1930." Master's thesis, University of Wisconsin–Milwaukee, 1977.

Anderson, Harry H., and Frederick I. Olson. *Milwaukee: At the Gathering of the Waters.* Tulsa: Continental Heritage Press, 1981.

Basilica of St. Josaphat, Milwaukee. *The Conventual Franciscan Fathers, the Franciscan Sisters of Hamburg and the Congregation of Saint Josaphat Celebrate Seventy five Years of the Basilica Church Dedicated July 21, 1901.* Milwaukee: The Bicentennial of the United States of America, 1976.

Borun, Thaddeus, comp. *We, the Milwaukee Poles: The History of Milwaukeeans of Polish Descent and a Record of Their Contributions to the Greatness of Milwaukee.* Milwaukee: Nowiny, 1946.

Bruce, William George. *History of Milwaukee, City and County.* 3 vols. Chicago: S. J. Clarke, 1922.

Bukowczyk, John J. *And My Children Did Not Know Me: A History of the Polish-Americans.* Bloomington: Indiana University Press, 1987.

Company K, 127th Infantry, History Committee. *History of Co. K., 127th Inf., 32nd Div. (Kosciuszko Guard), Wisconsin National Guard, 1874–1924.* Milwaukee: Company K, 127th Infantry, History Committee, [1925?].

Founding Industries of Wisconsin (survey project). Records, 1880–1993. UWM Manuscript Collection 41. University Manuscript Collections, Golda Meir Library, University of Wisconsin–Milwaukee.

Greene, Victor. "Poles." In *Harvard Encyclopedia of American Ethnic Groups.* Edited by Stephan A. Thernstrom. Cambridge, MA: Harvard University Press, 1980.

Gregory, John G. *History of Milwaukee, Wisconsin.* 4 vols. Chicago: Clarke, 1931.

Gurda, John. *Discover Milwaukee Catalog: Overflowing with Information about History, Homes, Character, Resources of Milwaukee and Its Neighborhoods.* Milwaukee: Milwaukee Department of City Development, 1986.

———. *The Making of Milwaukee.* Milwaukee: Milwaukee County Historical Society, 1999.

———. *A Separate Settlement: A Study of One Section of Milwaukee's Old South Side.* Milwaukee: United Community Services of Greater Milwaukee, 1974.

Gurda, John, and Byron Anderson. *The Near South Side: A Delicate Balance.* Milwaukee: Babylon Press, [1973?].

Kerstein, Edward S. *My South Side.* Milwaukee: Milwaukee Journal, 1976.

Korom, Joseph J. *Milwaukee Architecture: A Guide to Notable Buildings.* Madison: Prairie Oak Press, 1995.

Kuzniewski, Anthony J. "Milwaukee's Poles, 1866–1918: The Rise and Fall of a Model Community." *Milwaukee History: The Magazine of the Milwaukee County Historical Society* 20 (spring 1997): 27–40.

Kwasniewski, Roman B. J. Kwasniewski family papers, 1892–1953. Milwaukee Manuscript Collection 22. University Manuscript Collections, Golda Meir Library, University of Wisconsin–Milwaukee.

———. Photographs, 1907–1947. UWM Manuscript Collection 19. University Manuscript Collections, Golda Meir Library, University of Wisconsin–Milwaukee.

Landscape Research. *Built in Milwaukee: An Architectural View of the City*. Milwaukee: City of Milwaukee, Henry W. Maier, Mayor, and the Department of City Development, William Ryan Drew, Commissioner, [1981?].

Milwaukee Department of City Development. *Milwaukee Ethnic Church Tour: The Rich Heritage of Immigrant Architecture*. Milwaukee: Department of City Development, 1994.

——. *Milwaukee Landmarks*. Milwaukee: Milwaukee Historic Preservation Commission, [1982].

100 Years: St. Stanislaus Centenary, 1866–1966. South Hackensack, N.J.: Custombook, 1968.

Otis, John P. Church histories collection. UWM Manuscript Collection 8. University Manuscript Collections, Golda Meir Library, University of Wisconsin–Milwaukee.

Poles in Wisconsin. Madison: State Historical Society of Wisconsin, 1979.

Still, Bayrd. *Milwaukee: The History of a City*. Madison: State Historical Society of Wisconsin, 1948.

Sutherland, Laura Elizabeth. "The Immigrant Family in the City: Milwaukee's Poles, 1880–1905." Master's thesis, University of Wisconsin–Milwaukee, 1974.

Szalo, John R. B. *Poland's National Flag and Emblem*. Pittsburgh: Polish Falcons of America "Sokol Polski," 1972.

Taylor, Pegi. "A Shutter, A Doorway: Polish Milwaukee in Photos." *Wisconsin: The Milwaukee Journal Magazine,* October 27, 1991, 16–25.

Widen, Larry, and Judi Anderson. *Milwaukee Movie Palaces*. Milwaukee: Milwaukee County Historical Society, 1986.

Wisconsin State Board of Health. *Report of the Bureau of Vital Statistics for 1920 and 1921*. Madison, 1922.

Wolkenheim, Stanley E. Sylvester: *The Story of Maynard Steel Casting Company*. Milwaukee: Maynard Steel Casting Company, 1979.

INDEX